The art of the observer

I0804014

Manchester University Press

Anthropology, Creative Practice and Ethnography (ACE)

Series editors:
Faye Ginsburg, Paul Henley, Andrew Irving and Sarah Pink

Anthropology, Creative Practice and Ethnography provides a forum for authors and practitioners from across the digital humanities and social sciences to explore the rapidly developing opportunities offered by visual, acoustic and textual media for generating ethnographic understandings of social, cultural and political life. It addresses both established and experimental fields of visual anthropology, including film, photography, sensory and acoustic ethnography, ethnomusicology, graphic anthropology, digital media and other creative modes of representation. The series features works that engage in the theoretical and practical interrogation of the possibilities and constraints of audiovisual media in ethnographic research, while simultaneously offering a critical analysis of the cultural, political and historical contexts.

Previously published

Paul Carter, *Translations, an autoethnography: Migration, colonial Australia and the creative encounter*

Lorenzo Ferrarini and Nicola Scaldaferri, *Sonic ethnography: Identity, heritage and creative research practice in Basilicata, southern Italy*

Paul Henley, *Beyond observation: A history of authorship in ethnographic film*

David MacDougall, *The looking machine: Essays on cinema, anthropology and documentary filmmaking*

Christian Suhr, *Descending with angels: Islamic exorcism and psychiatry – A film monograph*

In association with the Granada Centre for Visual Anthropology

GRANADA CENTRE FOR VISUAL ANTHROPOLOGY

The art of the observer

A personal view of documentary

David MacDougall

Manchester University Press

Copyright © David MacDougall 2022

The right of David MacDougall to be identified as the author of this work has been asserted in accordance with the Copyright, Designs and Patents Act 1988.

Published by Manchester University Press
Oxford Road, Manchester M13 9PL

www.manchesteruniversitypress.co.uk

British Library Cataloguing-in-Publication Data
A catalogue record for this book is available from the British Library

ISBN 978 1 5261 6534 3 *hardback*

ISBN 978 1 5261 6535 0 *paperback*

First published 2022

The publisher has no responsibility for the persistence or accuracy of URLs for any external or third-party internet websites referred to in this book, and does not guarantee that any content on such websites is, or will remain, accurate or appropriate.

FSC
www.fsc.org
MIX
Paper from responsible sources
FSC® C013056

Typeset in Garamond
by R. J. Footring Ltd, Derby, UK
Printed in Great Britain
by TJ Books Ltd, Padstow

Contents

Figures

Preface

THIS book was written for the most part during 2020–21 when there was little else I could do, since we were all to varying degrees immobilised by the Covid pandemic. I tried to take one or another aspect of filmmaking and say what I knew about it, returning more than once to my own filmmaking experiences. For this I can only plead that I know more about my own experiences than those of other filmmakers. In what follows, several of the same films and people crop up in different chapters, but I hope always within the context of that chapter's topic. My intention is that each chapter should stand alone as well as contributing to the book as a whole, and that examining certain films from several different angles may lead to a better understanding of how they were made. I have tried to work my way around most of the situations that documentary filmmakers are likely to face, together with the problems and pleasures of what is admittedly a rather unusual way of engaging with the world.

A few chapters deal with ethnographic film, but the underlying subject of the book is observational filmmaking and the ideas and practices surrounding it. We are all actors and observers in the world, and observational filmmaking attempts to translate this to the broader canvas of documentary cinema. In doing so, certain skills are required and, I would argue, the cultivation of a particular sensibility and set of filmmaking strategies. These involve an openness to what exists, but also, I believe, a deeper interest in how certain aspects of a subject are chosen and how they are presented to an audience. In this process the filmmaker's own presence becomes inscribed in the film, and the film's aesthetic and ethical stance becomes inseparable from the connections established between filmmaker and subject.

A film is made in the same sense that a chair or table is made. Whatever skills are employed, the grain shows through, and I have tried not to forget the primacy of the subject in all that we do, or the practicalities of engagement between filmmaker and subject. In the end a film is a product of that engagement and the chance circumstances that surround it. We can have no guarantee that our films will survive, for history tells us that most films do not. The most that filmmakers can do, I believe, amidst the pleasures and disappointments of filmmaking, is keep alive for a few hours or a few years what would otherwise be forgotten.

Acknowledgements

THIS book has been made possible by the support of many institutions and individuals. An Honorary Professorship at the Research School of Humanities and the Arts at the Australian National University has allowed me to continue my writing and film work in congenial surroundings. Much of the book concerns film projects undertaken in India, supported by fellowships and grants awarded by the Australian Research Council, without which those projects would not have been possible. I am also indebted to a number of institutions in India for their cooperation and generosity in assisting my film projects, including the Doon School, the Rishi Valley School, the Prayas Children's Home for Boys, Seva Mandir in Udaipur and the Delhi School of Economics at the University of Delhi. Not least, I am grateful to all those people in many places who were willing to accept my presence with a camera.

I wish to thank a number of colleagues and friends who, sometimes indirectly, have encouraged me in my recent writing. These include Minakshi Basu, Tom Dark, Faye Ginsburg, Anna Grimshaw, Frank Heidemann, Paul Henley, Therese Henningsen, Paul Hockings, Andrew Irving, Judith MacDougall, Alok Mathur, Rossella Ragazzi, John Shannon, Abhishek Shukla, Xu Han, Colin Young and Salim Yusufji. I should like particularly to thank Paul Henley for his careful reading of the entire manuscript and his many helpful suggestions. I should also like to acknowledge the patience and care that Tom Dark, Senior Commissioning Editor, has given this book and the excellent work of its freelance copy and production editor, Ralph Footring.

Several chapters in the book have appeared elsewhere, some in slightly different versions. For permission to include them here, I should like to thank The Taylor & Francis Group for: 'How the Visual Makes Sense', *Visual Anthropology* 33(1) (2020): 1–8; 'Observational Filmmaking: A Unique Practice', *Visual Anthropology* 33(5) (2020): 452–8; 'Clearing Customs', *Visual Anthropology* 30(1) (2017): 78–87; and 'Seven Types of Collaboration', *Studies in Documentary Film* 16(1), 2020: https//doi.org/10.1080/17503280.2020.1854150. I should also like to thank the Krishnamurti Foundation India for permission to use 'How Children See', *Journal of the Krishnamurti Schools* 22 (2018): 50–5. The chapter 'The Strangers Within Us' was originally written for the anthology *Strangers Within*, edited by Therese Henningsen and Juliette Joffé, forthcoming in 2022 from Prototype Publishing, London. It is published here with their permission. The illustrations from various films are either from the author's works or are used here on a 'fair dealing' basis. Other images are by the author.

Part I

1

The practice of documentary

In documentary films the observer usually remains invisible, unless caught by a reflection in a mirror. In Alfred Hitchcock's *Rear Window* (1954) the observer is fully visible, a photojournalist stuck in his apartment with a broken leg. The film returns to him again and again as he watches his neighbours, peering through binoculars and eventually using the telephoto lens of his camera to watch them more closely. In this way the film gradually builds up a composite image of people in the surrounding apartments, a whole urban microcosm. The observer, played by James Stewart, first looks casually, then with mild interest, and then with mounting intensity as he realises a murder is in progress (figure 1.1).

Although rarely seen, the filmmaker-observer of a documentary film is nonetheless present, looking at this, looking at that, and putting two and two together, much as the James Stewart character does in Hitchcock's film. This work is carried on by the viewer, for whom the film is constantly revealing new things as it unfolds. In structuring it, the filmmaker has created a path that viewers can both follow and deviate from, sometimes looking into things

1.1 James Stewart in *Rear Window*

1.2 Wife and husband in *The Angelmakers*

for themselves. The practice of documentary has thus always entailed a kind of uneasy dance between the mind of the observer and that of the viewer.

Astrid Bussink, the director of the documentary film *The Angelmakers* (2005), engages our attention much as Hitchcock engages us in *Rear Window*, but more obliquely. The film teases us with its apparently disconnected scenes, piling clue upon clue until we begin to see what is going on: old women dancing in a joyless public hall, some using walking frames; a ferry crossing the river; a half-abandoned Hungarian village, its derelict state set off by its pretty houses and flowers; a drunk in a squalid room; a school science lesson on the Periodic Table, focusing on As, or arsenic. A whole rural microcosm. We begin to realise that in this village women have been systematically poisoning their husbands (figure 1.2).

In commenting on the uses of the camera in anthropology, Margaret Mead once remarked:

> I think it's very important, if you're going to be scientific about behavior, to give other people access to the material, as comparable as possible to the access you had. You don't, then, alter the material. There's a bunch of film makers now that are saying, 'It should be art,' and wrecking everything that we're trying to do. Why the hell should it be art? (Bateson and Mead 1977: 78)

Why indeed? There is much in what she says that one could agree with. Why shouldn't we be given full access to what the James Stewart character sees, or what the filmmaker Astrid Bussink saw? How else can we come to a conclusion about what is going on? But consider this a little further. Suppose in the second case we were given all the footage that Bussink shot in the village, all the scenes of houses, of the schoolroom, of the swamps nearby, all the interviews, all the random conversations. I doubt if we would conclude much at all, still less gain an understanding of the forces that led the women to poison their husbands. It is the structure of the film that makes it possible, and this requires some art.

What Mead was advocating was a cinema of documentation, not meant to be viewed in the present as a film but studied as evidence later. Furthermore, it would ideally be the view of a camera without a thinking person behind it, recording what she maintained was 'what happened'. What bothered her was the attempt to prettify images or impose a particular interpretation on them, believing that this altered their truthfulness. Still, there is another way of looking at it. The art that she deplored was in fact the very limited and impoverished art of mere aestheticism, while the truthfulness that she advocated was limited to the truth of what the eye could see, what André Bazin, in his essay 'The Ontology of the Photographic Image', called the pseudorealism of appearances:

> The quarrel over realism in art stems from a misunderstanding, from a confusion between the aesthetic and the psychological: between true realism, the need that is to give significant expression to the world both concretely and its essence, and the pseudorealism of a deception aimed at fooling the eye (or for that matter the mind); a pseudorealism content in other words with illusory appearances. (1967: 12)

By 'illusory' I take Bazin to mean here both the visual illusion that photography creates of physical presence, but also, more important, the illusion that reality exists in what is immediately observable, rather than in more complex relationships, the sum of connected observations arranged in a strategic way. Mead, of course, understood that a variety of patterns could be seen within a single shot, provided one was familiar with the background. What she refused was a realism made more profound through the intelligent arrangement of different observations.

Almost every scene that one might film contains multiple objects of potential interest, but what the filmmaker chooses to emphasise depends on the overall purpose of a film. If, for example, there are several people present in a shot, we must ask: Which ones are relevant to the film being made? What aspects of their lives is the film pursuing? One of the most difficult skills to master in filmmaking is finding a position and framing that allow – and indeed encourage – the viewer to see a particular aspect of the subject. Even with this guidance, every filmed scene will still continue to contain many competing elements, all simultaneously present, some in the foreground, some in the background, and some within the ostensible subject itself.

Just as this is true for the individual scene or shot, it is also true for the film as a whole, although on a larger scale. Every film will continue to contain many elements, all presented within a coherent whole. It is the skill of the filmmaker in structuring the film that allows us to relate its various parts to one another in particular ways. Why does this require art? Although every film is a construction of some kind, if it is to be more than a simple document, the skills and experience of a filmmaker are needed to create a structure that gives meaning to its disparate parts.

As the theorist Bill Nichols has argued (1991), many filmmakers attempt to reveal the complexity and interconnectedness of life through a variety of structuring strategies. This contrasts with the assumption still lingering in the social sciences that structuring a film for a purpose (or more often, a set of purposes) somehow falsifies reality. It is perhaps the abstraction of the simple recording process, divesting life of its complexity, that proves more false. Preserving some measure of a subject's complexity will inevitably reveal ambiguities, for it tends to expose a nest of multiple connections. But as William Empson observed, 'ambiguity is a phenomenon of condensation' (1949: 31). If we can accept ambiguity as an inherent characteristic of complex systems, all the more reason to accept it in our efforts to represent the real.

The 1960s produced a variety of new approaches to documentary, one of which came to be known as observational cinema. It inspired many of the films mentioned in the following chapters. The basic idea had been present in documentary filmmaking from the start and had motivated many of its later practitioners, however different their films might appear. It was, in Joseph Conrad's words, 'before all, to make you see'. For Louis Lumière, according to director Bertrand Tavernier, it was to 'bring the world to the world' (1996). For Richard Leacock it was to produce 'the feeling of being there' (Levin 1971: 201). For Colin Young, who first gave observational cinema a name, it was to make a film 'as much like observation as possible; the finished film can represent the event observed'. Young added, however, that 'if you distinguish between using the camera as a surveyor's instrument and as a method of examining human behavior and human relationships in detail, you cannot afford in the latter case to stand back and get distant panoramas of human behavior – you have to be close to it and follow it intimately' (1975: 67).

One of the problems with an observation, taken by itself, is that although it may show the appearance of an event, it does not reveal its relation, if any, to other events. This must be done either by commenting on it or by comparing it with other observations. Its meanings are not self-evident except in the light of broader knowledge or some process of analysis. In didactic documentary films and numerous television programmes the analysis is provided in a spoken commentary – what Louis Marcorelles acidly described as 'talking a great deal during a film, with a commentary imposed from outside, in order to say nothing and to show nothing' (1973: 37). But in most documentary films, the meaning of each shot is created not only by what is said about it but by the shots that surround it. Thus in the 'city symphonies' of the 1920s, such as Walter Ruttmann's *Berlin: Symphony of a Great City* (1927), we come to understand, among other things, that the film traces the events of a single day. Equally so, in *The Angelmakers* the classroom scene about arsenic becomes significant only in light of other scenes showing the women's discontent with their husbands. Even in the British documentary films of the 1930s and 1940s, which are often criticised for the complacency of their voice-over narration, much of the meaning is still provided by the accumulation of connected and contrasting shots.

The new documentary approaches pioneered in the 1960s and 1970s, which included Direct Cinema and *cinéma-vérité* as well as observational cinema, largely avoided spoken commentary, but because of their intimate focus on human behaviour they arranged their observations either in a narrative form (as in the 1969 film *Salesman* by Albert and David Maysles and Charlotte Zwerin) or employed some other structure to make sense of the material. To explore such a complex system as the life of an institution, this might mean showing variations on a theme, an approach adopted by Frederick Wiseman in several of his films, or juxtaposing the features of an interconnected cultural system, as in Robert Gardner's *Forest of Bliss* (1985).

Each approach had its merits, but also its disadvantages. Emphasising a particular feature, for example, could give it an undue prominence, at odds with its more modest place in everyday life. It might also ignore how people actually experienced it, within the seamless flow of which it was a part. Narrative provided one solution to this problem, allowing the viewer to experience a series of connected events vicariously along with the film's protagonists. It was the strategy of most dramas and melodramas. Following World War II, the Italian Neorealist filmmakers Vittorio De Sica and Cesere Zavattini began applying it to quite ordinary events in people's lives in such films as *Shoeshine* (1946), *Bicycle Thieves* (1948) and *Umberto D.* (1952). Documentary filmmakers soon realised the same approach could be utilised in nonfiction, resulting in the narrative structures of such films as *Crisis* (1963), *Warrendale* (1967), *Salesman* (1969) and other documentaries of the 1960s and 1970s.

The problem with narrative was that it tended to restrict a film to the perspective of just a few protagonists. An alternative approach was to try to use a multi-layered structure, focusing on more general patterns observable in human society. In fact, many filmmakers began combining narrative and multi-levelled elements in the same film. This was consistent with the search to find structures more commensurate with the complex texture of life itself. Bill Nichols posed this as a problem of magnitude. 'What structure', he asked, 'might documentaries have that will conjure or restore for the viewer those orders of magnitude appropriate to the full dimensionality of the world in which we live and those who inhabit it?' (1991: 230).

If achieving this complexity was in a sense an unattainable ideal, the idealism often remained as filmmakers cast about for different ways of representing human experience. One approach, discovered early by Robert Flaherty in *Nanook of the North* (1922), was to explore the broader tapestry of society through an individual life, just as novels and biographies had done for centuries. Some portrait films, such as *Jane* (1962), *Lonely Boy* (1962) and *Don't Look Back* (1969), were fairly straightforward accounts of a few hours in their subjects' lives, sometimes supplemented with interviews. A few others attempted more complex structures. Writing in 1993, Peter Loizos pointed to the innovative approach of Jorge Prelorán's film *Imaginero* (1970), a portrait of Hermogenes Cayo, a shepherd and maker of religious images living on the remote Puna plateau of Argentina. He praised it for providing

> enough material for further reflection, so as a narrative it is 'open' and suggestive, rather than wholly closed-off, definitive and restricting. That is one important difference between a non-expositional film (relying on narrative and poetic juxtapositions, rather than conceptual, analytic argument, for its effects), and a logic-driven written text. (1993: 70)

What Loizos particularly noted was the multifaceted construction of the film, combining contemporary and historical images of Cayo's existence with both the religious images he created and his spoken reflections on his life. Prelorán continued to employ this strategy in later films, notably in *Zerda's Children* (1978), in which he employed several further devices.

The question that Prelorán approached obliquely in *Imaginero*, of how to convey the fullness of a life, was tackled head-on by Jean Rouch and Edgar Morin in their film *Chronique d'un été* (1961). The film explicitly asked its participants: 'How do you live?' To explore the question further, it assembled a 'cast' of young Parisians (mostly friends of Morin) and ranged across their daily lives, using dinner-table discussions, scenes from their work, experimental monologues and intimate interviews. Rouch was an anthropologist and Morin a sociologist, but their approach was more self-conscious and improvisational than that of much social research, at one point mocking the inanity of the on-street survey.

Chronique d'un été had a stimulating effect on the next generation of filmmakers, showing that it was possible to break free of many of the constraints of traditional documentary form. At once more personal and revolutionary than previous documentaries, it ignored the assumption that the filmmaker should remain anonymous, or that the viewer should be shut out of the filmmaking process. *Chronique* was also posed as an enquiry into the reach of documentary cinema itself. The idea that a film could ask what a film could actually achieve was almost without precedent. In his book, Loizos described it as 'an important film because of the way it went about engaging more directly with real lives and real issues' (1993: 59). He went on to look at several films that tried to develop similarly innovative forms, using the earlier films of Rouch, the films of Robert Gardner and the film *Maragoli* (1976) as examples.

The search continues. In recent years, the innovations have included combining documentation with performance, varied forms of collaboration with participants, and a flood of autobiographical films, aided by digital technologies such as mobile phone cameras and new internet platforms. Some approaches combine different filming styles, others more varied content. Common to these efforts is a heightened concern about the disparity that exists between what filmmakers have experienced and what they have been able to convey in their films. There is a sense that although they may never fully close the gap, they can at least draw closer to what the writer and film editor Dai Vaughan characterised as a film that is not equivalent to what it records but 'still perceptibly of its density and of its mass' (1999: 114).

With the historical development of documentary film and its elaboration of different styles and approaches, an important shift has occurred that might be called the 'unfreezing' of the filmmaker-observer. Filmmakers have gradually emerged from behind the scenes, becoming more present as the authors of their films. It was once assumed that a film director, like the director of a play, would remain in the background as a kind of god-like figure. The film's stamp of authority demanded it. But this has slowly changed. Jean Rouch and Edgar Morin's appearance in *Chronique d'un été* is but one example of the change. In Michael Rubbo's *Waiting for Fidel* (1974) the objective of the film was to conduct an interview with Fidel Castro, but this is put aside and replaced by the filmmakers' activities as they wait in vain for the interview to take place. In Ross McElwee's *Sherman's March* (1985) the film's subject is, from the very beginning, the filmmaker.

The unfreezing of the filmmaker has also taken a more physical form, with the filmmaker's body becoming registered in the very fabric of the film. This has happened in large part because of changes in filmmaking technology. The very first films, such as those made by the Lumière brothers, were shot with a fixed camera, since early tripods were not equipped with a movable head. As soon as the camera could be panned horizontally or tilted vertically, the hand and mind guiding its movements became evident in an immediate and tangible way. An erratic or hesitant move conveyed either a lack of skill or indecision. A panning movement that went beyond its subject and then moved back to correct itself came to be derided as an 'excuse-me' pan.

When sound was added to films in the 1930s, voice became an essential element in most documentaries, in the form of spoken commentaries. This was yet another level of embodied presence. As camera equipment became more manoeuvrable, and smaller crews were required, documentary films started to be made by just two or three people. Finally, with the arrival of digital video, they could be made by only one. Once the camera was hand-held by the filmmaker, its movements became even more closely tied to the filmmaker's body, evident (when badly done) in what critics sometimes disparaged as 'wobblyscope'. Thus unlike the 'frozen' observer of *Rear Window*, figuratively and literally tied to one place, documentary filmmakers could now move freely among the people they were filming, giving a vivid sense of their connection to them.

Over the years documentary films have changed in one additional way, linked to the more noticeable presence of the filmmaker. Documentaries had once been presented as definitive statements, products of extensive research carried out before they were made. Their use of a photographic process also suggested that they presented nothing but the facts. Dziga Vertov's early newsreels of *Kino-Nedelya* (1918–19) and *Kino-Pravda* (1922–25), for example, were founded on the premise that they brought the facts of the new Soviet nation to the people. Even Vertov's later film *Man With a Movie Camera* (1929), which disclosed many of the tricks of filmmaking, was not so much questioning the truth of the images as revealing the mechanics of producing them. Documentaries with sound, such as the American *March of Time* newsreels, were also constructed as official reports, often reinforced by the commanding, even hectoring tone of the narrator. By contrast, there was something refreshing and direct about the more amateurish popular travelogues of Osa and Martin Johnson and Lowell Thomas, their makers journeying about the world looking for something exotic to film. Earlier, in *Nanook of the North*, Flaherty had also seemed to be searching for an informality that would bring his subject to life. It was this directness that endeared Flaherty to Jean Rouch, who considered him his 'master'.

The same carefree spirit of enquiry can be seen in Rouch's own films, made not so much to report on a subject as to discover and celebrate it. For Rouch, prior research was not a precondition for filming; the filming itself was a research process. In his films he was always ready to change direction, led by what he called the 'strange choreography' of the subject (2003: 184). 'We enter the unknown', he said, 'and the camera is forced to follow' (2003: 149). In one of his early films, *Bataille sur le grand fleuve* (1952), he hurls himself into the midst of a hippopotamus hunt to convey its excitement, later improvising his own spoken commentary as if experiencing it anew. In *Jaguar* (1968), about labour migration in West Africa – a subject of his earlier research on the Songhay – he created, in Paul Henley's phrase, an 'adventure of the real', becoming the companion and amanuensis of three young men travelling from Niger to the mines and markets of the Gold Coast.

By becoming more present in their films, documentary filmmakers have shifted the perspective of the viewer, who is more likely to regard films as personal creations. Their authors at once appear more contingent and fallible. Although some filmmakers have remained a kind of ghostly presence in their films, with their agency only implied, others, particularly in films that are observational or autobiographical, have moved to centre-stage, as witnesses sharing their perspective with the viewer. Given the changed conception of documentary that this produces, viewers are likely to judge its images more independently. And although the emergence of filmmakers from the shadows has perhaps reduced their authority, it has arguably at the same time increased the viewer's trust in them.

Faced with describing an institution such as a hospital, prison or asylum, a sociologist might write an essay about its rules and social structure. A philosopher or historian might describe its inmates and administrators, or its systems of power. A novelist might plunge the reader into the nightmare world of Bedlam or a debtors' prison. A doctor might produce a *Gray's Anatomy* of the place. For each of these efforts a specific art would be required.

As a filmmaker facing a similar challenge in describing an institution, I have had to employ still another expressive language. One such institution was a shelter for orphans, juvenile detainees and homeless boys on the outskirts of New Delhi, the Prayas Children's Home for Boys. It was the third institution for children I had studied in India, beginning with an elite boarding school for boys in the north and then a progressive co-educational boarding school in the south. What methods and cinematic language would be required to portray such a place?

To begin with, the methods would have to be very different from those required of a writer. Although we might both be confronted by the same overwhelming sights and sounds, the same general clamour and range of human emotions, and although I might make written notes each night, during the day I had to make sense of it by the way I used the camera. Moreover, these would be more than just notes, for anything I filmed might eventually form part of the finished film. Indeed, I was constantly aware that the film could *only* consist of what I had recorded. I could make no explanations or excuses to the audience for what I had missed.

Looking back on the filming, the thinking and the editing that went into the film, I have had to consider what is required to make almost any film, and in this case particularly what is required to make an observational film. For films of this kind depend on spending a sustained period of time with one's subjects, responding to events as they occur and eventually constructing the film out of a selection of carefully observed scenes. This demands certain arts, of which the first is the art of observation, accompanied or followed by what I would call those of adaptation, construction, allusion and (for want of a better term) performance.

The art of observation

It could be said that observation is an art in itself, quite apart from its role in filmmaking. What one chooses to observe and how one observes it is often highly individual and idiosyncratic, as in Walter Benjamin's Arcades Project or Oliver Sacks's lifelong observation of neurological disorders. Observing may require a degree of discipline and creativity comparable to that required of a visual artist. This leads to the conclusion that there could possibly be an artist who actually produces nothing.

Observing with a camera differs from our usual practices of observing others and their physical surroundings. Normally we see these things within the broader continuum of our lives, but observation of that sort does not by itself endow them with any significance. By contrast, the view of the camera is selective, and its choice of a particular frame both excludes a broader view and implies that what it shows has some meaning. In effect, each shot asks the viewer to deduce why it is important and how it might be connected to previous shots or other elements in the film. For the filmmaker, framing something with the camera thus carries a responsibility to justify why it has been selected and why it is framed in a particular way. If the viewer's expectations are not met, by discerning either some meaning or some physical connection, the shot will appear accidental or gratuitous and disconnected from the rest of the film. If viewers are shown too much that seems irrelevant, they will begin to lose trust in the filmmaker and the film. The film's cohesion will begin to fall apart, every new irrelevancy undermining it still further.

For the filmmaker, it is not just the placement of a shot within a film that conveys its intention, but the way it is framed, its emotional tone and the very act of having chosen it from other shots possible at the time. Moving with an observing eye, the filmmaker gives meaning to the film's various shots by emphasising one person or another, by its timing or degree of intimacy and by connecting one person's actions and expressed emotions to those of another. The art of observation lies in this delicacy of choice, in which the use of the camera indicates the filmmaker's understanding of the situation and directs the viewer towards a fuller understanding of it. The play of the camera can thus equal the suppleness and subtlety of a dance or a piece of music.

The early stages of a film generally indicate where the filmmaker's interests lie and what its subjects will be. Apart from the people filmed, its view takes into account the setting and the objects within it, their possible importance and the atmosphere surrounding them. The filmmaker may return repeatedly to certain places, routines and physical details that define the world of its human subjects. There is a kind of reciprocity in this, for although the filmmaker chooses the images, the images also reach out to make their claim on the filmmaker.

When I filmed at the Prayas Children's Home for Boys, I tried to see it primarily through the boys' experiences, for at one level an institution can be said to exist in the perceptions of its inhabitants. What was it like to grow up in such a place? I began by observing the lives of individual boys in their collective life, for the experience of each could not be disentangled from the surrounding presence of other boys (figure 1.3). These observations included

1.3 Waiting for food in *Gandhi's Children*

recording the daily routines of key places, such as the dormitories where they slept, the canteen where they ate and the washrooms where they bathed, used the toilets and washed their clothes.

In my filming at the children's home, I used a high-definition video camera for the first time, and this influenced the way I observed the life of the institution. I realised that it was capable of producing much more detailed images than had been possible with film or ordinary video. There was, in effect, more to look at in each image, and one consequence of this was that shots that might otherwise exhaust what could be perceived in a short time could be held on the screen longer and allow the viewer to take more from them. I often used frames that included several individuals, since the expressions on each face could be seen quite clearly. My sense of the importance of the boys' physical surroundings in their lives encouraged me to pay more attention to this than in previous films, exploring its details and the overwhelming presence of the building in which they lived.

The boys had come to the home by different paths, and it was important to show the varied reasons that had brought them there. I therefore set out to record the personal histories of at least four or five of the boys and found several who were anxious to speak about what had happened to them. Some were orphans, some had been abducted, some had committed petty crimes, but nearly all had ended up on the streets, from which they were finally taken into the home. New boys continued to arrive and others left or simply disappeared. I filmed newcomers being interviewed by the staff, these interviews providing further insights into their backgrounds. But the greater part of the filming concerned the boys' relations with one another and with the adult staff, as well as the physical presence of the home's prison-like building. By living there myself, I was able to connect some of my own personal experiences to those of the boys, and this became an important strategy in my filming.

The art of adaptation

The filmmaker's acts of observation and filming do not take place in isolation but in places shared with others, and making a film requires the ability to move among them in particular ways. A talent for making images would be nothing in the absence of this social sense. People being filmed generally come to understand and accept the filmmaker's reasons for being there. But if a film is to portray events with more than approximate accuracy, the filmmaker must avoid disrupting the subtler social interchanges of people's lives. This means being alert to their feelings and adapting to their moods and movements. It means knowing what position to adopt in any situation and sensing when the filming may be oppressive or annoying. In some respects this is nothing more than ordinary courtesy, but the circumstances of filming are not ordinary. The presence of an outsider, the presence of a camera, the awareness of being filmed – all these produce responses which may alter over time and vary with each situation.

Where to place oneself when filming often means resolving conflicts between one's filming strategy and the need to respect social conventions. As a filmmaker one may want to be close to a person, observing their responses to what is happening around them. At the same time, it may be difficult to occupy a suitable position for this, for moving there may attract unwelcome attention or inhibit what other people are doing. There can be no simple solution to this, but with experience a filmmaker learns how to anticipate the need to be in a particular position and move there unobtrusively. It may even require shifting to several intermediate positions before actually filming. This kind of social navigation requires a heightened awareness of others, and often compromise. The sense of privilege that documentary filmmakers once assumed as their right has no place in observational filmmaking.

Problems of movement and positioning are only one aspect of the filmmaker's behaviour while filming. People who are being filmed tend to see the filmmaker both as an individual and as someone with a specific role to perform. From the filmmaker's perspective, balancing these two perceptions requires skill and experience, but it is also a reflection of the filmmaker's personality. How filmmakers present themselves to their subjects determines to a large extent what they will be able to film. If they are trusted, they are more likely to be given access to personal exchanges that would normally be closed to outsiders. Trust must obviously be earned over time, but there are specific ways in which the filmmaker's behaviour influences the outcome.

The way the camera is handled is one of these. Interacting with others easily while holding a camera depends on knowing the camera intimately, so that turning it on and off, adjusting for light, focus and framing are all done with a minimum of disturbance. Ideally, the filmmaker should do all this instinctively, with the confidence of regular use, as a musician handles an instrument or an artisan a familiar tool. Any attention people pay should be to the filmmaker, not the camera. For the filmmaker too, it is preferable that the camera be ready for use at any time, not brought out laboriously for every shot. Many filmmakers prefer interacting with others with the camera always in the filming position, as an extension of their everyday presence. In this way the filmmaker is able to live alongside others for extended periods of time, almost incidentally recording what he or she observes along the way.

Many of the things I filmed at the Prayas Children's Home I first saw through the viewfinder of the camera. The decisions to film or not film became part of an extended continuum of personal experience while living continuously with the camera. Shots were often triggered by something that began unfolding as I watched and then continued to follow. On many occasions when an event began, I was already filming a particular person, and it was this that determined my position and framing at the time. At other times I was involved in a more deliberate way, as when I was filming boys speaking about the events that had brought them to the home. Apart from eliciting specific material of this kind, which often produced lengthy monologues, I was careful to avoid directing anyone I was filming. This followed a fundamental principle of observational filmmaking, for once a filmmaker directs a person to do anything for a film, they will expect to be told what to do next. Apart from this as a practical matter, directing someone in an observational film undermines its basic premise and contract with the audience: to show as closely as possible only what happens of its own accord in the presence of the filmmaker.

The art of construction

Even as a film is being made, it is being shaped and constructed in the filmmaker's mind. Furthermore, it has already been partly defined by the ideas and circumstances that led to it being made. During the filming the filmmaker is constantly assessing and reassessing how the materials will go together, based on what has been filmed, what has been discovered in the process of filming and the aims with which the film began. As the filmmaker learns more, new ideas and interests will emerge and others will be put aside. The film's construction is thus a continually evolving process. Without this shaping and reshaping the film is likely to emerge as either too rigidly or too loosely made.

A film may combine a number of protagonists, events and thematic concerns, all arranged in a linear system which will make certain demands on the memory of the audience. Nothing remains on the screen very long, and an understanding of the subject must be built up piecemeal in the mind of the viewer and added to progressively as the film continues. It could be said that a film has not really been seen until it is over, and then it is too late to go back.

One of the primary requirements in the construction of all films is the skilful exposition of essential information. Providing information is normal throughout a film, but it is especially crucial in the first few minutes. Here the film has a great deal to accomplish, not simply in engaging the interest of the audience but in providing a foundation on which the film can progress. Here a number of immediate questions must be given some sort of answer. What kind of film will it be? What is its subject or particular interests? Where was it filmed? The opening images announce at least provisional answers to these questions. Some answers are provided in a straightforward manner, others more obliquely in order to provoke further questions in the mind of the viewer. In general, a film at this stage will at least indicate what genre it belongs to, whether fiction or nonfiction, whether narrative, expository, personal essay and so on. It will also introduce elements of its cinematic style, clues to where it takes place, the sorts of persons involved and some of its principal themes. If there are key protagonists, they are likely to make an appearance here.

If a film deals with a series of events, their inclusion must observe a certain logic, whether they follow a particular chronology or are related to one another in some other way. A simple chronology often provides the basic structure of a film, but as most events cannot be shown in their entirety, deciding how they are positioned and what elements of them are shown is essential. The same applies to introducing the protagonists and developing their character. In filming at the children's home, I faced a situation in which there was no overarching narrative but rather a series of individual personal histories. It was important to position these within a more general account of the routines of the institution, which profoundly affected the life of the boys.

Several of the personal histories were self-contained, but others developed more gradually and had to be threaded through the film. One boy waited for his brother to come and rescue him, and this happened quite soon. But another had been brought forcibly to the home, and we saw him slowly adjusting to it as he began helping other, more distressed boys. Still another boy had been abducted from his village. He seemed lost and in an almost catatonic state until he realised he might eventually be taken home. The grandfather of another boy came to have him released, but first there were legal obstacles that had to be overcome. A suitable place had to be found for each of these narratives in the film, for they could not all be developed at once. At one point over 200 boys arrived unexpectedly, released by the police from working in a factory. For a few days they had to be housed and fed, disrupting the usual routine. Unexpected events like this often occur, and filmmakers have to be ready to take them into account. In this case, the event enriched the film by adding a further narrative element and raising questions about the role of child labour in India.

Beyond developing linear narratives, films generally provide a sense of progression towards some destination or conclusion. This may be nothing more than the gradual fulfilment of the audience's curiosity, or it may be movement towards the outcome of a conflict or crisis. Whatever its basis, the audience must perceive some purpose in the film's unfolding, a sense that the filmmaker has an intention in mind. The filmmaker and critic James Blue used to refer to a film's plot elements as its 'transport mechanism', but he insisted that this was always secondary to the film creating a deeper understanding of the subject.

Many of the principles of construction that apply to a film as a whole also apply to the individual scenes within it. Here too there must be a sense of time and progression, as well as the creation of a consistent screen geography. The way the film is shot determines part of this, but editing can also delineate how people and objects are placed within a space. Just how one person relates to others may be shown through a fluid camera style or through the logic of cutting from one person to another. Similarly, the presentation of events must take into account cause and effect, such as how the actions of one person are registered in the responses of others. Individual scenes may be placed out of actual chronology provided they do not misrepresent these causes and responses and make sense in the film's overall logic.

The art of allusion

In what I have written above I have said little about another aspect of film construction, the way in which different elements in a film are interconnected in an underlying structure of allusions. This structure consists of pervasive themes, recurring images and metaphors that refer to meanings beyond those of the immediate moment. In making such connections, some consciously and others implicitly, filmmakers reveal further dimensions of their subject and in some cases how these are linked to their own conception of it. Most are internal to the film, but there may be others that refer to written or visual works and traditions outside it.

In some films the connections are already obvious and present in the subject, and the filmmaker simply conveys them to the audience. Objects such as locks and keys that are already saturated with meaning, carrying their symbolism with them. But there are always choices to be made, and the filmmaker can choose to underline certain meanings at the expense of others. This may be done consciously, but more often, I think, as they emerge slowly from within the material. Certain objects function, in T. S. Eliot's terms, as 'objective correlatives' or mute expressions of individuals' feelings, such as in the Prayas home the looming presence of the building and the bareness of its galleries and corridors.

Some connections or parallels are recognised immediately during the filming, but it is not uncommon for a filmmaker to recognise others only in the final stages of editing. These may be strengthened in some explicit way or simply left as secondary meanings that will be grasped by some viewers but not others.

Much of this secondary order of meaning is to be found in a film's thematic structure and in specific details that have attracted the filmmaker's notice. These may take on further significance in the light of the experiences of the people filmed and often have a soundly material basis. Among the themes that emerged at the children's home were those of waste, disease, and dirt and its counterparts of bathing, clothes-washing and cleaning. The children waged a constant battle against the dust and dirt that blew into the building, the human waste they produced themselves, and such diseases as scabies that resulted from unsanitary conditions. The home was surrounded by refuse and by a system of canals that channelled sewage into the pumping station next door. At one level, these conditions were simply symptomatic of living in an impoverished neighbourhood and institution, at another level as a reflection of the children's own status as the cast-offs of Indian society.

The themes of the clean and the unclean, order and disorder, recur continually in the film and become part of the institution's pervasive presence in the daily experience of the boys. Food became another recurring theme: the long lines of boys waiting to be fed, the scooping of food onto their steel plates, the boys seated on the floor as they ate, one small boy being refused when he asks for more (figure 1.4). Other themes centre around isolation and vulnerability, the general unreliability of adults, the boys' longing for home, their solidarity and their resilience. Several boys speak proudly of the jobs they have

1.4 Amit asks for more in *Gandhi's Children*

done and their ability to earn money. They often refer to others in the home as their brothers, having no other family. But beneath their independence is a strong sense of abandonment and a longing for security, expressed in their treasuring of their few possessions and in the importance of their clothing, lockers and beds.

Material objects such as these come to have added importance, even as they remain firmly tied to daily reality. Whenever dirt and waste or clothes-washing and bathing appear they make implicit reference to similar scenes elsewhere in the film. The same is true of the beds and bedding with their connections to sleep, and the ambiguous meanings of clothing. At one point a pickpocket ends up making pockets for other boys' uniforms. None of these details are particularly singled out, but their presence in different contexts contributes to the metaphorical undertow of the film. This kind of repetition would appear to be a key factor in the allusive structure of many films. Very few items rise to the level of explicit symbol – in this case, perhaps only the bars on doors and windows, a locker that one boy has made into a shrine of his dreams, and the pipes of the pumping station that repeatedly spew out sewage into the surrounding wasteland (figure 1.5).

1.5 The sewage pumping station in *Gandhi's Children*

The art of performance

Finally, one should not overlook one of the most important arts required of the documentary filmmaker. Performance in this sense does not refer to social performance, or acting, or the re-enactments that are now often used in documentary films. Here I mean specifically the performance of the filmmaker in addressing the audience. This includes everything from giving overall shape to a film, to controlling its internal dynamics of pacing and rhythm, to the management of mood, to the ways in which the filmmaker creates and directs the viewer's expectations.

Performance is partly a matter of a film's construction, but the construction must be underpinned by a kind of musicianship, or what Andrei Tarkovsky (in a free translation of the title of his book) called 'sculpting in time'. It ranges from knowing where to start or end a shot, to how to develop a sequence, to when to introduce a film's protagonists. Sometimes it involves the classic dramaturgy of conflict, crisis and resolution. But primarily it is the rhetorical means by which a filmmaker communicates a firm grasp of the material to the audience.

I have mentioned the importance of a film's first few minutes in establishing what kind of film it is and how it is likely to proceed. A similar rigour is required throughout the film to manage its variations in energy and develop its themes. A film can easily go off track. Some filmmakers cannot resist the seduction of their own material and tend to repeat it to a wearying degree. Others are tempted to make their material carry more weight than it can bear. Although there are many different styles of filmmaking, each film establishes its own specific set of conventions for the audience, and if it strays too far from these the filmmaker is likely to lose the viewers' confidence.

This can happen in many ways. Some films change their style or tone part of the way through, as if wishing to become a different kind of film. They may strike a poetic note too late, when it seems mawkish, or provide too facile an ending, or use music too obviously to manipulate the viewers' emotions. Other films may be tightly constructed at the start but then begin to wander. Some do not know how to stop and tail off in multiple endings, as if in search for the most resounding one.

In the end, the filmmaker is a performer, and on this stage there are many pitfalls. Some may be unavoidable, for they are caused by unexpected shifts or breakdowns during the production. Many of the rest can be avoided, given a little experience on the part of the filmmaker. Certain films, of course, are flawed from the start by laziness or sentimentality or dishonesty. Others are simply 'difficult' because they attempt something new and untried. Among these last it seems invidious to single out those that fail, for often they are honourable failures, and filmmakers, like all artists, have a right to fail.

Asked why they have made a film, documentary filmmakers are likely to refer to the importance of the subject, or some objective interest in it, or launch into a story of how the film came to be made. Later they can sometimes be induced to divulge more personal reasons, some of which they may not have fully recognised at the time. A certain modesty also prevails, for after all a film is simply the product of a filmmaker's work. In reality, however, the film usually looms much larger than this in the filmmaker's life, for it may have taken years to complete and exposed them to new and difficult situations. It may even have altered their understanding of themselves, providing a mirror for reflection and self-examination. What, they may sometimes ask, were they doing there?

The reasons are likely to vary from one filmmaker to another. Some, like Jean Rouch, were there for the adventure, the stimulus and the companionship that the film could afford. For others the film was a sacred rite or duty, or even an act of love. There were also those (myself among them) for whom film was a means of engaging with others and becoming more deeply immersed in the fullness of life. Nearly all experienced the heightening of the senses that filmmaking brings, as they encountered the world afresh through the eye of the camera.

And then there was the art of it.

2

How the visual makes sense

THE use of visual images in anthropology observes many of the same principles that apply in other contexts, although there are occasions when different principles come into play, as in using images to make precise measurements. Photographs and films (or video) require the viewer to be familiar with certain cultural conventions, apart from being able to 'read' them as referring to some external reality (in itself partly a culturally acquired ability). Among these conventions are those of time and space – for example, understanding that an unbroken shot represents an unbroken period of time, whereas several shots cut together may indicate gaps in time, or continuity in time if there is continuous sound on the soundtrack. Movement of the camera within a shot indicates that although the framing changes from beginning to end, the shot was made within a single space. Conventions like these are employed to create a coherent sense of cinematic geography and temporality in the mind of the viewer, a construct usually made up of multiple images.

These conventions reflect a process of thought in the filmmaking which the filmmaker hopes will be communicated to the viewer. The mind of the filmmaker is guiding the viewer in what to see, but it is also necessary for the mind of the viewer to make sense of it – in effect, to read the filmmaker's intentions. Much of film viewing requires the ability to make connections, such as understanding that if someone in a film points to an object, or speaks of it, and this is followed by a shot of an object, the chances are that this is what the person had in mind. A kind of rudimentary grammar links the various shots. This tells us that if there are three shots of someone doing something, we accept that the actions occurred in that order. The rules can be broken, of course, but this only underlines what is the norm.

Still photographs also have their conventions, such as assuming that objects extend outside the frame, that images are presented right-side-up, that black and white stands in for colour, and so on. As with films, photographs also have conventions of time and space. In realist photography those of space are derived from Renaissance perspectival art, the design of lenses and human vision itself. The conventions of time owe more to the human imagination. A landscape may appear timeless, but dark storm clouds on the horizon may evoke a narrative of change and time passing. A photograph of a person in the midst of an action immediately suggests a narrative of what led up to this moment and what will happen afterwards. Photographs therefore have their own dynamism, and groups of photographs can conjure up connections similar to those produced by the shots in a film.

Anthropologists attempt to interpret human actions and interactions in varied material settings and within a range of largely invisible systems – political, economic and ideological. At the same time, they know that many aspects of these systems have certain visual manifestations. Economics becomes visible in a marketplace or a bank. Politics is expressed through electoral campaigns, parliaments and public debate. Much of what anthropologists learn they learn through visual observation – how members of a family treat one another, how a technical process is performed, and so on. This knowledge can be recorded and interpreted in words, but it is clear that important parts of it escape the encoding process. For example, you can describe a facial expression or the steps in making something, but the reader might find it very hard to reproduce either accurately from a verbal description.

The power of description

Film has a power of description different from that of texts, and in some ways superior to them. Most obviously this lies in its ability to delineate objects, people and events within an image, which a text must do by replacing objects and their qualities with words and then communicating this in a linear fashion. Importantly, the image of an object in a film is presented all at once rather than progressively. A corollary of this is the power of film to communicate *co-presence* – that is, the coexistence of several things in a particular space. Here, the visual makes sense through its ability to reveal relationships, or sometimes the lack of them. For example, within the same image two people may be talking about something in the foreground while two other people are having a fight in the background. These events may or may not be connected, but if they are, the connection may be important.

Corresponding to co-presence in space is simultaneity in time. In understanding social interactions and events, it is often essential to grasp several facts occurring at the same time, as a complex. Films can present this simultaneity very efficiently. In a film of which I was a co-author, *The Wedding Camels* (1977), there is a scene of men in an African pastoralist society singing while a sacrificed ox is being skinned. The two events are crucially interconnected as part of a marriage ritual. The words of the song comment on cattle and reflect larger cultural concerns. Later in the same film the young bride is brought to be blessed. Here four events are occurring simultaneously. The girl is crying from fear and the thought of leaving home. At the same time, her future co-wife is holding her hand to comfort her. Another person is blessing her by painting her with white clay. And her father, who has arranged all this, is looking on.

As this demonstrates, films make sense through the composition of their images and their arrangement in scenes. They also do so in other ways. One aim of ethnographic filmmakers is to convey the material surroundings in which people live – in effect, what they constantly see around them and experience with all their senses. It has been proposed that the tactile qualities of objects are best communicated through proximate, or close-range, vision, underlining the important role of the close-up in films (Riegl 1985). Bringing objects into close-up allows them to be touched, as it were, by the eye, and their surfaces more intimately inspected. This is the way we see the personal possessions that we handle daily. But as well, the close-up may allow for a curious kind of identification with material objects, much as in films we tend to identify with people when we see them at closer range. We do not actually feel that we become the object, but we feel we inhabit its qualities in some way.

Examples abound of how close-ups, often combined with sounds, contribute to our sense of the corporeal experiences of others. A close-up of hands shaping clay on a potter's wheel communicates the feeling of the clay's wetness and malleability. Sounds of water running and dripping enhance the effect. In broader terms, scenes like this can communicate something of the potter's habitual life. Extended still further, an enumeration of the details of people's lives can help to express the collective experience of a larger group. Anthropological films are particularly well suited to conveying the aesthetics (in the broadest sense) of social life – the particular blend of familiar objects, formal and informal rituals, colours, sounds and physical settings that are unique to each community – a task that would otherwise require the skills of a novelist. These aesthetic systems have a peculiar ability to perpetuate themselves and influence decision-making in community life.

The power of analysis

Anthropological knowledge is not just about observing events in themselves but making sense of the connections between them. Similarly, a film is not only about recording things happening but making an analysis of what it is recording in cinematic terms. A film cannot show everything, any more than an observer can observe everything, so filmmakers make certain choices and develop them according to their understanding of the subject.

How does this process take place in practice? Basically it occurs in two steps, in the filming and the editing. It is both an analytical and partly an intuitive process. Making sense of something happening in front of you requires the ability to decide very quickly what to emphasise and how to create a progression of images that gives the sense of it. This may be refined and deepened in the editing by uncovering further connections within the material. A hypothetical example: You are filming someone who has just suffered a minor injury.

Other people are looking on. You need to show their concern. But do you pan around with the intention of making a general shot, or do you focus on a particular person? The decision will be determined by what you already know, what you have previously filmed and what you are particularly interested in. This may involve the personal relations of those in the group or some larger set of themes about their lives. The choice of a particular person will develop one line of enquiry, the choice of several people a different one, creating a different emphasis. Later you may discover something you didn't know, such as that the person you chose is related to the person injured, or owes them money. How do you show this? You may have to wait until you can film a scene in which all this becomes evident. Or during the editing you may have to look for some other material that reveals it.

When making a film about the changing lives of mountain shepherds in Sardinia (*Tempus de Baristas*, 1993), I filmed a youth, Pietro, helping to kill a young goat. Apart from including the cutting of its throat, it was important to show his reaction to the act, so I moved the camera closer to show his face. In doing so, I was aware that just a few minutes before I had filmed him opening the pen of some baby goats and looking upon them with affection. All this was linked to a larger question posed by the film: how the shepherds' emotional life involved their livestock, which they had both to protect and at other times to kill. (Their livelihood depended on milk and cheese. As they could keep only a limited number of male goats, they often had to cull the rest.)

After the young goat is killed, Pietro hangs it up to be skinned. Also present is a young boy from the town, who has never seen this sort of thing before. My problem was where to position myself in order to show what Pietro was doing and at the same time register the responses of the younger boy. I was also interested in the fact that Pietro was now proud of showing off his proficiency to the older men nearby, despite his earlier repugnance at killing the goat. I took the only obvious camera position that would accomplish all this. Pietro skins the goat and guts it efficiently, and this serves in the film to show his growing competence and assurance in the tough exclusive world of shepherds, in contrast to the boy from the town. Meanwhile the young boy watches with both fascination and disgust, and the scene ends as he gives a shudder at the sight (figure 2.1).

In the editing, this scene is purposely followed by a scene in which older shepherds spontaneously discuss their feelings of sadness and distress at having to kill their animals. They refer to another shepherd who, they say, could never bring himself to do it. The conversation runs in part:

> Costantinu: When it's time to kill them, he goes somewhere else. He thinks, 'What horrible things we must do to our animals.' I don't know why he's like that.
> Miminu: I'm like that.
> Franchiscu: I feel sorry, but never as strongly as that.

2.1 Pietro skins a kid in *Tempus de Baristas*

Taken together, this material aims to reveal something about the world view and internal lives of the shepherds within the wider field of their economic and social life. It is linked to other scenes in the film that develop similar themes of youth, masculinity and relationships with livestock.

The power of interpretation

The visual makes sense literally, by showing how social systems operate and interconnect, and figuratively, by revealing patterns and layers of cultural meaning. In the example given above, the use of film is as much about revealing the values and poetics of Sardinian shepherd culture as the specifics of economic life. The killing of a baby goat becomes a metaphor for the relation of youth to age, among men as well as animals. Even if certain objects do not become explicit symbols (and I think they lose some of their force if they do) they nevertheless carry resonant meanings. Later in the same film, a shepherd carries a large forked piece of wood up a hill. Such pieces of wood are used to build the roofs of the shepherds' mountain huts, but they can be found only in the valleys. Some people have seen Christian symbolism in this scene, the burden of carrying the cross, but it could as easily refer to the myth of Sisyphus. Whatever its associations, it is still at base about the difficulties of shepherd life, a practical matter of getting the necessary timber to where it is needed. At the end of the film, Pietro's father is heard calling out across the valley, ostensibly to his goats. But his son has just left him to study in the town, and his calling out suggests a further level of meaning. It evokes a fact of contemporary shepherd life, the movement of youths from the countryside to the towns, forsaking the pastoral life of their fathers.

An ethnographic film from 1974 that I made with James Blue, *Kenya Boran*, provides another example of overlapping meanings. In north-eastern Kenya we filmed at a government primary school where each week the teacher assigned the children to one of four groups, depending on their marks. Those doing least well were put at the back of the room. The four groups were called Lion, Elephant, Hyena and Frog. It is not hard to guess how these were ranked. The names, however, also had special cultural significance in a cattle-keeping society familiar with wild animals. Later in the film a boy tells us, 'Lion is the President of Animals'. We filmed this same boy and a friend studying for a school exam at a waterhole where in the background elephants can be seen drinking. And in another scene, a senior man points to his elephant-ivory bracelet, saying it is worn only by those who have been brave enough to kill an enemy or a lion. Within the film these scenes create a confluence of interconnected ideas about the natural environment, social change, learning, proficiency and masculinity. Their presence in the film, however, depended crucially on our being aware of this cultural complex during the filming and editing,

The power of explanation

The visual also makes sense through the use of narratives and the power of narratives to explain. Narratives have come to have something of a bad name in critical theory, as artificial structures imposed upon the indeterminate realities of life. As Dai Vaughan put it, 'Film is about something, whereas reality is not' (1999: 21). To some critics, the movement towards closure implicit in narratives suppresses the objective facts of people's lives and tends to mask and 'normalise' the inherently unequal conditions of society. Whether or not this argument can be applied validly to narratives in non-industrial societies, there are some circumstances in which narratives neither provide closure nor necessarily banish indeterminacy. In anthropological films, narratives can have at least two useful functions: to show how complex social forces bear upon the individual at any one time and to provide explanations of social behaviour. To take the latter first, film narratives that follow existing situations of crisis and resolution help, in Victor Turner's view, to explain how communities maintain themselves through practices that heal, or seal over, underlying breaches and contradictions (Turner 1986: 39–44). Ethnographic films that focus on the crises implicit in social rituals – what Turner called 'social dramas' – fall into this category. Melissa Llewelyn-Davies's film *The Women's Olamal* (1984) and Kim McKenzie's *Waiting for Harry* (1980) exemplify this. Narratives that focus on individual experience are valuable precisely for showing that contradictions may never be resolved. By following particular persons through a series of events they can reveal the complex social forces that are manifest – as for example in a film about the degradation inflicted on a once-autonomous people (*N!ai, The Story of a !Kung Woman*, 1980) or about the pressures of consumerism pulling against those of limited job opportunities in Rahul Roy's *Till We Meet Again* (2013).

A different but equally important aspect of narrative is its ability to evoke the subjective experience – and at times the agency – of individuals in various cultures. The role of the individual in society has become of increasing interest to anthropologists as a counter to the view that societies are homogeneous, and that individuals simply fill the positions that others have vacated, a view that tends to neglect processes of social change. A focus on unusual individuals can often illuminate more about a society than a focus on those who are deemed typical. Atypical figures of this kind are the protagonists of *Lorang's Way* (1979), *Imaginero* (1970) and *Ika Hands* (1988). Films have also been important in highlighting the day-to-day experiences of women and their specialist roles, in a discipline that has often tended to focus more on the activities of men. The films of Margaret Mead and Gregory Bateson, made in Bali and New Guinea in the 1930s, were among the first to examine the role of women in society.[1] The increased interest in individual experience has had special importance for the anthropology of childhood. It has helped created a new awareness of children as social actors who make significant economic and cultural contributions to their communities. Furthermore, children are more readily seen as individuals in their own right, rather than uncompleted projects of socialisation, or passive adults-in-waiting. Films can reveal the unique personalities and unexpected abilities of children in ways inaccessible to texts.[2]

Finally, the visual has value in shifting anthropologists' perspectives and modifying their preconceptions. This dynamic aspect of visual research is a further way in which it helps to make sense of a subject. By being present with a camera, and using it to follow the experiences of others, one often sees things quite differently from the way a conventional participant-observer would see them. In my filming at a boarding school in northern India, the camera led me into situations I would never have witnessed otherwise, and through the camera I began to recognise repeated patterns of collective and individual behaviour that would have been invisible to me without it.

Notes

This chapter was published in slightly different form in *Visual Anthropology* 33(1) (2019), copyright Taylor & Francis, http://www.tandfonline.com, DOI: 10.1080/08949468.2019.1671746.

1 Later films include George Stoney's *All My Babies* (1953), the Maasai films of Melissa Llewelyn-Davies (such as the 1984 television series *Diary of a Maasai Village* and the television film *The Women's Olamal*, also 1984), John K. Marshall and Adrienne Miesmer's *N!ai, The Story of a !Kung Woman* (1980), the Jero films of Timothy and Patsy Asch, and Florence Ayisi and Kim Longinotto's *Sisters in Law* (2005).

2 See, for example, *Children Who Draw* (1956), *Beppie* (1965), *Naim and Jabar* (1974), *La Vie est immense et pleine de dangers* (1995), *Être et avoir* (2002), *The Age of Reason* (2004).

3

Observational filmmaking: a unique practice

THE first film I can remember seeing was Robert Flaherty's *Nanook of the North*. It was shown at my school, and I must have been about six or seven years old at the time. By then I had no doubt seen many other films, but it is *Nanook* that sticks in my mind. Of course by then it was already a famous film, but I did not know that.

I have often wondered why I remembered the film so vividly, compared with the many other films I saw around the same time. It lacked the production values of Hollywood films, with their colour and sounds and excitement, but I think even then I must have had a sense of the artificiality of those films. It also lacked the voice of authority that dominated most of the educational films we were shown at school. Perhaps I found those films suspect too, for I was a somewhat sceptical boy who did not believe everything he was told. I now think that what struck me most about *Nanook* was that it was observing the lives of real people, neither making them up nor telling me what to think about them. It was made from the viewpoint of someone who had actually been there.

Today I consider observational filmmaking to be a unique documentary film practice. It produces films that differ from most of the other documentary films that we see. It differs also in more subtle ways from similar approaches like Direct Cinema and *cinéma-vérité*, for it does one thing the others do not do. Instead of focusing exclusively on its subject, it puts the process of finding out about the subject at the centre of the film.

Several years ago I began a study of a famous boys' boarding school in northern India (described in greater detail in chapters 5 and 6). I was not particularly interested in the teaching methods of the school, but rather in what I considered to be the school's 'social aesthetics' – that is, how the particular physical and social environment that the school had created influenced the students' feelings and behaviour. In the end I made five films at the school over five years.

The students responded in two quite different ways to my filming project, depending on their ages. The first response came from the youngest boys in the school – eleven- and twelve-year-olds in their first year. When I first appeared with the camera they crowded around me asking what I was doing. It was difficult to formulate an answer, but finally I said: 'I am making a study of the school, but instead of writing a book I am writing it with a camera.' They seemed to find this explanation perfectly reasonable. When I began filming they were naturally excited and showed some self-consciousness, but they soon lost interest in the camera and accepted my filming as a matter of course.

At this same time I began filming another group of boys in their third year, aged between fourteen and fifteen. Their response was very different. Instead of asking me what I was doing, they began by asking me what I wanted *them* to do for the film. I realised that they already had very fixed ideas about what documentary films were and how they were made. Rather than expecting them to be about actual events occurring in the world, they expected them to be simulations of typical *kinds* of events, acted out for the camera. This took me by surprise, for I had come from a documentary tradition in which the whole purpose was to avoid fictionalising events and to show things happening spontaneously, to the extent that films can do this.

It took me some time to convince the boys that I did not want them to do anything specially for the film, but instead to let me film whatever they did or whatever happened around them, however it turned out. I think they eventually got the point. They began accepting my presence and my filming, although never with quite the carefree attitude of the younger boys. Once, when I said I would like to film them asleep and then waking up in the morning, one of them suggested they could stage this for me. But the others said, 'No, you should film us *really* asleep!'

What conclusions can we draw from this? One is that they believed documentary films almost always present themselves to their audiences as manufactured products – that is, from behind a screen of professionalism. The filmmakers, they felt, had no intention of confiding in them as viewers. On the contrary, they meant to conceal the realities of how their films were made, all the better to show their expertise at creating the illusion of reality. This reminded me of how in television documentaries, when a presenter is shown travelling in some distant part of the world, these scenes are based on the pretence that the presenter is travelling alone, even though a director and an entire film crew are standing off-screen, only a few metres away.

One can speculate why the boys held these assumptions, but the point is that in fact they were right: many so-called documentary films are indeed performances carefully staged for the camera.

The historical reasons for this are many, which I can only summarise here. They involve the technical limitations of camera equipment in the early days of sound films, when many documentaries adopted the methods of fiction filmmaking, using separate camera setups and directing each shot. They also have to do with the separation of filmmaking jobs into technical and creative roles, and the general conservatism of the profession. More recently they involve the strictures imposed by tight schedules and budgets, and the reluctance of producers to finance films whose outcome is uncertain.

In contrast to this approach, observational films tend to be more open and unpredictable, not pre-packaged works whose means of production are kept from the audience. Observational films are not the only films made from this general perspective. As already mentioned, they include the sub-genres of Direct Cinema and *cinéma-vérité*, which also try to show events as they occur spontaneously. But the emphasis of observational films is slightly different. They are based on a process of discovery. Implicitly or explicitly, at their centre is the filmmaker, an observer with a camera. The film then opens this perspective to the viewer. At the same time, the emphasis is not on the filmmaker as an individual (unlike the presenters of television programmes), but on what the filmmaker is able to reveal about other people's lives. An observational film doesn't claim to be comprehensive, covering every aspect of its subject, or what would have happened in other circumstances. Instead, it presents what has happened at certain times and places when a filmmaker was present.

It is reasonable to ask what observational filmmakers hope to achieve by these means. There are really two things. One of them is to analyse the situation they have come to film – the complexities in which the people being filmed are living. The other is to try to convey something of their experience, to bring the viewer closer to their lived reality. The filmmaker's motivation may also be to connect with other human beings through the sharing of a common experience. Beyond this it may simply be to do what most artists and scientists do, which is to try to understand, or define, or preserve something of importance in the world.

The prospect of making a film is always daunting. Even if filmmakers already know the people they want to film, it still requires courage and a measure of audacity to insert themselves into their lives. Filmmakers also suffer from the disadvantage that their subjects, unlike themselves, belong to the setting, they know their own community and one another, whereas the filmmaker is always to some degree an outsider and less knowledgeable. This is quite the reverse of what many critics have assumed about the position of power that filmmakers enjoy.

The starting-point for observational filming typically combines feelings of attraction to the subject with feelings of doubt and apprehension. It is often thought that before starting to film, filmmakers should undertake a period of research, gaining extensive knowledge of the people they will film; only then should they introduce the camera. I used to agree with this, but I have now come to think the opposite. Far better, I think, to introduce the camera at the beginning. There are both practical and ethical reasons for this. When you film, your behaviour towards others must inevitably differ from when you are simply socialising with them. If you introduce the camera late in the relationship, this shift in behaviour may well seem puzzling and discourteous to the people you have come to film. I also believe it is more honest to make your intentions clear right from the start, so that introducing yourself with the camera leaves no doubt about why you are there and what you intend to do. There is also another, methodological reason for starting to film from fairly early on. Filming should not simply be a follow-up to prior research but a research process in itself. Using the camera can be a powerful means of directing filmmakers along new paths and allowing them to see things from a different perspective.

Observational filmmaking often means working physically close to people as you film their conversations and other interactions. But if you ostentatiously pick up the camera to make each shot, or constantly draw attention to the filming, the camera will naturally remain the centre of attention. It is far better to behave unobtrusively, neither interrupting nor demanding anything, and treating the camera as a natural extension of your own body and senses. This can best be compared to playing a musical instrument, where the technique is completely subsumed into producing the music.

A filmmaker's emotions are closely linked to the filming process, and they feed back into it. These emotions may vary considerably, but I can suggest at least some of them. In observational filmmaking there is necessarily some personal involvement with the people being filmed. In observing people for long periods, the filmmaker becomes attuned to their expressions, their ways of moving and subtler aspects of their personalities. This hypersensitivity to others can be fascinating, but also tiring; and yet it is a crucial part of the filmmaker's ability to respond to what is happening, and to anticipate what is about to happen. There may also be a disconcerting sense of the people one is filming living autonomous lives in the present and yet at the same time becoming fixed forever in the film. This double perception can distance the filmmaker from the subjects. Yet filmmakers frequently feel a sense of humility in the face of reality, privileged to be witnessing what is happening. They may also develop a profound respect for those they are filming, while nevertheless having a sense that the course of their lives is somehow inevitable.

In contrast to this sharpening of emotions, observational filming can involve long periods of inactivity and waiting. There are times of irritation when one feels that nothing is happening, but also times of frustration when one feels one has missed something important. It is quite usual for filmmakers to feel in the wrong place at the wrong time.

It is also important to acknowledge that there is something acquisitive about filmmaking of this kind. A filmmaker is intent on capturing what is of interest, or value or beauty in the subject, and feelings of possession inevitably play a part in this process. To make films is to take fragments from the world and then return them to the world from a particular perspective. The filmmaker is at once acquiring and preserving, but also adding something personal to what he or she has seen.

Before the advent of video, actual film was costly, and this imposed a certain sense of economy on the filmmaker. When a shot was made, it was felt it should be for a purpose. If one was following a script, the purpose was usually clear enough. But later, when documentary filmmakers began working more often without scripts, they tended to think of how each image might figure in the finished film, and chose their shots quite carefully. With the arrival of inexpensive video, however, some filmmakers began to take the view that they could film as much as they wanted and work out how to organise it later. This frequently led to disappointment. They often discovered that if they had known what they wanted to film at the time, they would have filmed the subject quite differently. Many of us who began our careers using film have continued to treat video as though it were as precious as film – a useful discipline.

Filmmakers are always shaping the material by the way they are filming it. Because filming is selective, the film represents only a small part of what they have been able to observe. This means they must constantly be thinking about the material as they are recording it, considering how it will fit into the overall structure of the film. They must also consider the requirements of editing. Getting certain shots may be essential to the understanding of a scene – for example, showing what people are talking about, or establishing where people are physically positioned in relation to one another. The challenge is to keep such technical matters in mind while at the same time trying to concentrate on the larger issues of the film.

This kind of thinking is typical of what I would call a strategy of contextualisation. In order to make a scene comprehensible, it may be necessary to shoot another scene that helps the viewer to understand it. In traditional documentary filmmaking, this job of contextualisation could quite easily be done by giving the necessary information in a voice-over commentary. But in observational films, viewers can learn things only by piecing together the information presented to them. The ways of providing this information must therefore usually be found at the time of filming. At the same time, the filmmaker must engage with the feelings of the audience, not simply assume they will be interested in a subject because they themselves are.

Many things in people's lives remain unstated or unseen. This is the potential limitation of observational cinema. Often what people are talking about has already been stated, or is simply assumed and never actually mentioned by them. And yet, as in a novel, a fiction film or a stage play, filming connects the visible and the invisible, between what is openly expressed and what is known or experienced. In this lies its creative potential, and to a large extent its challenge. It is also where the logic of editing plays a major role, placing one scene against another to create the ideas and metaphors that resonate through the film.

One of the principles of observational filmmaking is that it responds to the particularities of the situation, always ready to adapt to them. Filmmakers very often find that what they thought were the important questions when they began are not in fact very important, and others soon take their place. Their priorities are more likely than not to change and evolve. This can become part of a conscious strategy, if filmmakers are willing to let the film lead them into new situations. It can be considered a method of voluntary self-dislocation, capable of producing significant changes of perspective and new kinds of knowledge.

The making of an observational film follows a general pattern which goes something like this. At the beginning the filmmaker feels bewildered by the many possibilities at hand and is often unsure which direction to take. As a direction establishes itself, this feeling is replaced by the work of following certain protagonists, themes and events. Almost always, at a certain point the filmmaker wonders if all this material will ever amount to a film, and a period of uncertainty and discouragement sets in. In my experience, this is gradually overcome when the filmmaker feels he or she has accumulated a sufficient critical mass of material to make a coherent film. From then on, confidence returns and the work becomes that of consolidating the film and filling in some of the blank spaces.

As the themes and priorities of the film become clearer, so do the personalities of the people in it. Very often at the beginning, filmmakers have no idea whom they will film. They may look for people whose lives illustrate certain aspects of a larger problem, or who as individuals seem particularly expressive. In other cases, it is particular people who inspire the film, and it takes shape around them. In the middle ground are those films in which the protagonists gradually emerge from the background. Undoubtedly some unconscious process takes place in which the filmmaker is attracted to certain people and recognises in them qualities that will prove relevant to the larger issues at stake. But whether this is done consciously or unconsciously, a documentary film is 'cast' just as surely as a Hollywood drama.

In what I have said, I have perhaps given the impression that observational filmmakers simply observe events and respond to them with the camera. This may be true of the most rigorous forms of observational cinema. But where there are close relations between a filmmaker and the people being filmed, it is natural for personal interactions to take place. Whether or not these are included in the film depends partly on the filmmaker's overall conception of the film and partly on the conditions of filming. Such interactions often have a way of occurring unexpectedly in a film. A group of people may, without warning, include the filmmaker in a conversation. Conversely, the filmmaker may consciously pursue an interactive mode of filmmaking, including interviews and informal exchanges with the subjects.

It is important to consider the final stages of filmmaking as well – when the editing is almost completed. My practice at this stage has been to show the film first to the main protagonists – either alone, or with friends they have invited to see it with them. This is both a matter of courtesy and a way of finding out if there is anything they find misleading or disturbing in the material. It is also an opportunity to get them used to seeing images of themselves on the screen – what I think of as a process of acclimatisation. If at this time there is potentially embarrassing material in the film, it needs to be discussed. But this does not mean that the filmmaker will necessarily agree to every change the people in the film might request. Very often, after discussion, they become willing for such material to be left in the film if they feel the film was made in good faith and gives an honest account of the events shown.

I followed this general procedure when I was completing the shooting for my films at the school in India. Usually two or more years had passed between the filming and the completion of the film, and the boys shown in them had changed in many ways. As a result, they were able to view them more objectively, even with feelings of nostalgia. For some, the film had become a precious document. One boy wrote to me, saying, 'Who is so lucky [as] to have a film of his school days?' Another said, 'When I look at myself [in the film], I feel like a different person now.'

One incident perhaps demonstrates some of these mixed feelings. After I showed one of the films to its main protagonists, I showed it to the larger group of boys from the same dormitory. As we watched, I saw one of the boys cover his face with his hands. Afterwards, I asked him what had happened. He said, 'Oh, I was so ashamed at how badly I behaved back then. I would never do those things today.' Then he added, 'But you must keep it in the film!'

Note

This chapter was first presented as a keynote address at the conference 'Ethnographic Filmmaking, Ethnic Memory and Cultural Heritage' held at Yunnan University, Kunming, China, on 15–16 December 2018. It was published in a slightly different version in the journal *Visual Anthropology* 33(5) (2020): 452–8, copyright Taylor & Francis, http://www.tandfonline.com, DOI: 10.1080/08949468.2020.1824976.

4

Ethnographic film: evolution of a concept

One often hears the question, 'What is an ethnographic film?' I have an answer to this, but the problem is that there are so many answers. For a field that has become increasingly prominent, with books, university programmes and festivals dedicated to it, one would think there would be some agreement. Instead a kind of cautious ambiguity reigns. Occasionally a scholar will argue for a particular definition or a filmmaker will claim their own practice as the only legitimate one, but, for most, defining ethnographic film hardly seems worth the effort. Karl Heider advised, 'It is probably best not to try to define ethnographic film' (1974:1).[1]

For all that, I think the attempt is worth the effort, if only to trace the confusing history of the term. Part of the confusion arises from the fact that the meaning of 'ethnographic' has been interpreted in several different ways. Generalists understand it in the broad sense of writing (*graphē*) about cultures or peoples (*ethnos*), a practice that goes back to Herodotus. This is how ethnographic film festivals have tended to use the word, applying it to a wide range of films on cultural and social topics, many not made by anthropologists.[2] Anthropologists, on the other hand, often tend to interpret it in the narrower sense of gathering precise scientific data on cultural groups. Here, however, a further complication arises. If an ethnographic film is to be defined strictly as a filmed ethnography, what concept of ethnography is being invoked? Is it the holistic ethnography of structural functionalism, or the ethnography of 'thick description', or the ethnography of psychoanalytic anthropology, or of cultural values or symbolisation? Some might argue that whatever the theoretical orientation of ethnography, the methods of collecting data remain basically the same. But can this really be true for such diverse forms of knowledge? Can the methodology of note-taking in the field, and the creation of texts, apply equally to the methods of filmmaking? Is there only one correct way to shoot and construct an ethnographic film?

Concepts of ethnographic film have largely paralleled the intellectual history of ethnography. Most of the earliest concepts, such as Félix-Louis Regnault's in the 1890s, focused on amassing collections. Regnault envisaged ethnographic film as a visual museum of the world's diverse cultures. That idea was still present in the 1950s with the creation of the *Encyclopaedia Cinematografica* at the Institut für den Wissenschaftlichen Film in Göttingen. The *Encyclopaedia* was conceived as a collection of short scientific films on a wide range of subjects, with examples of people of different cultures engaged in a variety of daily activities. Regnault's primary interest was in body movement (he filmed running, pounding maize, climbing trees, and the techniques of a Wolof potter at the Exposition Ethnographique de l'Afrique Occidentale in 1895), but for others the objective was collecting examples of indigenous technologies, agricultural methods, rituals, facial expressions, postures, gestures and so on. As late as the 1980s Alan Lomax was collecting films of dancers and agricultural labourers in an effort to chart the geographical distribution of movement styles throughout the world.

In parallel with this was the idea of extending the anthropologist's observations and fixing them in concrete form. Previously, anthropologists had relied on written descriptions, drawings and, later, photographs. Motion pictures now provided a means of documenting physical actions, including the techniques of making objects, the performing of religious rituals, and activities such as hunting, fishing and agriculture. The Cambridge Anthropological Expedition to the Torres Strait included a Newman and Guardia Kinematograph in its equipment in 1898. The project was multidisciplinary, combining the measurement of cephalic indices with linguistic research, folk tales, general ethnography and studies in the new field of experimental psychology: to 'gauge the mental and sensory capacities of primitive people' (Haddon 1901: viii). Only a few minutes of film material exist, shot by the expedition leader, Alfred Cort Haddon, or possibly Anthony Wilkin, another expedition member. It shows parts of a dance of the Malo-Bomai ceremony, a demonstration of fire-making and some indigenous dances from Cape York in Australia. Even then, the accuracy of the film documentation was being questioned. In the expedition reports, Alfred C. Haddon and Charles S. Myers noted: 'A cinematograph film was taken of the movements of the *zogo le*.... Strictly speaking, the Malu mask should not have been worn, as it never came to Kiam' (Haddon 1908: 306n1).

One of the primary attractions of film, apart from its potential to show ethnographic observations to others, was that it allowed the researcher to re-examine events after the fact. In advising Walter Baldwin Spencer to use a film camera in his Australian fieldwork, Haddon told him: 'It is an indispensible piece of anthropological apparatus.... I have no doubt your films will pay for the whole apparatus if you care to let some of them be copied by the trade' (Haddon 1900). Spencer took the advice and filmed ritual dances in Central Australia in 1901, later screening these films at Melbourne Town Hall to raise funds for further expeditions. The camera he used, a Warwick, he wrote later, was 'if not actually the first, was amongst the earliest cinematographs to be used in Australia. It was certainly the first used amongst the Aboriginals' (1928: 359).

As ethnography shifted towards the study of interpersonal relations, psychology and cultural values, so did ethnographic films. Margaret Mead and Gregory Bateson's filming in Bali and New Guinea focused on child-rearing practices and how these shaped personality. Their collecting was directed towards creating a set of examples of mother–child and sibling interactions for analysis and demonstration. Ideally, Mead would have liked to have filmed more extended examples, without the camera intruding at all upon the event. This basic idea of using the camera as an objective data-gathering device, unbiased by filming technology and theoretical or aesthetic objectives, has endured to the present day. It endures despite widespread acknowledgement that what and how one films is determined by particular interests, and that there are multiple ways of viewing and conceiving of even the simplest event. In effect, there is no single ethnographic reality that can be captured by visual documentation but, rather, multiple realities as defined by different observers taking different positions.

The ideal of an 'objective' ethnographic film was perhaps most concisely expressed by Walter Goldschmidt in an article in the *Program in Ethnographic Film Newsletter* when he wrote that it should consist of 'shots of people doing precisely what they would have been doing if the camera were not there' (1972: 1). Since then, however, most ethnographic filmmakers have accepted that films necessarily show what people are doing *in the presence* of a camera, and the consequences of this can vary greatly, nor are they always negative. In some situations the camera is welcomed as a witness or may be ignored for considerable periods of time; in others, its presence may stimulate people to reveal significant aspects of their culture.

Encyclopaedic collecting has also had staying power, particularly in the context of comparative and cross-cultural research and since the publication of George P. Murdock's *Outline of World Cultures* and his paper 'World Ethnographic Film Sample' in the 1950s. At about the same time, John and Beatrice Whiting launched the 'Six Cultures Study of Socialization' project. The project built on Margaret Mead's work and on psychoanalytic theory to compare the predictive effects of child-rearing practices in six different societies. But rather than making film records, it relied on extracting data from over 2,000 five-minute observation periods. In 1967 E. Richard Sorenson proposed the creation of an ethnographic film research programme and archive, eventually established at the Smithsonian Institution as the Human Studies Film Archives.[3] Inspired by Murdock's example, one of its aims was to create a world ethnographic film sample.

Optimism about the camera's ability to capture ethnographic data in some comprehensive way underpinned Karl Heider's book *Ethnographic Film*, published in 1976. Visual records equivalent to the anthropologist's observations in the field would provide new opportunities for anthropological analysis. Heider advocated filming 'whole bodies' and 'whole acts' as a means of ensuring the integrity and 'ethnographicness' of the films. 'In order to judge the ethnographicness of a film', he wrote, 'we have the need to know how much and to what degree reality was distorted' (1976: 7). Again, this presupposed the existence of a single objective ethnographic reality accessible to the camera or direct observation. It also presupposed a rather conventional range of questions that anthropologists might want to ask about an event, and that an audio-visual record would be sufficient to answer them. Perhaps Heider had not been altogether joking a decade earlier when he wrote, 'If only we could record everything about everything!' (1967: 464). As for the linguistic properties of film and theories of visual communication, Heider's book has little to say about them.

A not dissimilar view of ethnographic film was offered at about the same time by Jay Ruby, an archaeologist by training, in an article entitled 'Is an Ethnographic Film a Filmic Ethnography?' (1975). Its rhetorical title implied that it should be, but the article left the scope and intent of ethnographic research ill-defined. In its place it offered a methodology guaranteed by correct academic training. Like Mead and Heider, Ruby's ultimate objective (later qualified by him in the light of film theory) was to preserve and transmit a record of ethnographic reality largely independent of the process of observing it. This could be done not by filtering out the distortions introduced by filmmakers, but by subjecting those distortions to inspection and thus disposing of them. It was therefore incumbent on filmmakers to report their methods, biases, special interests and blind spots – a tall order even for the most scrupulously self-aware. By a kind of triangulation the viewer would be able to distinguish the truth from the bias. Only in this way could 'pictorial ethnographies' (2000: 239), as he called them, aspire to the professionalism of social science.

Most of these efforts to pin down ethnographic film assumed that a consensus existed about what constituted anthropological knowledge, based on a set of classic parameters. There was thus little need to pursue such epistemological questions further. But that assumption ignored a swathe of new anthropological interests that had widened the field and were widening it still further. There were ethnographies of sound, ethnographies of aesthetics, ethnographies of performance, ethnographies of the senses – all focused on increasing our understanding of the pervasiveness of cultural systems in human life. In such a context there could be no single methodology that fitted all cases. The cinematic strategies necessary to explore them would vary, and if they did not already exist would have to be invented.

Before the 1970s it was generally assumed that an ethnographic film would be a kind of illustrated lecture, not very different in approach to an ethnographic monograph and stylistically similar to the so-called 'educational' films of the period. Films such as *Mokil* (1950), *The Hadza* (1966) and *Miao Year* (1968) followed this general pattern. Several alternative approaches had begun to appear, however, employing narrative, interactive and more multi-layered structures. John Marshall had tried a narrative structure in *The Hunters* (1958), although he later discarded it in favour of films focusing on discrete episodes of human interaction. In *Kenya Boran* (1974), James Blue and I explored social and economic change in a community through the experiences of four different protagonists. In *Forest of Bliss* (1985) Robert Gardner aimed to convey the complex symbolic structure underlying Hindu mortuary rituals in north India. The film created a network of interrelated scenes, grounding their symbolic meanings in the sensory and material world. Unsurprisingly, some anthropologists found this approach opaque – a 'jumble of incomprehensible vignettes' according to Ruby (1989: 11) and 'not an anthropological document' in another critique (Moore 1988: 3).

The intellectual climate in France was somewhat different, although it is also true that some anthropologists like Jean-Dominique Lajoux took an obsessive interest in recording the ancient rituals, music and technologies of Europe, an approach consistent with the folkloric orientation of much European anthropology. At the same time a strikingly different approach to ethnographic film was flourishing, exemplified in the work of Jean Rouch. In making his 'ethnofictions', Rouch took the position that culture existed as much in people's dreams and aspirations as in observable reality, and *Moi, un Noir* (1960) and *Jaguar* (1968) explored this domain of culture with the creative collaboration of his subjects. While American anthropologists were worrying about the degree of distortion the filmmaker introduced into the ethnographic record, the Belgian anthropologist Luc de Heusch was writing, 'It is pointless … to dream about the fallacious advantages of the invisible camera; we must rather look boldly into the possibilities which the participating camera opens up for sociological description' (1962: 75).

De Heusch, along with French anthropologists at the CNRS (Centre National de la Recherche Scientifique), who included Jean Rouch and Germaine Dieterlen, were already conceiving of ethnographic filmmaking not as a method of producing uncontaminated visual documents but as part of a more ambitious research process. Among those who soon took part in this effort were Marc Henri Piault, Colette Piault, Éliane de Latour, the Swiss ethnomusicologist Hugo Zemp and Jean-Paul Colleyn, another Belgian and former student of de Heusch. By using a camera, these ethnographers sought to enter into a dialogue with the subject, seeking new forms of understanding. In a sense, the ethnographic films produced were by-products of these encounters.

In considering the filmmaker's role, Edgar Morin (Rouch's co-director on *Chronique d'un été*) described the situation this way:

> The truth which the cinema may achieve cannot disregard the observer or the seeker; in other words, it cannot avoid the abstractive operation which the human mind applies to reality in order to understand it. Understanding always involves linking reality to the structures of the human mind and the structures of the human mind to reality. (Morin 1962: 3)

In a striking example, *Akazama* (1985), a film by Marc Henri Piault, the thoughts of the ethnographer are put foremost (in this case, on the soundtrack) in a process that Piault called 'ethnography in the first person' (*auto-ethnologie*). In the film the ethnographer-filmmaker tries to make sense of the enthronement of a West African king, an event that had not taken place for forty years and was thus, in a sense, being reinvented.

One possible reason for the divergence between European and Anglo-American anthropologists, apart from different philosophical traditions, was that for the Europeans ethnography emphasised quite different aspects of culture. To be sure, there was the folkloric tradition, focusing on European peasant customs, which bore some resemblance to material culture studies elsewhere, but there was also great interest in the domain of the human imagination and emotions, as they influenced both ritual events and daily life. While many anglophone anthropologists were preoccupied with the visible, Europeans regarded filmmaking as a newfound means of exploring the invisible dimensions of culture. In an oft-quoted declaration, Morin defined this as 'the most difficult' area of ethnographic research:

> There is the rest, the most difficult, the most moving, the most secret: wherever human feelings are involved, wherever the individual is directly concerned, wherever there are inter-personal relationships of authority, subordination, comradeship, love, hate – in other words, everything connected with the emotive fabric of human existence. There lies the great *terra incognita* of the sociological or ethnological cinema, of cinematic truth. There lies its promised land. (1962: 4)

Morin's conception of ethnographic cinema was partly a response to the new means becoming available in documentary cinema. With the transformations of technology in the 1960s, ethnographic film had entered a new phase. The immediacy created by synchronous sound filming caused filmmakers to rethink what documentary films could be, leading to the development of *cinéma-vérité*, Direct Cinema, *cinéma direct* and like movements. Characteristically, Jean Rouch was at the centre of these developments.

One of the variants was observational cinema, which from the start was specifically associated with ethnographic film (Grimshaw and Ravetz 2009). The appeal of synchronous sound filming to anthropologists was clear. It closely resembled their practice of making observations during fieldwork, and at the same time it fixed those observations as a form of evidence. Like observation, it was selective, but it was also more enduring, giving the viewer a chance to share some aspects of the filmmaker's experience. In its immediacy it showed the anthropologist's relation to the subject, for the film's production methods were no longer concealed from the viewer. But it conveyed the anthropologist's observations without explicitly conveying the thought processes underlying them. These had to be inferred from the manipulation of the camera, the film's structure, its choices of material or by some complementary means, such as a text.

Observational cinema was often taken to be the ideal model for ethnographic filmmaking because it combined ethnographic enquiry with recognition of the observer's position at the time of filming. This immediacy was felt to guarantee a degree of authenticity. In 1975 Colin Young expressed the objective in this way: 'to record actuality in a form which, when replayed, allows a viewer elsewhere to have a sense of experiencing the event' (1975: 70). The approach was soon adopted by university ethnographic film programmes.[4] Paul Henley, the founding director of the Granada Centre for Visual Anthropology at the University of Manchester, while acknowledging that observational cinema had a number of other uses, wrote that it was the most suitable filmmaking style for ethnographic films. Simulating the perspective of the traditional anthropologist, it gave viewers an opportunity to examine ethnographic evidence for themselves and experience the personal engagement involved in fieldwork. 'Observational cinema', he wrote, 'has much in common with the ethnographic method of participant observation that is conventionally one of the defining features of anthropological research' (Henley 2004: 110). Later, in his book *Beyond Observation*, he was to describe it as 'an invitation to the audience to consider the film-maker's own experience of the life of the subjects as a sort of open channel through which they too could have an experience of that life' (2020: 299–300).

The other attraction of observational cinema was its narrative potential. In contrast to the didactic approach of the illustrated lecture film, it allowed a film to follow a chain of events, preserving the unities of time and space, both within shots and in the chronological arrangement of the film as a whole. This seemed to promise greater opportunities for conveying the experiences of the people being filmed as well as those of the fieldworker.

Narrative, however, can also be regarded in different sense, as a way that a filmmaker organises the materials of a film to provide a pathway through them for the viewer. Thus there can be narratives of ideas, just as there are narratives of events. Here the filmmaker creates a progression, the logic of which is not temporal but thematic or analytical. In making *Doon School Chronicles* (2000), for example, I found no single character or chain of events on which to base the film. Although there is some degree of progression over a school year, the guiding structure of the film is a series of thematic chapters that focus on different aspects of school life and the experiences and attitudes of several students. By the end of the film the viewer has traversed a certain terrain, but one of accumulating cultural connections rather than events in time and space.

As Henley noted, the challenge for anthropological filmmakers working within the observational tradition 'is to develop editorial strategies that will enable them to provide an appropriate interpretive context for the worlds they represent whilst at the same time ensuring that these do not fatally undermine the distinctive contribution that observational cinema can make' (2004: 120). By this, I take him to mean that observational cinema does not automatically produce a methodologically 'pure' form of visual ethnography, nor depth of understanding. While observational films should follow the principle of showing events from the perspective of an actual observer, they could at the same time arrange and juxtapose scenes in more complex ways.

Despite this, there were those who believed that this amounted to tampering with the evidence – or, as Toni de Bromhead put it as recently as 2019, 'fictionalising' it. This echoes Mead's remark made over forty years ago that it introduces 'a variation into it that is unnecessary' (Bateson and Mead 1977: 78). In her book *Muddied Waters: The Fictionalisation of Ethnographic Film*, de Bromhead examines ten films, noting particularly the extent to which they depart from the chronology in which they were shot. In her view, 'material should not be moved out of its original order to serve some concept or narrative' (2019: 22). Instead, it should follow an 'exploratory camera style [that] allows viewers to travel alongside the film-maker in the journey that is the film' (18).

This is all very well, and it is a style of filmmaking with which I have much sympathy and have sometimes followed myself.[5] But the problem is that it seems locked into the flow of an individual's real-time observations, a kind of anthropological investigative journalism. It elevates that style above all others as a guarantor of truth. I would argue that observational cinema has greater potential than this, and in developing its other possibilities has more to offer anthropology.

A narrative approach, in the chronological sense, serves ethnography particularly well when a sequence of events is being followed, such as the steps in a ritual, but it is less useful when thematic, comparative or qualitative enquiries are being undertaken. In de Bromhead's formulation, narrative tends to limit the practice of visual ethnography to a form of reportage linked solely to the field experience of the filmmaker. In considering the films I have been involved with, maintaining a chronological narrative was appropriate to a film like *The Wedding Camels* (1977), which focused on the preparations leading up to a marriage, but it would have made no sense in the companion film *Lorang's Way* (1979), which examined personal agency, character and the life trajectories of individuals in Turkana society. Nor was it appropriate to an earlier film, *To Live with Herds* (1972), about the predicament of Jie herders in the face of government policies. It would be hard to argue that these last two films are any less ethnographic than the first because they are less chronological. If ethnographic cinema consisted only of narrative investigations, it would exclude many valuable ethnographic films of recent years. I am reminded of

Colin Young's dictum: 'Representatives of one approach are racist about all others. This is obviously a waste of time. If different languages are being used, we just have to learn their rules to avoid confusion' (1975: 79).

Among the early reservations voiced about observational cinema – including my own – was its tendency to avoid showing the direct interactions of the filmmaker with the people filmed. From an anthropological standpoint, this seemed to leave out one of the most important components of fieldwork, which included conversations, interviews and other direct forms of enquiry. Many of these films seemed to be simply looking and listening. This did not occur so much in *cinéma-vérité*, which made a point of the filmmaker provoking the subject, but in Direct Cinema and its variants it suggested a detached and objectifying stance on the part of the filmmaker. It was, however, a characterisation that missed the point. It assumed that observational films could be made in the absence of a personal relationship between the filmmaker and the people filmed. The misconception was spread further by critics who had never themselves experienced the realities of filmmaking. It also misconstrued the act of observation itself, which far from signifying distance and indifference more often reflected a deep respect for what was being observed. Colin Young, in his earliest formulation of observational cinema, had made the point quite clearly, that it should 'be based on an intimate, sympathetic relationship between the filmmaker and the subject – not the eye of the aloof, detached observer' (1975: 76).

Feeling the brunt of this criticism, and despite the reciprocity already implicit in observational cinema, some filmmakers began self-consciously filling the perceived gap with reflexive gestures. These included glimpses of the filmmakers and their equipment and the use of direct interviews, already a mainstay of television journalism. But the convenience of interviews, particularly as a way of conveying information efficiently, all too quickly became a trap and a lazy option for filmmakers. Scenes that revealed important information but were difficult to film could simply be replaced with interview material. When interviews began to dominate observational films, it seemed almost like a step backwards to the verbal domination of voice-over commentary. The effect was to narrow the range and ambitions of ethnographic cinema. Granada Television's series *Disappearing World*, for example, developed a formula that became increasingly dependent on interviews, partly because television crews had very limited time in the field. When independent ethnographic filmmakers began imitating this, it introduced a certain vacuity into the genre.

Many found the resulting films flat and anthropologically superficial. Jay Ruby said he wanted to see no more of them, having seen the 'same old tired conventions' repeated endlessly at ethnographic film festivals.[6] The challenge for others was how to construct films that were more analytical and multifaceted without abandoning the principles that had drawn them to observational cinema in the first place. To the extent that films were simply informational and descriptive, they could not go much farther intellectually. One response, without trying to distil ethnographic filmmaking into some ideal form, was to explore structures that might serve as models for the future. If observational films could be structured in more complex ways, they might fulfil their long-awaited promise of making original contributions to anthropological knowledge.

It is significant that two of the most prominent supporters of observational cinema, Paul Henley and Anna Grimshaw, creators of the first visual anthropology programme at the University of Manchester, insisted on the need for it to evolve new forms. According to Henley it was essential that observational filmmakers be 'imaginative in renewing observational cinema by adapting its principles to meet both present and future needs' (2004: 125). Grimshaw went further, asking: 'How might observational work challenge established ways of conceptualizing the anthropological project?' (Grimshaw and Ravetz 2009: 130).

One of the strengths of film is its ability to show the co-presence of objects and actions within the same scene and even the same frame. They may be connected in some way or there may be no obvious connection between them. When there are connections, these may be visible (such as a cause and its effects) or more broadly cultural, such as the relation between a person's clothing and their occupation – for example, a chef's white uniform and cooking. One of the problems for observational filmmaking, however, is how to represent connections that are not co-present in such obvious ways but are still significant. This is perhaps the price film pays for being a linear medium. A filmmaker may aim to present several overlapping cultural patterns and show how they connect vertically, as it were, but this is difficult in a structure that is essentially horizontal and temporal. It may demand a strategy that expresses the links between several different registers of meaning. These might be links between objects and their attributes (such as colour) or merely the ideas and associations attached to them. Certain clothing, for example, may be connected to a particular activity (such as a sport or religious ceremony), but colour and clothing may also be connected to the wearer's status or affiliation within another quite separate cultural system, such as class or nationality.

This is a comparatively simple example, but in social life there are much more complex cultural overlappings and homologies. The picture is further complicated when emotion, personal agency and specialised knowledge are taken into account. A film about an individual's social experience may therefore require locating them within a cultural web that connects widely divergent elements – social rules, technology, beliefs, symbols and aesthetics. In order to establish these interconnections the filmmaker may have to combine several different approaches – narrative, thematic and sensory – and their interconnections may have to be implied rather than stated explicitly.

As the analytical frameworks of anthropology have expanded, it is reasonable for filmmaking practices to follow them. But to do so they must go beyond the basic modes of data collection. Observational cinema has made this possible in many ways, not least by situating the anthropologist-filmmaker more centrally in the ethnographic process. Yet the difficulties of exploring different forms of anthropological knowledge have increased. It could be said that although the technology has remained relatively static since the advent of portable synchronous sound in the 1960s (and digital video in the 1990s), the intellectual demands of ethnographic filmmaking have not. In response, observational cinema, along with other research methods, has had to evolve.

In many cases this has meant simply extending and reconfiguring elements already present in observational cinema. For example, communicating the immediacy of social situations (what Richard Leacock called 'the feeling of being there') has accompanied an increased anthropological interest in subjective experience. Dealing with it has been aided partly by the use of long takes and partly by exploiting observational cinema's evocative and 'haptic' qualities. One can see these developments emerging in such films as Ilisa Barbash and Lucien Castaing-Taylor's *Sweetgrass* (2009) and J. P. Sniadecki's two films *Demolition* (2008) and *The Yellow Bank* (2010). A similar interest is evident in Sergei Dvortsevoy's *Bread Day* (1998), Stéphane Breton's *La Montée au ciel* (2009) and Florian Geyer's *Sulfur* (2005). At the extreme, filmmakers have employed just one or two long takes to convey the immediacy of an event, as in Jean Rouch's *Tourou et Bitti* (1971).

In these works the temporal and sensory possibilities of film have been extended, but it is possible to identify at least five areas altogether in which such extensions can take place: in the *temporal* and *sensory* realms, as described above, in the uses of *narrative*, in a film's *thematic* elements, and in combinations of these in *multidimensional* structures. Inevitably there will be some overlap among these categories and some ambiguities within them. Sensory experience, for example, seems to be broader than is accounted for by the five traditional senses of sight, hearing, smell, taste and touch. It would be hard to say whether the sensation of spaciousness is enhanced more by movement through a space or by a sound such as an echo, or even whether movement through a space is more a narrative or a sensory experience.

In ethnographic films the sense of following a narrative of events has long played an important role in conveying the relationship of individuals to their environment and to other people, from *Nanook of the North* (1922) to *Grass* (1925) to *The Hunters* (1958). Some films have followed the lives of individuals for years, others their daily routines over shorter periods. Narrative has been the main driver of many of Jean Rouch's African films, from *Jaguar* (1968) to *Cocorico! Monsieur Poulet* (1974) to *Madame l'eau* (1992). Each of these films follows the course of a journey. Gary Kildea's *Celso and Cora* (1983) is a narrative of a poor family's life in the Philippines over several months, but the focus is more on the intimate details of their day-to-day survival.

Some film projects cover much more extended periods of time, such as Ilkka Ruuhijärvi and Ulla Turunen's films shot year by year from 1985 to 1991 about a group of Finnish school children, or the film *Être et avoir* (2002), which covers an entire school year. The format of the television drama series was successfully adapted to nonfiction in the twelve-part television series *An American Family* (1973) and the British documentary series *The Family* (1974), directly inspired by it. Probably the best-known longitudinal television project has been Michael Apted's *Seven Up* series, which returned to the same group of individuals every seven years, following the *World in Action* programme in which they first appeared in 1964. Although none of these series involved an anthropologist, they suggested a possible model for ethnographic filmmaking, given enough time in the field. The project that probably came closest was Melissa Llewelyn-Davies' five-part series for the BBC *Diary of a Maasai Village* (1984).

One advantage of a narrative approach, which has a parallel in ethnographic oral histories (e.g. Oscar Lewis's *Children of Sanchez*, 1961, and Marjorie Shostak's *Nisa*, 1981), is that it allows ethnographic filmmakers to show how individuals respond to major disruptions in their social lives. One of the clearest examples of this is John Marshall and Adrienne Miesmer's film *N!ai, The Story of a !Kung Woman* (1980), which traces N!ai's life from childhood in a self-sufficient hunter-gatherer community to adult life in a squalid 'relocation' camp.

Taking a *thematic* approach to observational filmmaking may mean largely dispensing with narrative as a chronological sequence of events. Such films can centre around anything from a physical object, a concept or a specific cultural practice. The filming may be narrowly focused, comparative or accumulative. A typical accumulative approach can be seen in Frederick Wiseman's films about public institutions. Wiseman's dominant theme has long been the fate of individuals at the hands of administrators, prison guards, the police, hospital workers, teachers, judges and others in similar positions. Instead of following a single narrative, his films tend to present multiple examples of people's experiences in the institutions he studies, much as a lawyer (which he also is) might present forensic evidence.

Such films work by juxtaposing substantial bodies of observational material, viewing them comparatively while at the same time revealing their interconnections. This allows observational films to harness the intellectual potential of cinematic montage while preserving the immediacy and continuity of individual scenes. By re-arranging large blocks of material in this way the filmmaker can explore a wide range of cultural links and associations. The adjacent segments reflect on each other and resonate with material located elsewhere in the film. By forsaking a purely linear structure, filmmakers are also able to focus the viewer's attention on the meanings generated by the placement of the scenes. Even if the film retains some narrative elements, its ability to create such compound structures makes this a particularly versatile form.

One approach to the thematically based film is to focus on a physical object and its social context, as expressed in Arjun Appadurai's phrase the 'social life of things' (1988). Valerie Hansch's *Sifinja: The Iron Bride* (2009) is one such film, showing how a whole industry has grown up in Sudan around transforming English Bedford trucks into tougher, more desert-worthy vehicles. Judith MacDougall's *Diya* (2001) centres on the production of terra cotta lamps in India, showing them being made in a family household, sold in the market, used in Diwali ceremonies and then finally thrown away. In a slightly different vein, our film *Photo Wallahs* (1991) focuses on the meanings and practices of photography in an Indian hill town, examining how photographs function both as idealisation and evidence in family life, public administration, tourism and arranged marriages.

Another version of the thematically based film is organised around an idea or custom rather than a physical object. Agnès Varda's *The Gleaners and I* (2000) follows her quest to find out what has become of the ancient practice of salvaging the remains of harvested crops. Varda's research into this adds a narrative element to the film's thematic focus. Adela Peeva goes on a similar quest in her film *Whose Is This Song?* (2003), tracing the many fraught claims to ownership of a song widespread in the Balkan nations. These examples are also typical of films that create a *multidimensional* or hybrid structure. The film that perhaps most obviously inaugurated such a mix of different approaches was *Chronique d'un été* (1961), which begins like a fiction film, includes a pastiche of *vox popoli* journalism, proceeds through several studies of individual lives, takes a journey to the south of France and ends up with a meditation on the future of documentary cinema.

Few ethnographic films have undertaken to create such complex amalgamations, although Gardner's often-derided *Forest of Bliss* (1985), with its combination of thematic, narrative and sensory elements, attempts to do so. Several films from the Sensory Ethnography Lab at Harvard University mix temporal/spatial, sensory and narrative approaches, including J. P. Sniadecki's *The Iron Ministry* (2014), about journeys on Chinese railways. In *Doon School Chronicles* (2000) my aim was to explore relationships between the school's ideology, customs and material culture and their combined effect on the experience of the students. Dealing with so many interdependent factors required a multidimensional structure of different themes and narratives.

Most of the films discussed above have been indebted to a maverick documentary film tradition that approaches its subjects in oblique and multifaceted ways. These films stand in sharp contrast to the majority of documentary films that value a simple declaratory style over complexity or allusiveness. One of the more 'ethnographic' of these idiosyncratic films is *Los Refrigeradores* (2012), which focuses on the household refrigerator in Cuba. By taking this single ordinary object as its subject, the film is able to range widely through Cuba's culture and recent history, including a quest to find the last kerosene-burning refrigerator in the country, and concluding with an indigenous religious ceremony. A similar mixture of disparate materials characterises Andrey Paounov's *The Mosquito Problem and Other Stories* (2007), a film that explores the possible links between pig hunting, mosquito eradication, construction of a nuclear power plant and a former Communist concentration camp in Belene, Bulgaria. The film approaches these themes through symbolism, narrative and pure visual pleasure.

One of the earliest examples of such a mixed genre was Dušan Makavejev's *Innocence Unprotected* (1968). Playful in spirit yet linked to the horrors of war, it investigated the social and historical context of making the first Serbian 'talkie', using the testimonies of the film's producers, wartime archival footage and re-enactments by the film's star, a circus acrobat-strongman. In a film that recalls Makavejev's hybrid approach, *The Act of Killing* (2012) employs re-enactments by the protagonists in a history of the political massacres of the Suharto era in Indonesia.

Irony pervades many of these films, in which the 'stories' emerge only gradually. *Theremin: An Electronic Odyssey* (1993) focuses on one of the first electronic musical instruments and its inventor, Leon Theremin. In 1938 he was kidnapped from his home in New York, probably by NKVD agents, and made to work on secret electronic devices in the Soviet Union. The film combines performances on his musical instrument, archival materials, accounts by his associates and finally an interview with Theremin himself, when it is discovered that he is still alive in Moscow, aged in his late nineties.

As can be seen from these examples, ethnographic filmmaking cannot easily be detached from its embeddedness in documentary cinema as a whole. Nor is it simply a recording technology to be employed for scholarly purposes, following a fixed set of rules. It may of course be used for that purpose when specific kinds of knowledge are being sought, but such films will say little about the surrounding social context. Ethnography increasingly requires a more sophisticated and analytical approach. Any quest to find a single anthropologically correct way of portraying the complexities of social and cultural life seems bound for failure. As H. L. Mencken reminded us, such solutions are likely to be neat, plausible and wrong.

Notes

1 Cited by Ruby (2000: 26).

2 Paul Henley opts for this approach when discussing early French filmmaking in Africa, taking ethnographic film to mean 'any nonfiction film that is concerned with customary sociocultural practices' (2020b: 32).

3 See Sorenson (1967).
4 These included those at the University of California at Los Angeles, the Granada Centre for Visual Anthropology at the University of Manchester, the University of Tromsø, the University of Sao Paulo, and others.
5 This is the style I employed in *Link-Up Diary* (1987), in which I followed three members of the Link-Up organisation as they attempted to reunite Indigenous Australians with their families, often after decades of forced separation by government policies. My aim was to provide an exact chronological account of my experience of one week's work, with no advance knowledge of what would happen.
6 In an entry titled 'Observational Dull' on the VISCOM email discussion site, 16 July 2008. VISCOM is an internet listserv created in 1994 by the Graduate Association of Visual Anthropologists at Temple University, Philadelphia. See https://listserv.temple.edu/cgi-bin/wa?A1=ind0807C&L=VISCOM (last accessed May 2022).

Part II

5

Structuring nonfiction films

It is an oft-told tale that Robert Flaherty, in the years before he made *Nanook of the North*, shot another film in the Canadian Arctic. When he was editing it the nitrate film caught fire from a smouldering cigarette and the whole of it was destroyed. There is a theory that Flaherty intentionally started the fire, for, as he said later, when he came to complete the film he was dismayed to find it was 'simply a scene of this and a scene of that, no relation, no thread of a story or continuity whatever' (Flaherty 1950: 12). If his problem was how to edit it, this was surely a drastic way to solve the problem.

Filmmakers are often faced with a mountain of material, and the question of what to do with it may seem insurmountable. Usually, unlike Flaherty at his first attempt, they have thought about it long and hard during the filming. But faced with the amount of film that has accumulated, the prospect may still be daunting. Film genres have become more settled since Flaherty's time. Many fiction films are prefabricated in the script to fit a particular model. In documentary films, however, the situation is more complicated. Often the contents emerge only in the shooting, and documentaries can be constructed in many ways, not necessarily observing a fixed chronology. Some rely on narratives or argumentation, others on character, theme or archival sources. Documentary films are also difficult to categorise. Critics tend to think of them in varied ways, depending on whether the critic is more interested in theory or subject matter, or whether they tend to see the filmmaker's position more in relation to the audience or to the subject. Some divide documentary into didactic, narrative, discursive and poetic categories, while others such as Bill Nichols (e.g. Nichols 1991) favour the expository, the observational, the interactive, the reflexive and so on.

Much in how one views a film depends on whether one looks upon it as a fixed, self-contained work or the outcome of a process. In the latter case, questions are likely to arise. Did the filmmaker begin with a clear structure in mind, or did the structure develop while engaging with the subject, or later, in the editing? Did it follow a structure found in the subject or in an idea preceding it? Films that follow a chain of events tend towards a narrative structure, but if more concerned with ideas, towards an essay style. If a film is about impressions and feelings, it may result in something poetic and associative. Yet these tendencies are by no means absolute. Many films turn out to be hybrids in which a variety of approaches are used.

From didactic to observational

Many of us in the 1950s were subjected to what were called educational films. They were perhaps merely the more banal examples of the broader category of informational documentaries. They were typically constructed as lessons for the viewer, based on a spoken commentary about the subject and illustrated with images shot expressly for the film or gathered elsewhere. They tended to be dominated by the speaker's voice, reading from a written text. The source of the text and identity of the speaker generally remained unspecified, implying that the film was a definitive presentation of the facts. Most films of the British documentary movement in the 1930s conformed to this model, although some departed from it by including enacted scenes or varying the commentary in some way, such as including passages in verse. Most employed a musical score.

What is clear about these films is that they left little space for the viewer. They were institutional statements, carefully crafted from behind the scenes and presented with an air of professionalism that discouraged criticism. Although a few used visual images daringly, the images were not primarily what advanced the film, but rather its verbal argument. The images were not intended to show anything specific, but examples of the types of events the film was concerned with. These films therefore gave an abstract impression of reality, filtered through the sensibilities of the filmmaker and put together as a kind of collage. As the images were supposed to be representative, they tended to be interchangeable and were often drawn from previous films, as in such famous films as *The River* (1938) and *Listen to Britain* (1942). An image of a farmer in one film could just as easily stand for a farmer in another (figure 5.1).

The didactic film has had many reincarnations, most obviously on television. Television was only a short step away from radio, which was necessarily text-based, and it was a medium in which, at the beginning, the image quality was poor but the sound every bit as good as radio. Television had at its command an almost inexhaustible supply of visual material, and it made great headway in the post-war era when vast amounts of military footage became available. One of the most successful series was *Victory at Sea* (1952–53), which ran to twenty-six episodes, all composed of wartime footage.

Many of us who began making films in the 1960s were intent on producing films of a new kind, but we were just as determined not to make films of the old kind. We rejected the authoritarianism of didactic films, which told the audience exactly what to think about a subject. Accordingly, part of structuring these films meant either avoiding voice-over commentary altogether or at least substituting for it a specific, identifiable voice. The motive force was now

5.1 A farmer at work in *Fenlands*

to be based on the images and accompanying sound, not on a spoken text. All this was made possible, and indeed propelled, by the availability of newly developed filming equipment, which allowed filmmakers to record an event with synchronous sound as it happened. In using this advanced equipment, however, filmmakers had to confront the question of how to structure the new kind of material it produced.

One possibility was to construct documentary films like fiction films – although as a model the fiction film also had its drawbacks. Like the voice of the traditional documentary, the eye of the fiction filmmaker remained anonymous. It could vary its style, but in most cases its view was omniscient, free to range anywhere it chose within a scene. It rarely took the position of an actual observer who might be constrained by the realities of time and place. Furthermore, in the *découpage classique* of most American and European films, scenes tended to be chopped up into shots taken from several different camera angles. These constructions were therefore not unlike the sequences in didactic documentaries, although put together to convey a feeling of narrative continuity. In the hands of a director such as Hitchcock they could produce bravura sequences of a hundred shots, no one shot like any other, but this required days of shooting using different camera setups. There was no way that narratives of real events could be filmed in such a style.

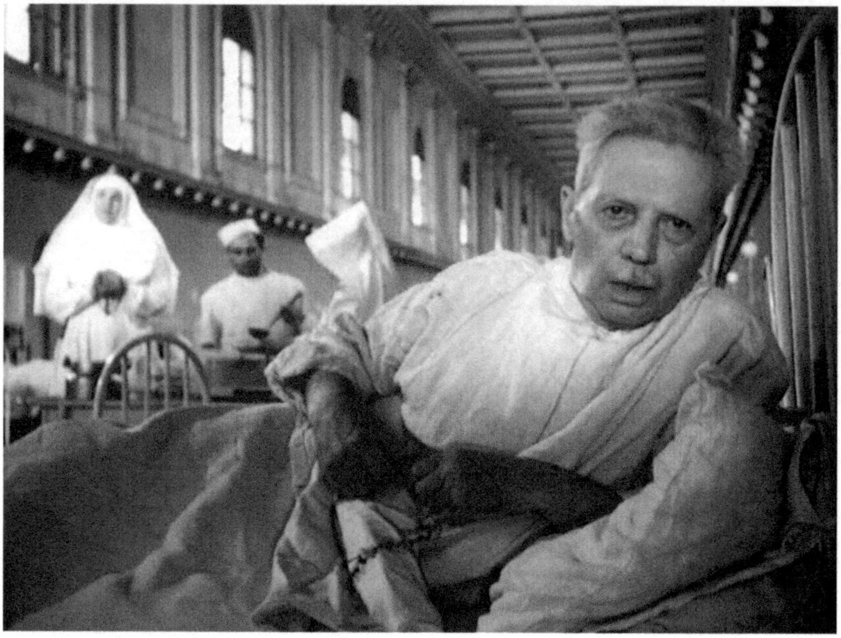

5.2 The hospital scene in *Umberto D.*

Many of us, as new documentary filmmakers, were determined to avoid the shooting and editing styles of fiction films as well as the didactic style of the traditional documentary. At the same time we were drawn to the narrative potential of fiction films. The inspiration came from the work of the Italian Neorealist directors, who used non-professional actors and real locations to tell stories about the lives of ordinary people (figure 5.2). With the new equipment, we felt it might be possible to apply the same narrative approach to nonfiction. Perhaps documentary films, instead of reporting on general topics, could follow the lives of real individuals, showing what life was like for them. In addition, these films could be made anywhere in the world.

The uses of narrative

Fictional dramas allow audiences to identify with characters as they deal with the needs and conflicts in their lives. In the process these films also frequently reveal the larger forces in society that affect them. Some documentary filmmakers reasoned that the same principles should be used to portray the experiences of living people. Robert Flaherty's films suggested what might be possible. From *Nanook of the North* (1922) to *Moana* (1926) and *Louisiana*

Story (1948) he created narratives around individuals, based on events he had observed in their lives. In the post-war period documentary filmmakers made further attempts, influenced partly by the films of Italian Neorealism, partly by a need to return to the values of ordinary life which had been upset by the war. One of these, which represents a kind of transitional moment between fiction and nonfiction, was Georges Rouquier's *Farrebique* (1946), a film that followed events in the life of a French farming family throughout the four seasons. After the recent traumas of the war and occupation, the film was decidedly nostalgic and conservative, looking backward to memories of the pre-war period. Although some of the events in the film were invented, such as the love story, most were true to the family's daily experiences on the farm and in the nearby village (figure 5.3). Its filming of bread-making was as thorough and detailed as any aficionado of material culture could wish.

By the 1960s the advent of more portable equipment gave further impetus to the idea of narrative documentaries. *Salesman* (1969), by the Maysles brothers and Charlotte Zwerin, was one of the first feature-length examples, showing the increasing disillusionment of Paul, a door-to-door Bible salesman. Other prominent narrative documentaries of the period were D. A. Pennebaker's *Don't Look Back* (1967), which followed Bob Dylan's 1965 concert tour in Britain, and Allan King's *Warrendale* (1967), structured around events that occurred in a home for emotionally disturbed children in Canada.

5.3 Men gather after church in *Farrebique*

A somewhat different approach was adopted in the films of Frederick Wiseman. Although his films were shot and edited like many other documentaries of the period, avoiding the filming and editing styles of fiction films, their narratives were more about institutions than individuals. Wiseman's interest was in how these institutions served their clients and inmates. Thus in his first film, *Titicut Follies* (1967), and in subsequent films such as *Law and Order* (1969) and *Hospital* (1970), there is no single protagonist or group of protagonists who are followed throughout the film. Instead Wiseman adopts a theme-and-variations structure in which he strings together a series of separate interactions between the employees of the institutions and those they are supposed to serve.

At this time most documentary filmmakers remained focused on their own societies, but some began to wonder why similar films could not be made elsewhere. Most ethnographic and anthropological films of the period were still produced in the didactic style, with a narrator explaining the life of another people, illustrated with shots of typical activities. If individuals were identified at all, they tended to be used to exemplify specific social roles. The films had titles that either spoke for an entire cultural group, such as *The Land Dayaks of Borneo* (1966), or recorded rituals specific to it, such as *The Honey Ant Ceremonies of Ljaba* (1956) or presented important members of it, such as *Haida Carver* (1964).

There were of course many good reasons why ethnographic films had been made in this way. They were often based on silent footage that an anthropologist had shot in the field, which was then turned into a film with an explanatory commentary. Furthermore, unfamiliar cultural practices would not necessarily be understood by an audience just by showing them on film, and they required an anthropological exegesis. There were also financial constraints. The equipment capable of producing synchronous sound was often considered too expensive or complex for ethnographic filmmaking. It was also believed by some that making purely visual records should be the first priority, as in the case of Ian Dunlop's *People of the Australian Western Desert* series (1966–70).

Direct Cinema and *cinéma-vérité* inspired a number of filmmakers to apply the same methods to ethnographic films. John Marshall, even before having access to synchronous sound equipment, began filming as though he did, roughly synchronising the sound he had recorded in the field, as in *An Argument about a Marriage* (filmed in 1958, released 1969). In a project filmed between 1962 and 1965, Asen Balikci applied Direct Cinema techniques to his series on a Netsilik Inuit community in Canada (*Netsilik Eskimos*, 1963–68), while from the mid-1960s Jean Rouch began shooting sequences with synchronous sound in a lengthy series of films about the ceremonial life of the Dogon of Mali, though he continued to overlay this with his own spoken commentaries in French. In 1968, however, Rouch made a film among a group of Songhay hunters in Niger, *Un Lion nommé l'Américain*, which was based entirely on synchronous dialogue without any voice-over commentary.

This film posed a problem that other ethnographic filmmakers of the time were also struggling with. If you recorded people speaking a foreign language with synchronous sound, how could they be understood? The answer to this question seemed obvious, but it took some time to be implemented. Fiction films from foreign countries had long used subtitles. Why not translate the speech of people in ethnographic films in the same way? Some filmmakers, including Rouch, rejected subtitles because they felt that they distracted from the image. For this reason, he refused to use them in *Un Lion nommé l'Américain*, but the result is that extended passages are incomprehensible to anyone who is not a speaker of Songhay.

Yet filming with synchronous sound clearly demanded subtitling, for it brought viewers into intimate contact with speaking, thinking individuals. In retrospect, the time lag in using subtitles in ethnographic films seems in many ways inexplicable. Although the first English-language ethnographic films to be released with subtitles are generally said to be those of John Marshall, it wasn't until the late 1970s that the practice began to be more widely adopted, and not until the 1980s that it became a matter of routine.

Structuring an ethnographic film

It was in this climate of cinematic change that Judith MacDougall and I began filming *To Live with Herds* among the Jie people of Uganda in 1968. We had come to Uganda as student members of a team from the University of California at Los Angeles to make a film on the initiation rituals of the Bagisu people, for which I was the principal cinematographer. Following this, we were allowed to keep the filming equipment for a few more months and had an opportunity to make several films on our own. We were particularly interested in pastoralist societies and travelled to the north-eastern part of Uganda, where we made *To Live with Herds* and two shorter films among the pastoral Jie. At this time we were still graduate students at the University of California and the film was intended to be my thesis film.[1]

We understood that using the new synchronous sound equipment might bring an audience into more intimate contact with individuals in Jie society, but it also required finding an appropriate camera style and learning how to structure such a film. As well as focusing on individuals, *To Live with Herds* ended up addressing larger questions of social and economic change, specifically the conflict between the development policies of the Uganda government, which were based heavily on agriculture, and the traditions of the Jie, who had strong economic, cultural and emotional ties to cattle herding.

The filming methods and final form of the film emerged only gradually. During the filming Judith operated a Nagra tape recorder and I an Éclair

NPR camera. We were linked together by a synchronisation cable. We usually looked for a single strategic position when filming an event or when filming in a Jie family compound. Occasionally, however, we adopted a second camera position. This was theoretically to provide greater flexibility in the editing. It was an approach based on long-established editing principles, but it proved to be misguided. It ignored the fact that filming a scene from two viewpoints would contradict our basic aim, which was to put the audience in a position very much like our own, witnessing events as they occurred. There was a basic inconsistency in the idea of intercutting material from two camera positions, a throwback to an older editing style more appropriate to a fiction film. When I came to edit the material months later, I realised that a real observer couldn't convincingly be in two places at once, so most of the footage from the second camera position had to be left out.

The overall structure of the film developed both during the filming and in the editing. For the Jie it was a time of drought and hunger. For most of the filming we remained in the area of the permanent Jie homesteads. There, people were suffering the hardships of being separated from their cattle, which had been taken to better grazing areas in the west. Towards the end we travelled to these cattle camps, thus creating a narrative line in the film. A second line was provided by the attempts of government officials to collect taxes, introduce farming, and induce the Jie to sell more cattle and send their children to school. All these practices were foreign to the Jie, since they relied on their herds, which had to be moved often, and they needed the help of children to look after them. In the film we observed how the official policies were being applied and how the Jie responded to them. Ending the film with scenes at a cattle camp signalled a temporary relief from these pressures. It also provided some measure of resolution for the film, but only in a very attenuated form. It was clear that interest in the Jie people's lives would have to take the place of a more dramatic narrative (figure 5.4).

During the editing I added several formal devices to give the film further shape. I divided the film into five chapters, setting out basic information in a few titles at the beginning of each chapter. The idea of using chapters was partly inspired by Basil Wright's film *The Song of Ceylon* of 1934. In that film the chapter titles had indicative meanings, and my use of titles signalled that the film would have a similar, essay-like character. Using titles also underlined the fragmentary nature of the film, as a personal and limited exploration of its subject, and far from definitive. The blocks of titles also had one further effect. They made the intervening scenes stand out more starkly as pieces of evidence presented, much as the black outlines surrounding the panes of a stained-glass window make them stand out more vividly. Although spoken commentary was anathema to us then, I finally added a few lines of personal commentary to each section as my own spoken observations, like entries from a diary or notebook, which in fact a number of them were.

5.4 Leaving for the cattle camp in *To Live with Herds*

I have gone into some detail about this film to make clear that constructing a film often means trying out one thing and then another before a final form is found. In this case the process also required finding ways of framing material that could otherwise have a number of possible meanings. Several additional things deserve pointing out. One is that filmmakers need not be tyrannised by the imperatives of dramatic structure, for it is possible to engage an audience in other ways. Much of a film's motive power can be created by the principle of answering questions that the film itself has raised. Formal devices, too, can help guide the viewer when the actual 'story' is quite limited.

Varying the structure

A process not unlike the structuring of *To Live with Herds* came into play in *Doon School Chronicles* (2000), the first in a series of five films I made about a famous boys' boarding school in India (see also Chapters 6 and 11). The series was the first phase of what eventually became a much longer project studying institutions for children in India. With *Doon School Chronicles*, however, I made many decisions at an earlier stage than with *To Live with Herds*, for by now I had more filmmaking experience. The film, as I envisaged it, would have no strong narrative line but would instead explore the culture of the school and some of the experiences of students growing up in it. I wanted the film to include general aspects of school life but also show the lives of several individuals. As with *To Live with Herds*, I decided to divide the film into chapters. These would be accompanied by quotations from the school's documents, each announcing a different theme. I was attracted to the idea of putting 'chronicles' in the film's title to forewarn the audience not to expect a single story but rather a series of smaller incidents. To make this even clearer, I gave the film the secondary title *A Study in Ten Parts* to suggest that it would be a kind of cinematic enquiry.

For protagonists, I eventually settled on four fourteen-year-old students who shared a dormitory room together, and then two others, one older at sixteen and one younger at twelve. It seemed to me that a key strategy in maintaining the momentum of the film would be to avoid introducing all the protagonists at once. I would bring them into the film at successive stages, so that each would start the film off in a new direction. This would also emphasise their different personalities and their different attitudes to being at the school.

Character, seen as a structuring principle, can play a part in documentary films different from its role in conventional narratives. It is not necessarily what happens to a person or the changes to a person's character that matter (for it may remain quite static) but the gradual revelation to the audience of what sort of a person they are, and what they represent. If interest in a film's protagonists does not already exist (and there is no reason to suppose it should) the film must create it. One method is to explore their interactions and relationships with others. Another is to show how others regard them. This has long been a technique in writing plays, where minor characters set the stage before the main characters appear.

This was a strategy we had already followed in an earlier film, *Lorang's Way* (1979), a portrait of a traditional camel herder in north-western Kenya.[2] In that case, the appearance of Lorang was purposely delayed. The film begins with his voice recounting episodes in his early life over scenes of a dust storm. A scene then follows showing him very briefly, at which point the film shifts to Naingiro, his sister-in-law, and an old friend, Ngimare, both of whom speak about his character and history.[3]

One problem in *Doon School Chronicles* was how to mix filming styles, formal devices and different types of material in the same film. This included using chapters, intertitles, school documents, still images, general scenes and scenes about particular students. If such a mixed approach was to be employed, it had to be made clear early in the film in order to accustom the audience to the shifts of content and style. The opening of the film therefore presents a kind of catalogue of the types of material that will be used. From a scene at the school laundry, the film shifts to a staff member explaining how school uniforms are organised, followed by an abstract sequence made up of names, numbers and pieces of clothing, boys lining up for a rollcall, and then a scene of a group of rowdy students whose heights and weights are being measured. This is followed by a quieter scene of four students eating biscuits in their room. Interspersed among these scenes are titles, intertitles and still photographs, all of which will become recurring devices in the film.

I hoped that separating the film into chapters would provide a pathway through this material, but I soon came upon an additional way of providing continuity. One of the four boys who shared a room was named Rohan. He was an intelligent and determined young man who looked out at the world through a pair of owlish spectacles. Near the beginning I filmed a long conversation with him. I found his comments on the school so perceptive that I decided to use them as a recurring commentary, for they combined an insider's thoughts and feelings with the kind of objective analysis one would expect from an outside observer. In the astuteness of his observations I felt Rohan had the makings of a sociologist.

The idea of gradually introducing information and protagonists is but one aspect of a larger principle that can be drawn upon in structuring documentary films. It runs counter to the impulse, particularly among educators, to deliver as much contextual information as possible as soon as possible. Instead of drawing viewers into a film, however, such an overload often simply dampens their curiosity. It also seems presumptuous for filmmakers to assume that viewers will be interested enough at this early stage to take it all in. Rather, their interest must be earned. Despite this, the images and sounds presented at the beginning of a film create an important framework and staging-point for what follows. Here the film provides a kind of guidebook for the audience about how to watch the film. Here they first encounter its filming style, its mode of address and indications of its mood and pacing. Simply supplying 'context' is not enough, for a viewer must be invited into the film. Part of the process involves announcing its main themes, either literally or metaphorically. Thus by starting *Doon School Chronicles* with the washing and sorting of school uniforms, the film immediately raises questions about what sort of institution this is, where it is, whose uniforms these are and what the uniforms are for. Soon they will be worn by students, and as the film progresses they will come to stand both as signs of order and regulation and as a more intimate presence in the students' lives.

Internal and external structures

In a nonfiction film the role of the director is not to direct actors but to direct viewers. Films necessarily consist of fragments, but the gaps between the fragments are not accidental. One of the skills of a filmmaker is to guide the viewer in creatively linking the fragments together. Some films literally invite the viewer on a journey, as in Harry Watt and Basil Wright's *Night Mail*

(1936). In other films it may be a journey of ideas or associations as the film tends towards an essay-like or poetic form. Man Ray's *Emak-Bakia* (1926), Jean Vigo's *À propos de Nice* (1930) and Alain Resnais's *Night and Fog* (1956) are all films of this kind. This approach is particularly suited to short films, since it is hard for a longer film to maintain a sense of direction without the impetus of a narrative. But there are exceptions. J. P. Sniadecki's film *The Iron Ministry* (2014), at some eighty-two minutes, has no particular drama or even destination, although it is about railway travel in China. Whenever it risks losing momentum, it overcomes this by varying its materials and exploring the details of different travellers' lives.

In Jean Rouch and Edgar Morin's *Chronique d'un été* (1961) a sense of a direction is provided by the question: How do you manage to live? In Chris Marker's equally probing film *Le joli mai* (1963) the question is expanded to how one resolves the tensions between personal and political responsibility. Agnès Varda, in *The Gleaners and I* (2000), asks viewers to join her in a quest to examine an almost obsolete economic activity in its implications for today. It is a personal quest, relying on Varda's active guidance but also on the force of her ideas.

This approach of constructing a film as a narrative of ideas often relies on the filmmaker taking a central role, as in many of Chris Marker's films. Some other well-known examples include Michael Moore's films such as *Roger & Me* (1989), *Bowling for Columbine* (2002) and *Sicko* (2007). Others are Nick Broomfield's *The Leader, His Driver and the Driver's Wife* (1991) and Ross McElwee's films *Sherman's March* (1985) and *Bright Leaves* (2003). In these films the filmmakers address the viewer directly, asserting their authorship. In films like Raoul Ruiz's *De Grands événements et des gens ordinaires* (1979) the director's intelligence, sometimes playful, sometimes grave, is always on show. In certain other films the authors display a more cloaked and baleful presence, as in Georges Franju's *Le Sang des bêtes* (1949) and Luis Buñuel's *Land without Bread* (1933).

When filmmakers were first experimenting with documentary styles in the 1960s, many looked for inherently dramatic situations on which to base their films. In part this was to compensate for the loss of commentary and music that they had vowed to abandon. Thus the Drew Associates film *The Chair* (1962) was based on an impending execution and *On the Poll: Eddie Sachs* (1961) on winning or losing a car race. Although this worked well for certain topics, it was sometimes over-confidently assumed that a film built on an existing event would automatically hold an audience's attention. *The Road to Button Bay* (1962), another Drew Associates film, about an annual girl scout gathering, was less successful. Ethnographic filmmakers have sometimes made similar assumptions when filming rituals, despite the fact that most rituals require extensive knowledge of their meaning to be comprehensible. One film that overcame this problem was Kim McKenzie's *Waiting for Harry*

(1980), organised not around the structure of the ritual but the politics surrounding it.

Many films seek to base their structures on a chain of events. The problem with this approach is often the lack of an ending, when the events extend beyond the filming. A film that stops at some arbitrary point feels incomplete. When making *Takeover* (1980), about a conflict between national and state authorities over administration of an Australian Aboriginal community, Judith MacDougall and I were determined to document the events in strict chronology, so that the film would stand as an incontrovertible record of what had happened. In editing the film, however, we faced the problem of how to shape the series of events, since when we stopped filming the conflict was still unresolved. One solution was to intersperse the scenes with radio news broadcasts that we had recorded each day during the conflict. As a further device, we used shots of aircraft landing at the local airstrip, bringing in waves of politicians and journalists in an almost comical procession. The film ends with an Aboriginal leader expressing his disillusionment with all politicians, at best a very provisional conclusion.

In this case, strict chronology was followed for historical accuracy, but it can be dictated by other factors. Another film in my long-term project about institutions for children in India, *Gandhi's Children* (2008), was made at the Prayas Children's Home for Boys, a juvenile detention centre and children's shelter in New Delhi. I wanted to maintain some flexibility in arranging the scenes, for the film was organised more around themes of the children's experiences than specific events. One event, however, greatly limited this flexibility. Halfway through the filming several boxes of red and blue jerseys were donated to the shelter by a wealthy businessman. From then on nearly every boy wore one of them. This created in the film an absolute point of reference. A scene was clearly shot either before or after the arrival of the jerseys. Later scenes could not be placed before earlier ones without an obvious discontinuity. This imposed a partial chronology on the film, even though the film did not otherwise require it. It made more evident the fact that most audiences unconsciously assume a film's scenes to be in chronological order unless the director makes an explicit point of altering it.

A dual structure

Gandhi's Children presented several further structural problems, for the film had two linked objectives. The first was to present the physical aspects of the children's life in the institution. This required a complex overview of its routines, its staff activities, the prevailing atmosphere and actual physical conditions. The second was to show why children ended up in such a place. I felt this could only be done by presenting the histories of a number of boys, for the reasons were extremely varied. Some boys were orphans, others had been abandoned or lost, others were former child labourers, and others were living on the streets or had been arrested for minor crimes. Some came from distant villages, some from the city. The film finally included the histories of seven boys, as each described their experiences. When combined with the first objective, this took considerable time. In the end the film ran to just over three hours.

The question then was how to make the film acceptable at such a length. The narratives of the boys were distributed through the film, embedded in the other material. This meant their entries were staggered, creating new points of departure as the film progressed. To some extent this irregularity mirrored the unpredictability of life at the home, for although many boys spent years there, others appeared and disappeared unexpectedly. Some ran away, some were taken in by relatives or were sent to other institutions, and a few managed to go home. As the institution was also a juvenile detention centre, many were serving a sentence and had to await formal discharge by a court or magistrate.

A further strategy was to divide the film into chapters, as in *Doon School Chronicles*. Each of the twelve chapters in the film thus bears an identifying title, sometimes referring to specific individuals, sometimes to particular themes or events. Several of the boys' cases run throughout the film, while others appear in only one chapter. Weaving together these narratives with the other materials helped maintain the film's momentum. Towards the end of the film several events coalesce and produce a partial resolution, although clearly the problems of many of the boys will never be resolved.

The dual structure of this film was made necessary by its content. It might have been possible to divide its two objectives into two shorter films, but to grasp the boys' situation properly it was important to embed their separate stories in the daily life of the institution, which was a major subject in its own right. Thus the film gives close attention to the routines of eating, sleeping, dressing and bathing as well as the physical setting, with its bare walls, broken plumbing and echoing spaces.

An episodic structure

Although films like *Gandhi's Children* are episodic, one can envisage other films that are equally so, but with a different premise. These films might provide a set of variations on a theme, as in Wiseman's films, or narratives linked to an historical event. In making *SchoolScapes* (2007), also an episodic film, my aim was more tentative: to see if a film on the theme of observation could be made in which each scene consisted of a single shot. This film also formed part of the long-term project about institutions for children in India. It was shot at a school in South India founded by the Indian thinker Jiddu Krishnamurti, who urged students to learn by observing rather than by precept or by accepting received wisdom. By presenting a set of simple scenes of school life, I hoped to emphasise both the idea and the act of observation.

The idea for the film originated in the early films of the Lumière Company, each of which was a single shot lasting about forty seconds. These films pioneered various ways of using a camera and were adroit at presenting a place or an event in less than a minute. Working in time as well as space, they brought a new public consciousness to the framing and observing of images. Like the Impressionist paintings of the period, they were also notable for their emphasis on the details of everyday life. In *SchoolScapes* I attempted to stimulate a fascination with looking similar to that which greeted the Lumière films of the 1890s. Almost as important to me as observation itself was examining the reality of how we experience it.

The challenge presented by the film was how to determine what shots to make and how to organise them. I reasoned that some scenes should have their own internal structure while the aim of others should simply be to invite the viewer to look at some ordinary event or object more attentively. The scenes might last from a minute up to six minutes. In one scene of the first kind, with a clear internal structure, a pile of shoes lies in the foreground as distant sounds can be heard. Gradually the sounds become louder, and then a crowd of students descends on the shoes and puts them on in a flurry of activity. The sounds diminish as the students disperse, leaving silence and the frame entirely empty (figure 5.5). In another scene, it is early morning and a boy lies in bed asleep. He is awakened by an adult and then slowly dresses, but finally he decides to get back into bed again. The structure of each of these begins before an action, shows it commencing and then follows it through

5.5 Shoes awaiting their wearers in *SchoolScapes*

to a conclusion. Each thus has a classic beginning, middle and end. Similar scenes show a haircut, a music lesson and an argument between two students.

In other scenes almost nothing happens. These include such subjects as a landscape at early morning, bedcovers drying in the sun and an empty classroom.

In structuring such a film it was important to control both the pace and the subject matter in order to hold the audience's interest and suggest that something unexpected might follow at any time. Scenes with similar subjects or a similar tone were not placed close together, as variety was essential. Some scenes are humorous, others not. Some are from fixed vantage points, but in one the camera moves continuously. Some scenes refer to other scenes in the film, creating a network of internal connections. There is one concession to conventional form: the film gives the effect of following the course of a day, from morning to evening. It also suggests the passing of a school term, for the film ends with examinations, packing and the students leaving for their holidays.

This film had no central characters, no real narrative and no obvious theme. In attempting to make a virtue of its episodic structure, it directed the audience away from more usual ways of looking. There is nothing new in this strategy. It is little different from picaresque tales like *Don Quixote* and *Tristram Shandy* (or a picaresque film like Jean Rouch's *Jaguar*), each offering a series of new adventures. Here the viewer becomes the traveller, the filmmaker offering up the new sights to be explored.

Engaging the viewer

Whether films are organised by ideas, poetic association or the dramas of people's lives, all require insight into the minds of potential viewers. Not all viewers will respond to a film in the same way, nor should they, but films with a sufficient density and logic in their construction can speak to a variety of audiences. Some viewers may see the humour in a film; others, untouched by the humour, will respond to its plot or its visual details. Films that reflect the complexity of human experience are capable of being understood in multiple ways, whereas those made to deliver a single message are often discarded like yesterday's newspaper. Some films produce unexpected responses. Our film *Lorang's Way*, referred to above, has been seen by a variety of audiences. Academic audiences generally see it as a study of patriarchy and pastoral economics. But when we showed it to an Australian rural audience of farmers and cattle-breeders, one man in the audience exclaimed, 'Lorang is just like my father!' He saw, in this almost naked man, with a dark skin, spear and painted headdress, someone perfectly recognisable. Lorang, through the medium of film, had crossed the cultural divide.

Notes

1 The two shorter films were *Nawi* (1970) and *Under the Men's Tree* (1973), the first of which in fact served as my thesis film, as it was completed before *To Live with Herds*.
2 See also the discussion of this film in Chapters 9 and 10.
3 Similarly, Ibsen's *Hedda Gabler* opens with a scene in which Hedda and her new husband George are discussed at length by George's aunt and a servant. It was a device also used by Shakespeare, notably in the opening scenes of *Macbeth*.

6

Filming in a closed community

FILMMAKERS are frequently called upon to film in small communities, where the objective may be as much to convey a sense of the community as the individuals within it. The more enclosed the community, the more likely it is to have developed its own unique character, which has intensified over time as people's manners, habits and preferences have become set and enmeshed with their physical surroundings. I have filmed in a number of communities in which my sense of them as living organisms was particularly strong, but none more so than in a traditional boarding school in India. This experience forced me to look more closely at how the personal, physical and social aspects of people's lives were intertwined, and to try to register this on film. What follows is an account of how the project came about and the shape it ultimately took.

One day in 1993 I received at my office in Canberra a note from a graduate student at the University of Sydney. He was Sanjay Srivastava, a young anthropologist who was writing his PhD thesis on three elite boarding schools of northern India. He was from Delhi but had come to Australia to complete his studies. His research interests lay in class, gender and the creation of post-colonial elites. He asked if I thought a boarding school would be a suitable subject for ethnographic filmmaking.

I had gone to a boarding school myself, and I knew that anthropologists were taking an increasing interest in communities other than the remote, small-scale societies they had traditionally studied. The sociologist Erving Goffman had been writing for some years about what he termed 'total institutions' – hermetic places like prisons, hospitals and asylums (1962). Why not consider boarding schools as well? I was intrigued by Srivastava's suggestion.

These were the days of posted letters and fax messages. I replied to Srivastava by fax, proposing that we should meet to discuss the idea. We met the next time he came to Canberra. He proved to be a confident young man, neat in his movements, with serious eyes and a closely trimmed beard. He was cheerful, but there was also something brooding in his manner, as if he was a little distracted by looking into the future. In fact at this time he was wondering what to do after receiving his PhD, and he was hoping to find a teaching job at an Australian university. This meeting between us was to be the first of many over the coming years.

At this time I was about to undertake a filming project about mountain shepherds in Sardinia, invited there by the Sardinian ethnographic institute, ISRE.[1] Further discussions with Srivastava were therefore delayed, although we kept in touch during the following year. Our first meeting had established a common interest in boarding schools as enclosed institutions and as training grounds for political and social elites. Sanjay's fieldwork had taken him to three prominent schools: Mayo College in Rajasthan, Lawrence School in Sanawar and the Doon School, located some 200 kilometres north of Delhi. Of these, Doon School was the most influential, a boys' boarding school famous throughout India. Later I was struck by how many of the middle-class Indians I met had friends or relatives who had gone there. Although the tag 'the Eton of India' had been applied to a number of schools, including Mayo College, it was most often applied to Doon.

Having agreed that filming at an Indian school was an idea worth exploring, we went on to discuss the options. There was an unstated understanding that we would collaborate on the project, although what role Sanjay would play remained vague, other than bringing his Indian background and anthropological knowledge to it. At first we considered making three films, one on each of the schools he had studied, or a single film comparing all three schools, or only one of them. Another possibility was to look at other, quite different sorts of schools, such as those for children from very poor families, or schools with a specific focus such as music or religion. We even considered the 'wrestling schools' of northern India, athletic clubs each run by a wrestling guru. Over the next two years we continued to explore these ideas by fax, email and in person.

There was also the question of money. How were we to fund such a project? As time went on and our ideas narrowed, we took the more conservative view that it would be best to stick with one of Sanjay's original three schools, and preferably Doon, the school he knew best and where he had some family connections.

In November 1994 I wrote to David Wason, the commissioning editor of *Disappearing World*, a long-running anthropological film series produced by Granada Television in Britain. I mentioned Sanjay's research and proposed making a film about one of the schools he had studied. Although I told him that Sanjay's interest was primarily in how these schools had prepared middle-class students to become leaders in postcolonial India, I also mentioned my own interest in how students developed intellectually and spiritually in such a 'hothouse' environment. I was more interested in their personal interactions than the school's educational system. I suggested that the film might be particularly suitable for *Disappearing World* at a time when the series was trying to move away from its earlier focus on remote and exotic societies. With Sanjay involved, it would remain faithful to its practice of creating collaborations between filmmakers and anthropologists.

Nothing came of this overture. A few months later I wrote a three-page prospectus for a possible film about Doon School. It combined Sanjay's and my interests and stated that it would 'explore Doon School's special ethos – its vision of a modern citizenry and nation-state, and its unique influence on Indian society'. At the same time it would focus on the 'living experiences of boys at the school'. By this time Sanjay had received his PhD and I had completed my Sardinian film, which had appeared as part of the BBC Television series *Fine Cut*.

I developed the proposal further in 1994 and 1995. By December 1995 I had secured an agreement in principle from the Australian Broadcasting Corporation and BBC Television to co-fund a film titled *Boys of the Doon*, which was to be part of a new BBC series, *Under the Sun*. I must have had doubts about the durability of the agreement even then, however, for I made a similar approach to Channel Four Television in Britain and to Westdeutscher Rundfunk and Südwestfunk in Germany.

That the ABC–BBC agreement might fall through, or was at any rate precarious, became apparent in April 1996 when Alan Bookbinder, the commissioning editor of *Under the Sun*, informed me that he was leaving his position at the BBC. As this was during the British summer, his replacement would not be appointed for several months. The axe finally fell on 5 August, when the newly appointed commissioning editor of the series, Nick Fraser, sent me the following fax:

> Dear David. Sorry – but I don't feel *Boys of the Doon* is my sort of project – there have been films about British equivalents, and they never really seem to work – I just don't feel the subject is energising enough.

Thus came my dismissal, and ultimately my liberation from broadcast television. For without the BBC's funding, the ABC could no longer support the project. It was only in retrospect, of course, that this appeared as a liberation. At the time it was a severe blow. But if the project had in fact gone ahead, the film would have had to be shot on 16 mm film, the preferred medium for broadcast television, and this would have entailed great expense and multiple layers of supervision and responsibility. I would have had two broadcast companies and two commissioning editors looking over my shoulder. Mixed with the disappointment, I therefore felt some sense of relief. But Sanjay and I were on our own again.

It is hardly worthwhile reporting the other avenues we tried, for at this time several new factors profoundly altered the situation. One was that I applied for a research fellowship for a proposed study of the field of visual anthropology. Another was that Sanjay had found a university teaching job in Australia. The third was the arrival of affordable, high-quality digital video.

I had perhaps already been anticipating the difficulties with television when I applied for the fellowship, for it was the Doon School project in a new guise. It was funded by the Australian Research Council and was ambitiously titled 'Reconsidering Visual Anthropology: Towards a Theoretical Framework for Anthropological Visual Research'. It was to be hosted by the Centre for Cross-Cultural Research at the Australian National University (ANU). The Australian Research Council had little past history of funding film projects, considering them somewhat outside the scope of legitimate academic research. My strategy in proposing the project was to question the methodology of visual anthropology, which remained a somewhat ill-defined discipline. What sort of activity was it, and what problems did it face? I proposed developing new and better models for the field. Included in the proposal was the idea that the study would include 'field projects designed to demonstrate these principles in practice'. Among them would be a project with Sanjay Srivastava 'linked to his doctoral work at Sydney University'.

Somewhat to my surprise I was awarded the fellowship, which included an annual research grant for fieldwork and equipment.[2] Thus the project could finally go ahead. In the end, I made five films at Doon School over the next five years and published a number of journal articles and eventually two books, *Transcultural Cinema* and *The Corporeal Image: Film, Ethnography, and the Senses*. To explain how this came about, however, I need to go back to some of the earlier factors at play.

By this time Sanjay had secured a teaching post in anthropology at Charles Sturt University in Bathurst, New South Wales. He was to go on to several higher posts at Deakin University in Melbourne. His teaching commitments meant that it no longer seemed feasible for us to collaborate in the field, although he would continue to be a valuable advisor to the project. If I were to do the filming at Doon School, I would have to do it on my own.[3]

Perhaps the most important of all these changes was the arrival of digital video. For the first time it had become possible to make high-quality moving images very cheaply. In contrast to filming with 16 mm film, which could cost as much as US$1,500 per hour, the cost of filming for an hour in digital video was about $15. A film could also be made by one person working alone, without the need to change film magazines every twelve minutes and have a second person to operate a tape recorder. Editing was also becoming progressively simpler and cheaper, with several computer editing systems coming on the market. I was thus no longer dependent on 16 mm and television funding. With the fellowship's research budget I could purchase the necessary equipment, get myself to India and back, and film as much as I wished.

There still remained the question of whether I would be permitted to film at Doon School or, failing that, at some other school. In August 1996 I visited Dehradun, about twenty-five kilometres from Mussoorie, where in 1988–89 Judith MacDougall and I had filmed *Photo Wallahs* (1991), about local photographers and their work. We had returned to visit the friends we had made when making the film and to show it to those who had not yet seen it. We had often been to Dehradun, as it was the terminus of the railway line from New Delhi and was situated at the start of the road that made its circuitous way up to the hill station of Mussoorie. We knew Dehradun well, and it was here that Doon School was located. By now I had written to its headmaster, John Mason, describing my connection to Sanjay and explaining the idea of filming at the school. I asked if I could visit the school when I came to Dehradun and discuss the idea with him. He agreed, and an appointment was set for 7 September.

I approached this meeting with some anxiety, for I was well aware that institutions, and perhaps especially schools, were highly protective of their reputations and might well feel threatened by the prospect of anyone filming in their midst. There were many cases of films about institutions that had started out in a spirit of cooperation but had ended in disagreement and discord. Given that history, it was no wonder they were cautious. Roger Graef, who had pioneered making films about public and private institutions in Britain, had approached as many as a hundred large corporations before one of them, British Steel, allowed him to film its decision-making activities. He had met similar rebuffs trying to film at other institutions but had somehow managed to gain access to the offices of the European Union, the United Nations and Thames Valley Police.

I was therefore much surprised by the reception I received at Doon School. My visit coincided with a term break, when the students were away on school expeditions. Without the students present the school seemed eerily empty. But the grounds were magnificent. My first impression was of a leafy park, with giant trees and broad green playing fields. These grounds had in fact originally belonged to the Forest Research Institute, and the campus was still a splendid botanical garden.

John Mason ushered me into his office in an old brick building dating from the Forest Research era. At first glance he appeared to be European, with fair skin, European features and a balding head with fringes of hair over the ears. This was misleading, for he was from an Anglo-Indian family who had lived in Bengal for several generations. When he spoke it was with an Indian accent.

I repeated my well-worn description of the proposed film project, emphasising that although it was linked to Sanjay's research, I would be filming alone and pursuing my own research interests at the school. These revolved around the students' daily lives and how students from different backgrounds interacted with each other. Mason was at once positive about the idea. My filming, he said, would give the school a valuable new perspective on itself. At the same time, my presence and filming at the school would stimulate the students to think more deeply about the role of visual media in their lives. He felt that although the boys consumed a lot of visual media, they thought very little about it. In short, if I wanted to stay at the school, the school would give me a place to live, I could take my meals with the boys and I could film what I wished.

I admit I was taken aback by this reception: having walked into his office assuming the idea would be met with suspicion, I had walked out an hour later with the project all but approved. I had even been given *carte blanche* to film what I wanted without censorship or supervision. Mason said that the project would have to be put to the school's board of governors, but he gave me the impression they would agree to it.

It's one thing to have a project in mind, another to have to think seriously about implementing it. It was now up to me to decide when I would arrive, what equipment I would need, what other practical problems would have to be solved and not least how I was going to set about it. Although I had certain general objectives in mind, I immediately resolved to come to the school with no fixed plan as to the number of films I would make, or their lengths or what exactly they would be about. I wanted my encounter with the school to determine these things.

At this time my thinking was still focused on a concept of the school as a crossroads of students from different geographical, religious and linguistic backgrounds, a concept partly influenced by my connection with the ANU Centre for Cross-Cultural Research. The school drew its students from all over India, a mixture of Sikhs, Hindus, Muslims and even a few Christians and Parsis. There would be Hindi-speakers, Bengalis and Punjabis, as well as boys from as far away as Bangalore and Madras. The school also made a point of its simple style of living and its opposition to distinctions of wealth, class and caste, although inevitably most of the students were from middle-class and upper-class families who could afford the school fees. Nevertheless, a boy from one of the wealthiest industrial families in India might share a dormitory room with one whose parents were modest civil servants. Given this variety, I wondered to what extent the boys would bridge the differences between them. Would they make friendships across the boundaries of language, class and culture? I had yet to learn that most of the linguistic differences would be smoothed away by the exclusive use of English at the school, and perhaps even more by the school's own distinctive culture, which was later to become a major focus of my attention. First, however, I had to confront a number of practical and social challenges. One of these was the great gap in age and cultural background between me and the boys of the school.

Among my interests was the then very current topic of personal and group identity. To what extent did children identify with their home communities when thrust into a new environment? I assumed that the boys' responses would be fairly uniform in this regard, but I was soon to learn how varied and forceful their individual personalities could be, even at an early age. In order to clarify my thinking, I began to keep a daily journal about the project. In the very first entry I wrote:

> Whereas Sanjay's concern is with broad swathes of history, mine must be with the revealing moment, the dawning of a new idea in my subjects' consciousness,

> the flow and counterflow of a relationship. I am interested in acts – of generosity, of courage, of rebellion – and the manner in which a person performs them. I suppose I am interested in the discovery of the self – the discovery of what one is capable of being. (7 April 1997)[4]

All this was well enough, and it did influence what I did later, but I was still largely stuck on the idea of charting broad social and cultural differences across an institutional terrain.

On the morning of 9 April 1997 I took the train from New Delhi station to Dehradun. I was met by a car and driver from the school. I had a brief word with John Mason, who then put me in the hands of one of the teachers. I was taken to the school guest house and given a small furnished flat, with windows on one side overlooking one of the first-year dormitories and on the other offering glimpses of the great central playing field. My first day was spent in a fog of disorientation and crowding impressions – the sheer number of boys, their clamour suddenly replaced by order at the ringing of a bell, teachers turning up unexpectedly and introducing themselves. I was never quite sure how to explain my presence, as the headmaster had let it to be known that I was there to share my knowledge of visual media with all and sundry. However, quite soon I began saying that I would like to make a film about the school. I realised this would be known very soon in any case, and it provided a simple explanation for my presence. That I had little idea what the film would be about, I kept to myself.

From the beginning the school struck me as a kind of theatre. A drama was being enacted, with choreographed movements and colours. Bells would ring and boys would appear, all dressed alike. Later another bell would ring and they would reappear dressed in a different uniform. The day was made up of a series of acts and ebbs and flows. In the afternoon, the boys' games uniforms could be seen as flickerings of blue through the green foliage. In the morning the boys appeared in sober grey (figure 6.1).

My first visit in April 1997 was a preliminary one lasting only two weeks. I had brought with me one of the first small digital video cameras, which I intended to use primarily as a note-taking device. I filmed scenes of the school grounds, the boys having their meals, early-morning physical exercises and a rehearsal of a Shakespeare play, along with a considerable range of other activities, some public and some more private. They included boys cheering at a cricket match, a meeting of boys with their house tutor, the youngest boys playing with a broken shower pipe, a boy having a haircut and a punishment called 'change-in-break'.[5] Although the video camera had only a one-chip receptor (unlike the three-chip camera I used later), the high quality of digital video eventually allowed me to use a number of these early scenes in the finished films.

6.1 Crossing the main playing field in *Doon School Chronicles*

I was particularly taken by boys' speech, how articulate many of them were, and the fact that I heard nothing but English. They were quick to speak to me, a trait promoted by the school, which encouraged the ability to speak confidently to anyone. This was bolstered by their awareness that they belonged to the most prestigious school in the country and that this would undoubtedly benefit them in the future. Each boy was assigned a number that he kept until he left the school, when it was then given to another boy. These numbers had many uses in the school's operations and the boys, rather than feeling dehumanised by their numbers, seemed to value them, many eventually incorporating them into their email addresses. I observed how busy the school kept them as they followed a demanding schedule, having scarcely any time to themselves. It increasingly seemed to me that they were like the parts of a larger organism. On my second day at the school I wrote: 'The steps of the dining hall are a sea of blue and grey uniforms and brown legs as we go in to lunch. The boys are a little like a colony of insects' (10 April 1997).

I was absorbed very quickly into the activities and social life of the school. I was appointed one of the judges for a one-act play competition. I met with the school's Video Club. I was asked to conduct a workshop at the school's Teachers' Centre, talking to teachers, mostly from other schools, about using video cameras in their classes. The Centre's director, Minakshi Basu, later became a friend and astute guide to the school and appeared in several of the films I made.

The headmaster and his wife invited me to have tea and dinner with them as they entertained other visitors. I began to make the acquaintance of the teachers, particularly the younger ones, who would meet for drinks and meals at one another's houses. Theirs seemed like a separate social world, set apart from the more serious business of the school. One young teacher briefed me on the school's finances, saying that the teaching staff were badly paid but in compensation were given free accommodation and free tuition if they sent their sons to the school.

During this first visit the openness and candour of the students allowed me to get to know several of them individually. Some of those I spoke to later became figures in the films I made. These included Karam, a protagonist in two films, and Arjun and Veer, who represented contrasting ages and personalities in the first film I made, *Doon School Chronicles* (2000). This suggests that first impressions are more important than filmmakers realise and often influence their later decisions. In my journal I wrote:

> Lunch at the head of a long table of boys from, I think, Kashmir House. The boys are a little shy but put themselves out to make conversation. They are friendly and invariably polite. I meet on my left Arjun, a new boy. (10 April 1997)

The next day, I added:

> Boys wander by, including Arjun. I make a remark and call him by his name.... We go in together and I sit at his table again with some other boys I recognise from before.... I bring out the video camera and take a few shots, then continue outside where a very capable-seeming Sikh boy is organizing a tennis competition. (11 April 1997)

On the fourth day I met Veer, whom I later filmed as he was rehearsing the part of Hamlet in a school play.

> They are stumbling through a scene, then go on to the 'To be or not to be' soliloquy.... Veer takes it too fast and too vehemently, but there is no doubt he commands attention.... During all of this I have been using the video camera.... I am also interested in Veer – how he moves in and out of his part and the contradictory qualities of his manner. (12 April 1997)

It happened that I had come to the school just when a new group of first-year students arrived, and many were struggling with homesickness. On the second evening I was sitting outside in the dark with a young teacher who had befriended me. There was supposed to be a comet in view that night.

> We look for the comet but can't see it. A new crescent moon rises over Kashmir House, turned yellow by pollution or moisture in the air. Strange sounds come out of the darkness. A group of boys comes across the cricket ground, one of them crying miserably, the others trying to reassure him. 'A new boy,' my friend

> says. 'He's been crying all day.' I watch the little party move off into the night, the older boys giving words of encouragement to the younger one. Already, I'm beginning to feel connected to this place. (10 April 1997)

By the time I returned to the school five months later I had revised my thoughts about what I wanted to film there. I saw the school now not as a crossroads of difference but as a much more homogeneous community, with a distinctive character that had been created and consolidated over the years. This character – or aesthetic, in the broadest sense – was a combination of features that included its daily rituals, habitual modes of behaviour, speech, clothing, material objects and physical setting. If you were to take a former Doon student and set him down blindfolded in the school today, he would immediately sense where he was. The sounds and smells alone would suffice. I had come to the conclusion that I wanted to explore the nature of this distinctive character and its effects, both practical and emotional, on the students. How was it modified and reinforced as it was passed on from one generation of students to another? What was it like to grow up in such an environment? How did it influence the decisions and character of both staff and students?

The question was where to begin. How could one film something so pervasive and yet so elusive? 'I know there are a hundred possible films here,' I wrote, 'all with the potential to fulfil or exceed my hopes and imaginings' (21 September 1997). I had already considered several films, one about the lives of newcomers to the school, another featuring Veer, possibly to be made in collaboration with him. Another might be about 'a group of boys who share a room in one of the houses – their hopes, ideas and friendships' (21 September 1997). As it turned out, I incorporated all these ideas in the first two films I made. The best opening strategy, I decided, was to spend several days in some of the school's dormitories and main houses. I would look for likely groups and situations, and eventually suitable protagonists.

This is hardly a novel approach when searching for a film subject. I had experienced it several times before. The difficulty was how to approach the underlying theme, which I was now calling the 'social aesthetics' of the school. How could one film something that was ever-present and part of every aspect of the school's culture yet was in a sense invisible?

I began searching through the school's written records and documents, looking for expressions of the institution's guiding principles. Many were to be found in the school newspaper, *The Doon School Weekly*, run by the students continuously since the school was founded in 1935. More appeared in its yearbooks and other school publications. There were also several published histories of the school as well as Sanjay's forthcoming book about the school, most of which I had already read in manuscript.[6]

Much of the way the school had evolved could be traced back to its founding fathers. The school had been created by a group of moderate Bengali nationalists, many of whom had been educated in Britain. The aim was to establish a school on Indian soil modelled on the British public school. Here India's future leaders would be trained to step into the shoes of British administrators following Independence. Many of the school's founders, including its chief promoter, S. R. Das, were members of the so-called Bengali Renaissance, a movement which espoused reformist politics, religion and the arts. At its heart was the ideal of the rational, 'scientific' man who would liberate Indian society from centuries of superstition and weakness under colonial rule. Key features of the school's ethos, which I often encountered in its documents, were appeals to scientific reasoning, measurement, secularism, human equality and physical prowess. As Sir Jagdish Prasad, one of the school's board of governors, put it in 1937: 'The aim of this school might well be to give you the physique of the savage and the cultivated brain of the civilized man.'[7] The school would preserve the best of British education, moderated by modern Indian values. Instead of adhering to divisions of class and caste, the boys would be trained in egalitarianism and social service. Instead of learning Latin and Greek they would learn Sanskrit and Urdu.

I saw these aspirations mirrored in many of the school's customs and activities. There was a commitment to order and measurement, expressed in such things as periodically recording the height and weight of each boy, as well as in the regimes of school uniforms, numbering and scheduling. Quite early on I filmed both a military-style 'march-past' and boys with burning torches practising for a night-time 'Torchlight Tattoo'. I filmed one of the school's many linen rooms in which the boys' clothing was arranged by type and student number. I also filmed a physical training exhibition in which the boys competed in choreographed gymnastic exercises, forming blocks of different colours representing their different houses. Each of these scenes featured in the first film, *Doon School Chronicles* (2000). It was organised in chapters, each of which treated a specific theme and opened with a quotation taken from the school documents.

Perhaps because it was the first film I made, *Doon School Chronicles* focused extensively on the school's ideology and rituals. At the same time I tried to convey the sensory aspects of the school's atmosphere – the appearance of its buildings and grounds, typical objects in the boys' lives and the physical presence of the boys themselves. Clothing was a key element in this. *Doon School Chronicles* begins at the school laundry, with school uniforms being dried in the sun. Each day the students made five changes of clothing, from their nightwear to the uniforms worn for morning physical exercises, to uniforms worn in the classroom, to games uniforms in the afternoon, to white kurtas in the evening, and then back again to their nightwear. Changing clothing was also a key feature of the punishment system called 'change-in-break'. It struck me that this relationship of the boys to their clothing, with its intensely personal associations, was one of the most persistent and unforgettable aspects of their lives. It shaped their consciousness of the school in multiple ways, through its textures, colours and its ritualistic and symbolic meanings.

As well as paying attention to these more formal aspects of school life, my aim in *Doon School Chronicles* was to convey the experiences of individual boys. Interspersed through the film, and providing a thread of continuity, are the observations of Rohan, a fourteen-year-old student with whom I recorded a conversation early in my filming. In it he comments on the school's 'deliberate' artificiality, its pressures upon students to conform, and the personalities of the three boys with whom he shares a room. This forms a counterpoint to the more extended attention I give to Arjun and Veer, two of the boys I had met on my first visit to the school.

I focused on these protagonists because I wanted to explore how different students responded to being at the school. Rohan and his roommates were aged about fourteen. Arjun was twelve and Veer sixteen, thus being amongst the younger and older students in the school. Their personalities were in sharp contrast to each other, as were their attitudes. Arjun was keen on cricket and other sports, through which he achieved popularity and success. He appeared to accept at face value everything the school espoused and had to offer. When I asked if he thought the school might ever admit girls, he regarded the idea with astonishment. 'But the school was designed for boys', he said. 'It would never work' (figure 6.2). Veer, on the other hand, was independent and sceptical by

6.2 Arjun in *Doon School Chronicles*

temperament and was determined to make a success of the school on his own terms. He had little interest in sports and was ready to challenge the school's customs and ideology. He was forceful in debates, directed and acted in school plays and was widely respected. He became an editor of *The Weekly* and was eventually made a house captain (figure 6.3).

When Veer spoke to me, he made it clear that he rejected many of the school's values and traditions. Among them was bullying, which had evolved from the British public school tradition of giving older students power over younger ones, allowing them to award punishments and demand 'favours', which was Doon School's version of the British fagging system. Although the school officially discouraged bullying, it was widely tolerated as an inevitable part of school life. Veer told me:

> [It] gets quite nasty sometimes. And the worst thing is that it's sponsored … I mean, it's endorsed by the school. It's allowed. So … it's like school-sponsored bullying almost, because the school allows it.[8]

As for himself, Veer made it clear that he was determined to achieve success at the school, not by the usual means but through his own personal and literary skills. He told me:

6.3 Veer in *Doon School Chronicles*

> I found very early on, I took the attitude that, 'I'm not going to play a sport, but I'm definitely going to survive.' And … you can. It's all about being at rhythm with yourself, being at peace with yourself. Not really caring about if you're popular amongst ninety per cent of your classmates or not. I mean, it's very important to have your friends and your soul-mates, and the people who you can really talk to, which you sometimes desperately need in school, but … no, I don't think it's a hard-and-fast rule that if you're sensitive you can't survive in school.[9]

Veer described the school practice of 'scoping', by which students in their penultimate year attempted to ingratiate themselves to the teaching staff and headmaster by assuming important responsibilities, with the hope of being appointed house captains and prefects in their final year. As Veer admitted, he was scoping himself.

In my efforts to portray the school comprehensively as an institution, I found it difficult to film the bullying, because most of it took place behind closed doors. This was also true of many of the punishments, which were carried out secretly in so-called house 'common rooms', which younger boys in particular were forced to attend. Boys could be beaten with hockey sticks or cricket bats simply for losing a house match. Although many admitted these things occurred, they were afraid to talk about them. I filmed several instances of verbal bullying and older students demanding unreasonable 'favours' as well as official punishments supervised by older boys, such as the 'change-in-break', given for being late, not shining shoes, having uncombed hair and the like.

At one stage Veer became interested in making a film himself, and did so using a video camera borrowed from the headmaster. He chose bullying as the subject and organised several of his housemates to act in it. Fortunately for my purposes, he allowed me to film him directing a scene of bullying, which I later incorporated into *Doon School Chronicles* as a kind of film within the film. In this way I was able to approach, at least in a roundabout way, what had proved a difficult topic.

Still more difficult was the sexual life of the school, for virtually all of it naturally occurred in private and few boys would talk about it openly. It was widely known that some older students sexually abused younger ones, and during my stay one young boy ran away from school because of this. I never found a way of dealing adequately with this subject. In part this was because I believed the film should focus on presenting actual events, not merely reports of them. In the end about all I could do was suggest the atmosphere of sexual potential present among adolescents in such an all-male environment.

Even while filming *Doon School Chronicles* I realised that representing the complexity of the school might call for additional strategies. This ultimately led me to make four more films. I had already filmed some of the younger boys, the eleven- and twelve-year-old D-formers, on several occasions. This suggested another way of approaching the life of the school. For the first year the D-formers lived in two separate 'holding houses', after which they moved into one of the school's five main houses. During their first exposure to the school they were expected to learn its customs and fit into what was, for them, an alien environment. I reasoned that if I followed their lives closely during this period, the audience would learn about the school in the same way as the students learned about it.

I began filming occasionally in Foot House, one of the holding houses named after the school's first headmaster, A. E. Foot. By the fifth week I began filming there regularly. This was the genesis of *With Morning Hearts* (2001), the second film I made about the school, its title taken from a prayer by Robert Louis Stevenson that was often repeated at school assemblies.[10] I thus found myself shooting two films at once, while keeping the two films quite separate in my mind.

My approach to this second film was quite different to that of *Doon School Chronicles,* although it explored some of the same themes. The everyday experiences of the new boys became its main focus. While the first film had ranged throughout the school, this film remained almost entirely within the confines of Foot House, for it was this enclosed world that I wanted to examine. At the heart of the film were certain dominant questions. Coming from a background of family life, how did the boys adapt to living with others in a new place? What was their experience of it? What kind of social order did they create among themselves? I wanted the film to convey aspects of both their physical and their emotional lives, and their feelings of living closely together.

With Morning Hearts contained many scenes of the boys' collective life, but it could render the experiences of only a few individuals. I began looking for boys who stood out from the rest for some reason. Karam was one of these. He was among the smallest in the group and one of the most vulnerable. He seemed to express what many of the others were feeling but were not revealing so obviously. He stood out for other reasons as well. He had a dramatic flair and an expressive face that commanded attention (figure 6.4). I had already filmed him on my first visit, when he seemed lost and miserable during early-morning physical exercises.

Another boy, Anant, stood out for very different reasons. He impressed me as a capable boy who dealt with others in a mature and composed manner. He was respected by them and assumed the role of a natural leader. I had first filmed him in a music class, where it was clear he possessed musical ability and the best singing voice in the group. Gradually several other boys emerged to become prominent in the film, in part through their relationships with Karam and Anant. Thus slowly the film assembled its cast of characters.

With Morning Hearts charts the boys' life in Foot House through the year. Most of the filming took place during the middle and latter part of it. The

6.4 Karam in *With Morning Hearts*

first days were covered by some of the scenes I had filmed on my first visit, plus Karam's account of his arrival at the school and the observations of several adults connected with Foot House. Among these was Minakshi Basu, the Foot House tutor, whom I had first met as the head of the Teachers' Centre. She had been observing the boys' lives from the start, and I included her comments at various points throughout the film. This gave it a further perspective, different from what I was able to show directly. The film ends as the boys are leaving the house and are about to move into the main houses. They are clearly upset by the move. Initially I put this down to their being forced to leave Foot House, to which they had become attached, but an historian friend argued persuasively that they were more upset at being separated from their friends. During the year they had created a new communal life among themselves, different from any they had known before.

The next film, *Karam in Jaipur* (2001), could be considered a footnote or sequel to *With Morning Hearts*. It is shorter than the other films and follows Karam into his new life in Jaipur House, named for one of the school's benefactors, the Maharaja of Jaipur. Along with several other boys from Foot House, Karam begins to learn more about the school at first hand. He works to find a place for himself and achieves this partly through his aptitude for gymnastics. In this film I was able to create a more individualised portrait of him than had been possible in *With Morning Hearts*.

6.5 A boy arrives with his parents in *The New Boys*

With this third film it was clear that a pattern was emerging in my filming of the school. Each new film was an outgrowth of the previous one, and in a sense a response to it. The fourth film, *The New Boys* (2003), demonstrates this clearly. I decided to film the next group of students to arrive at Foot House, which would allow their experiences to be compared with those of their predecessors. As they came from similar backgrounds, I wondered whether their life would be similar or different to that of the previous group. In contrast to *With Morning Hearts*, I started filming from the day of their arrival as they first appeared with their parents, dragging their trunks and suitcases into Foot House (figure 6.5). I filmed as they unpacked and looked around nervously, wondering what they, or their parents, had got them into.

I was also curious to see how the parents of the new boys would react to my filming. Surprisingly, they appeared to find it perfectly normal, perhaps assuming that a school with Doon School's prestige might well host a visiting filmmaker. Most were aware that other films had had been made about the school, and over the years there had been occasional television news features about it. Several parents seemed pleased by the attention being paid to their sons. Those whom I spoke to directly were more curious than surprised. Some asked what I was doing, and when I told them they simply nodded in agreement, saying it sounded like an interesting project. As the filming had been permitted by the headmaster and approved by the school's board of governors, the school was in effect acting *in loco parentis*. In this sense, I was benefiting from the trust the parents placed in the school and the school's prominence and influence in Indian society. It is more than likely that if today's academic research protocols had been in place then, the project would not have been possible, and the films would never have been made.

After these first exchanges, the parents became preoccupied with getting their sons settled, and they largely ignored me. I filmed them as they helped the boys unpack and conversed with other parents. I had a strong sense that they felt themselves part of an elite community, with much in common. Several of the fathers had been students at the school. One father said to another, 'This was our *toye* [study] room.... At least they have new fans'. A mother asked another, 'Your husband is an old boy?' She replied, 'No! He's from Mayo [College]. We committed the ultimate in treason. But I don't think there's any comparison at this point of time. Doon's doing much better. Definitely.'[11]

Most of the parents spoke English, although a few spoke Hindi to the housemaster and staff. I tried to gauge their reactions by observing them with their sons. Later I managed to send copies of the filmed material home with some of the boys for their parents to see. I also met a number of the parents again when they visited the school later in the year. Several expressed pleasure at being able to see, through film, how their sons were growing up so far away from home, something they were unable to see directly. One mother, however, expressed anger at how her son was bullied by other boys, declaring that if she had known about it earlier she would have taken him out of the school.

Differences soon appeared between the new group of Foot House boys and the previous group. Instead of appearing unified they tended to break up into smaller clusters, based on social class or having come from the same city, such as Mumbai. Some gave the impression they felt they were better or more sophisticated than the others. A few were viewed as socially inept. Casual bullying of at least one boy began, and this continued through the year. Overall, the group seemed to lack the ability of the previous group to develop its own effective social system and code of conduct. It lacked leaders like Anant, who had set an example of fairness and tolerance.

It was possible to film these fractures and discontents by showing the fights and instances of bullying that frequently broke out, but it also required being continually present and ready to film whenever they occurred. The bullying of one boy finally caused the housemaster to call a meeting of all the boys to ask them to desist. There were further expressions of unhappiness, of a kind that had been less apparent the year before. Karam had spoken of his homesickness, but I had not seen many other examples of it. This year it was pronounced, with one boy quite often in tears. After the evening study period I sometimes asked groups of boys to talk about some topic that interested them, and I filmed a number of these conversations. One heartfelt discussion was about homesickness, another about the causes of conflict in the house. One boy declared that competitiveness in sports led to divisions in the school and in society, and ultimately to warfare between nations like India and Pakistan.

By the end of the first term the lack of cohesion in the group had become obvious. The boys seemed tired and ready to go home. The two films about Foot House had exposed the development of two very different social dynamics, suggesting the fragile basis on which harmony in small groups so often depends. At the same time, they demonstrated that children acting on their own, and in the right circumstances, have the capacity to construct their own effective social order.

Each of the films so far had been made in response to the one before it, and this pattern was to continue. The filming had grown organically rather than according to some overall plan. The final film was no exception. As I filmed the arrival of the second Foot House group, one boy caught my attention. He was a small, slight boy with neatly combed hair, who appeared self-contained but also looked around him in obvious wonder. His parents, I noticed, spoke to the housemaster in Hindi. I learned they were from Nepal, and their son, Abhishek, was therefore something of an outsider in the group. At this time I was fully engaged in my filming of *The New Boys*, and I assumed Abhishek would play a part in it. He often engaged me in conversations, many of which I filmed at length. He told me about his life in Kathmandu, what his former school was like (run by Jesuits with a high regard for scholarship), books he had read, films he had seen and his ideas about teaching and learning. He was perhaps a little eager to impress me, but I recognised in him an unusual intelligence and maturity of thought. The material I was accumulating about him was steadily growing out of proportion to the rest. Although I could include a small amount of it in the film, I felt this would not do justice to the extent of it, or to Abhishek himself. It was at this point that the idea of making a film portrait of him began to take shape, and this eventually became *The Age of Reason* (2004). (A more detailed account of my filming of Abhishek is given in chapter 11.)

The making of this fifth film confirmed several shifts that had taken place in my ideas about Doon School. The first shift had been from thinking of the school as a cultural crossroads to thinking of it as a closed and self-fashioning community, with its own specific culture. A further shift had taken place in my ideas about children and childhood. It was the first time I had filmed children at close range. Like many people I had accepted the view that children were unfinished adults, in the process of being socialised in the culture of their elders. Until fairly recently even most social anthropologists had subscribed to this view. They had focused primarily on children's upbringing and, in certain cases, on their initiation rituals. Less attention had been paid to the economic and cultural contributions they made to society or their thinking and agency as individuals.

Meeting so many children and observing them intently had forced me to think of childhood in new ways. For one thing, children appeared to possess an innate sense of fairness that could not be ascribed to moral teachings. They seemed able to translate this both into moral judgements and into organising themselves effectively in groups. The first Foot House group had been particularly adept at this. In Abhishek and others I began to discern a capacity for experimental thinking quite different from the more habitual thinking of adults. In certain ways children seemed to lose rather than gain capabilities as they grew older and as they adapted to the dominant culture around them, just as they gradually lost the ability to pronounce the sounds of other languages.

Part of my interest in Abhishek lay in his autonomy as an individual, which seemed to embody the autonomy of children more generally. I encountered in him, and in others such as Anant, a fully formed personality, as serious in his thinking as many of the adults I knew. I gradually became less able to think of children and adults in separate categories, seeing them more in terms of their personal qualities. I found a statement by John Locke about the independent spirit of children, and I used it as an epigraph for the final film.[12] The decision to title the film about Abhishek *The Age of Reason* was thus both an acknowledgement of the abilities I had discovered in him and a reference to the ideas of Locke, Thomas Paine and other Enlightenment thinkers.

Completing this fifth film was a matter of recording further conversations with Abhishek, his thoughts and aspects of his daily life at the school. But there was another question that needed to be addressed. I was worried how he was fitting into the school, coming as he had from Nepal and being something of an outsider among the boys. As I watched him over the next few months this concern became a narrative element in the film. I realised that his relationship with me had provided a kind of refuge during his adjustment to the school. But as he grew closer to his classmates he also grew more distant from me, introducing a more sombre note into the film.

The Age of Reason became a composite of scenes showing Abhishek's interactions with those around him, including me, and a narrative of him finding his place in the school. I filmed him reading aloud an essay he had written about his first two weeks at the school. Later he spent some time in the school hospital with viral fever. He tried his hand at making model airplanes, and he learned how to swim. Perhaps the strangest scene was his visit to the school's natural history museum, where he wandered among the glass cases of skeletons, stuffed animals, jars of snakes and a human foetus preserved in formalin. By then he seemed to have reached some sort of existential turning point in his life, from which he would leave part of his childhood behind.

Viewed as an evolving project, the series of Doon School films narrows in focus from beginning to end. Starting with an overall view of the school and its ideology in *Doon School Chronicles*, it moves on to the more enclosed world of first-year boys in Foot House. Finally it narrows to the portrait of Abhishek in *The Age of Reason*. In keeping with this, the style of filming also changes. *Doon School Chronicles* combines observational scenes with formal devices such as chapters, quotations, still photographs and Rohan's voice-over. Several protagonists represent different age groups and attitudes to the school. *With Morning Hearts* and *The New Boys* are intentionally limited to the more confined space of Foot House, emphasising its physical environment and how the boys' social relationships develop over time. Nearly all the material is observational except for those occasions when the boys address me directly. The emphasis placed on Karam and a few other boys is always in relation to the group as a whole. In making *The Age of Reason*, however, I employed a more interactive approach. Many of the scenes involve exchanges between Abhishek and me. These scenes would obviously never have taken place without my presence with a camera. In this film I also provide, for the first time, a personal voice-over commentary.

Except for the first film, each was made in response to an earlier one. This contrasts with projects in which all the parts are conceived in advance. There was a conscious effort on my part to connect the films with each other, sometimes in multiple ways. The two Foot House films, *With Morning Hearts* and *The New Boys*, form a pair, allowing one to see the experiences of two groups in successive years. *The New Boys* and *The Age of Reason* also form a pair, allowing one to see Abhishek as one of thirty boys in the first film and as a single individual in the second. Because of its more general view, *Doon School Chronicles* in certain ways encompasses the other films, but the five films can also be regarded as a multidimensional structure, allowing one to look at any of them from the vantage point of any of the others. From each perspective, the view will be different. It is impossible, for example, to see *The New Boys* in the same way if one has seen *The Age of Reason* first, and this is equally true in reverse.

As a study of an enclosed community, the project evolved from inside out, working towards a broader, cumulative view rather than providing illustrations of a pre-existing analysis. In this sense it was experimental, since it developed incrementally, step by step. Nevertheless, it looked for answers to certain general questions: How did the dominant culture of a community affect its inhabitants? What aspects of that culture had the greatest influence? What were the experiences of those who lived there? As time went on, another question emerged. What were the capabilities of children, and how did they differ from those of adults? I did not expect the films to answer all these questions, but to provide examples for further thinking on the subject. What interested me were not only the experiences of individual children but the ways in which groups of children were able to develop their own patterns of communal living. Were there any principles involved in this that might be applied to adult society?

In retrospect, certain images in the films stand out for me more vividly than others. Some images I remember as coherent scenes, but more often they are fragmentary glimpses, or the sounds of certain words spoken in a particular way. These live in the memory not because they are representative of any general truth, but because they are like an unknown object seen for the first time, or an expression on a face that seems to go to the heart of another human being. These small moments may pass by unnoticed by many viewers of the films, but in some ways they remain for me those that justify all the rest.

Notes

1 Istituto Superiore Regionale Etnografico. The resulting film was *Tempus de Baristas* (1993), discussed in chapter 9.

2 This was one of the Australian Research Council's Queen Elizabeth II fellowships. It was followed in 2002 by an ARC Professorial fellowship, which allowed me to conduct filming projects at two more Indian institutions for children, the Rishi Valley School in Andhra Pradesh and the Prayas Children's Home for Boys in Delhi.

3 Although Judith and I had collaborated on many films previously, in an all-male environment this did not seem practical. Furthermore, I believed that by working on my own with digital video it would be possible to explore a different and more intimate kind of filmmaking.

4 This and all subsequent quotations from my Doon School journals are identified, as here, by the date of the entry.

5 The 'change-in-break' punishment required a boy to run to his house during the mid-morning break between classes, change into his games uniform, run back, when he presented a chit to a prefect, and then return to his house, where he changed back into his school uniform. All this meant he got no tea and biscuits and risked being late for his next class if he did not do it quickly enough.

6 *Constructing Post-colonial India: National Character and the Doon School*, published in 1998.

7 *The Doon School Weekly*, 13 November 1937, p. 3.

8 Quoted from *Doon School Chronicles.*

9 Quoted from *Doon School Chronicles.*

10 Published in *Prayers Written in Vailima* (1910). The film's title is taken from the following verse:

> Go with each of us to rest;
> If any awake, temper to them
> The dark hours of watching;
> And when the day returns,
> Return to us our sun and comforter,
> And call us up with morning faces,
> And with morning hearts,
> Eager to labour, eager to be happy
> If happiness shall be our portion,
> And if the day be marked for sorrow,
> Strong to endure it.

11 Quoted from *The New Boys.*

12 The epigraph was taken from John Locke's *Some Thoughts Concerning Education* of 1693:

> Children have as much a Mind to show
> that they are free, that their own good
> Actions come from themselves, that they
> are absolute and independent, as any of
> the proudest of you grown Men.

7

Seven types of collaboration

THERE is a curious ambiguity in how we think about documentary films. On the one hand a film is all about the concreteness of its subject, but on the other it is all about itself. The two seem mutually exclusive, like those trick drawings that make us see from two different perspectives, or see two different objects in one. In viewing films, the ambiguity is not just about distinguishing their different levels: of seeing the subject in itself and through its rendering, which is one way of taking two perceptions into account. It can be a more productive kind of viewing, leading us to see the filmmaker and the subject as somehow fused, joined together at the moment of perception. From this stance, authorship becomes more than an act of communication, or of recollecting a previous reality in tranquillity. It becomes an encounter that is perennially alive, renewed at every viewing of a film. This is the case, that is, if it is the film of a single author. But what if the relationship between observer and observed is complicated by several levels of consciousness? It is here that we must think about the effects of collaboration and its ambiguities. How should we interpret a film that has been made not by one person but, as is quite often the case, by many?

Films come to us whole, as if predestined to be that way. That they are complex constructions, constantly worked over to reach their final form, should be no surprise. But most films strive to present themselves to us as *sui generis*, alive and organic. This, I think, is chiefly due to the professionalism of their production, which is at pains to conceal how they were made.[1] Filmmakers want their works to have a life of their own, detached from their humble beginnings, all the more to proclaim the autonomy of the world as it is. This is perhaps more true of documentary than fiction films, since the latter can at least receive some praise for their artifice. But in documentaries the concealment of art is often a kind of declaration that no art was really needed.

Most commercial films are made by teams of people, each doing a particular job. This is partly a legacy of the technology that was needed to make films in their early years. The difficulties were compounded when it became necessary to direct actors, and again when sound was added to the moving image. An industrial model of film production thus became the norm, as films became mass entertainment and as increasing sums of money flowed in. The director might assume overall responsibility for a film, but the actual work was shared out among various people, most obviously the director, writer, cinematographer and editor. Together they practised a type of filmmaking that I would call 'dispersed' collaboration.

The word collaboration can convey a number of meanings, some nearly opposite in connotation, and this makes it difficult to prevent one idea of collaboration from spilling over into another. For example, it can sometimes be hard to disentangle sponsorship from complicity and propaganda. Or if I say that you are a good collaborator, the statement may carry a hint of condescension, suggesting I am the dominant party. On the other hand, if I say that we collaborated well on a project, our positions appear more equal. Such minor differences can be put down as much to the context in which the statement is made as to the instability of the word itself. But collaboration has a history which we cannot ignore. A collaborator in 1944 France is quite different from a collaborator on the Manhattan Project, even if a certain opprobrium clings to each.

In nearly every case, collaboration in documentary filmmaking raises questions of dominance. Except perhaps when films are co-authored, there are likely to be significant differences in the relative positions of the collaborators. To say that a film is 'by' a particular author is to elide the contributions of others. Attribution of a film to one person therefore tells us little more than that this person bears final responsibility for the film. Documentary also nearly always involves disparities in the positions of the filmmakers and their subjects, if not in class, wealth or ethnicity, then in who controls the camera and means of publication. Theorists are concerned with the power differential this implies, but filmmakers must be concerned with the actual effects filming may have on the lives of those whom they film. Films that are about living human beings inevitably involve some degree of intrusion in their lives, with potentially both positive and negative consequences. Filmmakers thus face ethical dilemmas in recording many of the situations they encounter, when this could cause embarrassment or harm to their subjects. The safest approach would of course be not to make films at all, but if films of this kind are considered worth making, much depends on how they are conceived, the trust developed between filmmakers and their subjects, the subjects' commitment to the film and their participation in the decisions surrounding it. Without going so far as to make only anodyne films, or films with a prescribed outcome, filmmakers can still reach understandings with the subjects that include their participation in the film's making. The good faith of filmmakers cannot be guaranteed, but short of abandoning this kind of exploratory filmmaking, the development of ethical practices seems the most practical and realistic approach.[2]

Collaboration, particularly in fiction films, has long been viewed as fundamental to the art. Many writers on cinema take this as a given, and there is at least one book called *The Collaborative Art of Filmmaking* (Seger 2018). The assumption that films are essentially collaborative arose first from the theatre and then its successor, the film studio. From fiction films it spread to nonfiction, especially with the addition of sound in the 1930s. From then on, the techniques of feature film production were increasingly adopted by documentary film producers such as John Grierson. Nonetheless, there has been an alternative tradition. Throughout film history, starting in the earliest years of the Lumière Company, many people have made films alone, and since the advent of digital video the ability to do so has greatly increased. Many documentary films can be attributed to a single author, shot and edited by the same person. Films of this kind are typically associated with determinedly independent filmmakers such as Maya Deren, Chris Marker, Stan Brakhage and Robert Gardner.

My purpose here is not to reinforce the notion that all films are collaborative but to show that where there has been collaboration in the past, it has varied in kind and degree, just as the films it has produced have taken different forms. These collaborations have involved people in varied relationships, and we can sort them into several distinct types. Moreover, two or more types of collaboration may be present in the same work.

1. Dispersed collaboration

The first type, which I have called *dispersed collaboration*, is that with which we are most familiar, because it is almost universally employed in commercial documentaries and television productions. By this I mean the 'industrial' model I referred to earlier, in which specialised creative tasks are assigned to different members of a crew. The resulting films combine multiple talents and generally express a corporate rather than a personal perspective. It takes a strong director to override such a powerful system, which is perhaps why the *auteur* directors of Hollywood are held in such esteem.

Although many personal and experimental films were made in the silent era, the coming of sound required more complex equipment and increased the pressures to adopt the industrial model. The classic American documentary film *The City* was released in 1939. It was first outlined by Pare Lorentz. A scenario was then produced by Henwar Rodakiewicz, and the commentary was written by Lewis Mumford, but spoken in the film by Morris Carnovsky. Aaron Copland wrote the music. The film was shot by Ralph Steiner, Willard Van Dyke and three other cinematographers. It was edited by Theodore Lawrence. Although the actual direction was credited to Steiner and Van Dyke, one can see that this was very much a group effort.

Many of the films produced in Britain around this time were similarly collaborative, although the extent of the collaboration was often left unstated. *Coal Face* (1935) contained important contributions by W. H. Auden, Humphrey Jennings and Alberto Cavalcanti, although none are named in the film's credits

(British Film Institute 2008: 48). The British Film Institute lists the following makers of *Night Mail* (1936), one of the most famous films of the period (British Film Institute 2009: 40):

Directors (uncredited): Harry Watt, Basil Wright
Assistant director (uncredited): Pat Jackson
Cameras: Jonah Jones and Chick Fowle
Producers: Basil Wright, Harry Watt, John Grierson (uncredited)
Editing (uncredited): Basil Wright, Alberto Cavalcanti, Pat Jackson, R. Q. McNaughton
Script (uncredited): Basil Wright, Harry Watt, John Grierson
Sound direction: Alberto Cavalcanti
Verse: W. H. Auden
Music: Benjamin Britten
Sound recording: E. A. Pawley and C. Sullivan
Narration (uncredited): Pat Jackson
Poem spoken by (uncredited): Stuart Legg
Additional verse spoken by (uncredited): John Grierson

Night Mail might be called the holotype specimen for this kind of collaboration. Many of the films produced by John Grierson and the GPO Film Unit seem like family affairs, with various members pitching in where necessary to provide voices, music, sound effects and even small acting parts. Humphrey Jennings, later to make many of the most distinguished British documentaries, plays the part of a grocer in *Pett and Pott* (1934) and a postman in *The Glorious Sixth of June* (1934), both directed by Alberto Cavalcanti. Many of the GPO Film Unit films have a consistency of tone, despite trying out numerous experiments with image and sound. This may have resulted from Grierson's influence or the fact that they were made by a small group of people with similar views. There is generally a social message, a degree of experimentation in the camera work, sound and editing, and a commentary delivered in an authoritative voice. Perhaps because nearly all these films were made by left-leaning intellectuals but sponsored by government or industry, they tend towards a certain moral ambiguity, combining a measure of social criticism about living and working conditions with a generally positive view of British institutions.

Mixed authorship in documentary gradually became more orderly and routine with the coming of television. In most commercial productions each member of the production team had a defined role – as director, writer, cinematographer, sound engineer, lighting technician and so on. If the cinematographer encroached too much on the director's role, he or she was likely to be rebuked or not invited back. Yet the director was also careful not to encroach too much on the cinematographer's decisions. In most cases, this meant giving general instructions about the shots but leaving the exact framing to the cinematographer. In any case, in many of the events that unfold during the making of a documentary there is not enough time for the director to determine every shot. The visual sensibility of the cinematographer, like the conceptual sensibility of the director, becomes part of the film's overall design.

Consider the degree of collaboration involved in big productions like the multi-part British television series *The World at War* (1973–74), or the American series *The Civil War* (1990), which involved scores of participants and marshalled archival photographs and film footage from many sources. *The World at War* required twenty-seven producers and over 200 interviews shot by nine cinematographers. Producing *The Civil War* required at least 180 people, including twenty-one sound editors and forty-seven narrators. In some respects these television programmes can be considered 'editor's films', for they are elaborate collages pieced together out of a huge array of materials. Yet the writers and directors were also important, and many of the images they used had been produced by a still earlier generation of filmmakers and photographers.

2. Co-authorship

A second and perhaps equally familiar type of collaboration, *co-authorship*, characterises many recent documentary films. It is what most people imagine when they think of collaboration: two people working together to produce a single work. Here much more than filmmaking comes to mind: the operettas of Gilbert and Sullivan, the scientific work of James Watson and Francis Crick in describing the DNA double helix, the art works of Christo and Jeanne-Claude, the crime novels of 'Ellery Queen' and those of Maj Sjöwall and Per Wahlöö. Co-authorship is hard to find in fiction filmmaking but it is very common in documentary. An early example is *Grass: A Nation's Battle for Life* (1925), by Merian C. Cooper and Ernest B. Schoedsack (figure 7.1). Several of Robert

7.1 Cooper (left) and Schoedsack (right) during the making of *Grass*

Flaherty's films may also be considered co-authored, even though Frances Flaherty's contribution went largely unacknowledged at the time.

Indeed, documentary film history is notable for famous collaborations: Albert and David Maysles filming *Salesman* (1969); Wolf Koenig and Roman Kroiter making *Lonely Boy* (1962) and other films at the National Film Board of Canada; David Hancock and Herbert Di Gioia making the *Vermont People* series (1971–75); Jean Rouch and Edgar Morin making *Chronique d'un été* (often contentiously) in 1960–61. In this type of collaboration male–female partnerships abound, the partners often living as well as working together. The husband-and-wife team of Bob Connolly and Robin Anderson together made the New Guinea Highlands trilogy (including *Joe Leahy's Neighbours*, 1988), and Ilisa Barbash and Lucien Castaing-Taylor jointly made *Sweetgrass* (2009). Castaing-Taylor went on to collaborate on *Leviathan* (2012) and other films with Véréna Paravel.

I have been involved in co-authorship on a number of occasions. Judith MacDougall and I have made eighteen films together, of which we have co-directed eleven, including the films of the *Turkana Conversations* trilogy (1977–81), *Photo Wallahs* (1991) and *Awareness* (2010). In most of these films, but not all, I have done the filming and Judith has recorded the sound, a working arrangement typical of documentary filmmaking from the 1960s onwards. Decisions about what and how to film have been made jointly. In the editing, one or the other of us has tended to make the first cut of a scene once we have decided on its general outlines. Then we have met together to review and revise it. This process has not been without heated disputes and sometimes humour. Very often we have disagreed on a particular point, only to discover after lengthy debate that we have each accepted the other's argument.

Co-authorship involves certain complexities and limitations along with its benefits. Collaboration of any kind can be difficult, requiring much patience and deliberation. At its best it is exhilarating to exchange ideas and put them into practice, building on one another's knowledge and insights. At its worst it can create a clash between two personalities with very different conceptions of what the work should contain and how it should be made. Ethnographic filmmaking provides extreme instances of this. It was once assumed that bringing together a filmmaker with an anthropologist was an ideal combination, each contributing what they knew best to the film. But all too often the anthropologist had an agenda that upset the filmmaker's idea of how the film should be constructed, and the filmmaker's approach seemed to the anthropologist to impede much of what needed to be said. Happily, in other cases filmmaker and anthropologist have each absorbed enough of one another's ideas to produce a unified approach.[3]

One of the inevitable consequences of co-authorship is the need for constant consultation over how to proceed, which can sometimes stand in the way of risk-taking and spontaneous decision-making. It can also influence, for better or worse, the filmmakers' relations with the film subjects. For someone being filmed it is a very different matter to deal with two or more filmmakers than just one. Even two people constitute a social unit from which it is easy to feel excluded, whereas if you are dealing with a single filmmaker you may be able to have a one-on-one relationship. For filmmakers, however, there may be advantages in being part of a social unit. If the collaboration involves a man and woman, for example, the woman may in some situations take the lead and the man in others, widening the range of filming possibilities. In these cases one or the other may be allowed to be present at events where usually only a man or woman would be welcomed, the partner being accepted as a 'silent' or background presence. A similar diversity in age, ethnicity or class may benefit collaborations in other situations.

When co-authorship is working at its best the collaborators have a common understanding of their objectives; they often seem to know instinctively what the other is thinking and how he or she will act; yet at the same time each gives space to the other to take the initiative when this is advantageous. This is particularly important in documentary filming, since very often there is no time for consultation, for events are moving too quickly. Each member of the pair must then have confidence that the other will make the right decisions. The situation is rather different when it comes to editing the film. Here a great deal of discussion is called for, and a willingness to try varied solutions to problems, in the belief that the right one will eventually emerge. There must also be an acceptance that not all of one's most cherished wishes can be realised, and sometimes it is best to give way to the views of one's collaborator. In effect, co-authorship means combining two creative impulses, and this inevitably involves compromise.

3. Creative assistance

Another type of collaboration involving two persons might be called *creative assistance*. Here one of the pair takes a secondary role, helping the other realise his or her objectives while still making a substantial contribution to the work. An ideal example of this type of collaboration would be any of the films of Frederick Wiseman, such as *Hospital* (1970), directed and edited by Wiseman but filmed by William Brayne (figure 7.2). Brayne worked closely with Wiseman on most of his films of the 1970s: *Basic Training* (1971), *Essene* (1972), *Juvenile Court* (1973), *Primate* (1974), *Welfare* (1975), *Meat* (1976) and *Canal Zone* (1977). Brayne's contribution to these films was immense, for he shot all of them while Wiseman recorded the sound; and yet it was Wiseman who decided what to film and finally how to put the film together.[4] Wiseman had tried out this sort of combination on his first film, *Titicut Follies* (1967), with John Marshall as the cinematographer. In early prints of the film Marshall

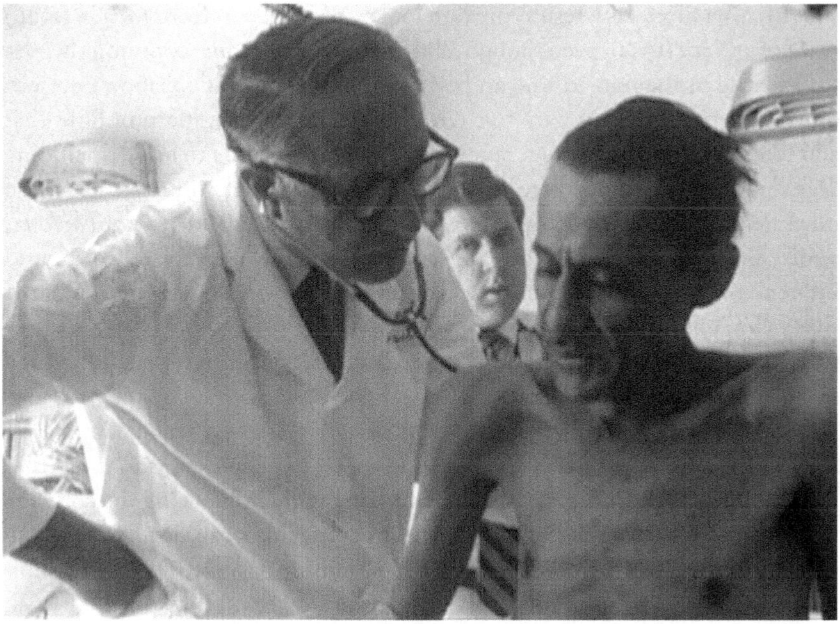

7.2 Doctors examine a patient in *Hospital*

is even given a co-director's credit. But this working relationship did not continue, and it is clear that Wiseman wanted to maintain a more dominant position and, in effect, to be considered the sole author of his films.

The role of the second person in this type of collaboration can vary greatly in kind and extent. In some films it may be as the cinematographer, in others as the editor or the director's assistant. The contribution is more than technical, but it is always supplementary to that of the director. Many cinematographers or film editors would argue that their creative contribution to a film has been as important as the director's and they should be considered the co-author – that is, a collaborator of the second type. It is also undoubtedly true that many an editor has 'saved' a film that has gone awry in some way, or that has been botched by an incompetent director. But if we blur the borderlines too much, or allow too many exceptions, we lose the point of making these distinctions. Where one person retains the final say, the other cannot be considered a co-author.

One can point to many films in which a filmmaker relied on the collaboration of another person for a creative contribution. Robert Gardner's *Forest of Bliss* (1985) is one of the most personal documentary films ever made, but it nevertheless relied extensively on Àkos Östör's knowledge and advice (Gardner and Östör 2001). Richard Leacock's distinctive camera-eye helped shape *Louisiana Story* (1948) by Robert Flaherty, a director who had previously always shot his own films. As a result, the film looks very different from *Moana* (1926) or *Man of Aran* (1934), even though all these films share some common themes.

The role of the film editor can be crucial in this type of collaboration, not only shaping the film in narrative terms but discovering important links that add to its complexity. Certain renowned film editors come to mind, including Dai Vaughan, who helped create the pioneering approach of British television documentary in the 1970s and 1980s and who, in *Portrait of an Invisible Man*, wrote about another film editor, Stewart McAllister, who exercised a profound influence on the films of Humphrey Jennings and other documentaries of the 1940s (Vaughan 1983). In *Listen to Britain* (1942), a film that is essentially a collage of images and sounds from varied sources, McAllister is justly credited as co-director along with Jennings.

In some cases the collaborator is not directly involved technically in the filming but acts as an intermediary, giving access to people and situations that would otherwise be inaccessible, thus fundamentally influencing the contents of the film. This has been the case in a number of ethnographic films in which an anthropologist has provided access to a community and the linguistic skills to communicate with its members. The more successful films of the British *Disappearing World* television series (1970–93) provide examples of this, such as *The Last of the Cuiva* (1971), *The Mursi* (1974), *Masai Women* (1974) and *Ongka's Big Moka* (1976). After making *The Mursi*, the anthropologist David Turton and the film director Leslie Woodhead went on to make a further five films about the same African people, an instance of this kind of collaboration working out for the best.

In my own filmmaking I have experienced creative assistance from the viewpoint of both director and assistant. When I filmed *Gandhi's Children* in 2005 I acted as director, cinematographer and editor, but I was greatly assisted by Siddhartha Kumar, a postgraduate student completing a degree at the Delhi School of Economics. While making the film I lived in the Prayas Children's Home for Boys, a shelter for orphans, street children and juvenile detainees on the outskirts of Delhi. Siddhartha would join me each day and many evenings as we filmed and interacted with the children. The children spoke Hindi and dialects of Bihari. As a Bihari himself, Siddhartha therefore had an essential role, as both translator and intermediary. It was he who conducted most of the conversations with the children I filmed. We had to agree on many things beforehand, and we constantly discussed the objectives and progress of the project. It was especially fortunate that our ideas coincided so closely, both about what we were doing and how we viewed the situations we encountered. That, of course, was one of the reasons I had chosen Siddhartha. Without his contribution I would still have made the film, but it would have been very different.

In some of the films that Judith and I have made together, one of us has acted as director with the other providing support and assistance. This was the case in *The House-Opening* (1980), for which I did the cinematography. Beyond that, I simply followed her direction, particularly as the film also involved a further type of collaboration, as described below. This pattern characterised our filmmaking from the very beginning when, as film students, she shot the first film I directed, *Km 400* (1966), and I then shot her thesis film, *Indians and Chiefs* (1967). She then recorded the sound for what was planned as my thesis film, *To Live with Herds* (1972).[5]

Mayank's Family (2014) may seem like an unusual example to give of a film in which I was the assistant, for at first glance it would appear that I had a greater role. Moreover, the director of the film, Mayank Ved, was only ten years old (shown second left in Figure 12.1). This film resulted from a series of video workshops that I conducted with groups of children in India, in which they made films in their own communities. At the beginning their knowledge of filmmaking was essentially nil, so whatever skills they picked up were the result of the workshops. The main skill they learned was how to use a video camera, but they also developed their own ideas about what to film, how to film it and in general how to organise the resulting materials. My role was as instructor, facilitator and, finally, co-editor.

To gauge the nature of my collaboration on Mayank's film it is necessary to describe more precisely how he made it. The workshop lasted two months. The first two weeks were devoted to my teaching the children video skills, such as how to hold the camera steady, how to get acceptable exposure and focus, and basic ways of connecting one shot with another. The idea was for the children to use the cameras as research tools to explore the topic each had chosen. Mayank's topic was his father and his father's work as a barber in the village (figure 7.3). But as time went on he told me he wanted to show more

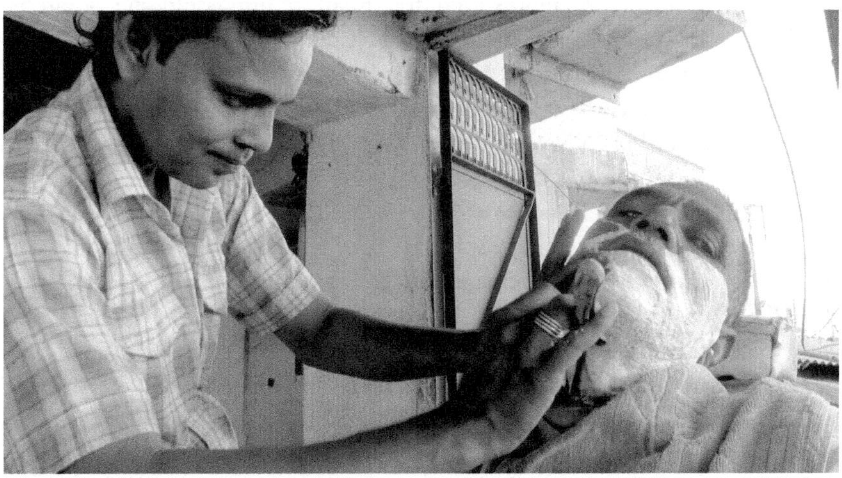

7.3 Mayank's father at work in *Mayank's Family*

about his father's life at home. Still later, he told me he wanted to show the parallel lives of his father and others in the family. Mayank loved using the camera, and he was very good at it. His filming gradually expanded to cover his father, his mother and his younger brother.

Together with a local assistant, I had taught Mayank some basic filming skills, but he seemed to know instinctively what to do with the camera. Day by day we watched his footage together. It was during this time that he developed the idea of alternating scenes at the barber shop with those at home. Towards the end of the workshop we reviewed everything he had shot and he decided which scenes to include in the film and what order to put them in. My main contribution was to help edit the material in this way and provide such technical assistance as adding the titles, subtitles and end credits. Mayank's film was among the more complex of those made in the workshop project, but it was definitively his own and no one had told him how to make it. Despite facilitating the production, my contribution was always secondary to his.

4. Subject collaboration

A film subject's collaboration in the making of a film, or what we might call *subject collaboration*, is as old as *Nanook of the North* (1922), which can also serve here as an example. The story of the film's production is well known and perhaps too often repeated. Allakariallak, Flaherty's protagonist, was one of the film's creators, suggesting to Flaherty at least one of its most notable scenes, the walrus hunt, as well as acting in it. Flaherty immediately embraced the idea as embodying one of his key themes, the struggle of man with nature. This is also the theme of the seal hunt scene and the blizzard scene elsewhere in the film. That the protagonist of a documentary film could collaborate in making it was a novel idea at the time, and it remained so for many years.[6]

Flaherty was much admired by the anthropologist Jean Rouch, who also invited his subjects' collaboration in many of his films, an arrangement that he termed 'shared anthropology' (*anthropologie partagée*) (Rouch 2003: 100–1). The collaboration took various forms. In one of his 'ethnofictions', *Jaguar* (filmed 1954, completed 1968), Rouch's subjects viewed footage of their travels, which Rouch had instigated, creating a soundtrack of reminiscences and dialogue in the studio in response to the images. In *La Pyramide humaine* (1961) Rouch carried out a collective experiment in race relations with a group of black and white secondary school students in Abidjan, capital of the Ivory Coast. And in *Petit à Petit* (1971) Rouch turned the tables on anthropology, persuading two of his friends (Damouré and Lam, also seen in *Jaguar*, *Cocorico! Monsieur Poulet* [1974] and several other films) to visit Paris and study Parisian life in order to improve their import–export business at home, as a kind of extended cinematic joke.

Rouch used the term 'shared anthropology' not because he and his collaborators were conducting anthropological research in a strict sense (*Petit à Petit* is a send-up of anthropology) but rather to insist that ethnographic knowledge should not be the private preserve of Western scholars and should instead become a dialogue between ethnographers and members of the culture they studied. By recording shared experiences, something new about the perspectives and social lives of individuals might be revealed. The collaboration involved a high degree of reciprocity. He and his subjects all gave something of themselves to the project, and all in the end benefited from it in some way. At least that was how Rouch perceived it. Who benefited most can be disputed, for Rouch always saw his life and practice in mythic terms. But there is little doubt that these films provide some of the most comprehensive examples of subject collaboration in filmmaking that we have. Rouch's collaboration with Damouré lasted for more than sixty years, from 1941 until Rouch's death in a car crash in Niger in 2004 at the age of eighty-six. Damouré was travelling in the same car, but as he was in the back seat he was not seriously hurt.[7]

A different kind of collaboration emerged in the 1960s in the National Film Board of Canada's *Challenge for Change* programme, conceived as a way of using film and video to initiate social change. Directed through most of its existence by George Stoney, the programme produced over 200 films in which marginalised Canadian communities interacted in varied ways with filmmakers, responding to footage as it was produced, creating video footage themselves and speaking of their concerns on camera. This participatory approach inspired many later community film and video projects, which were often shown on local or cable television channels, one example being the three-part series *Who Killed Fourth Ward?* (1977), produced by James Blue in Houston, Texas. A participatory approach also underpinned many of the films that Judith and I made with Aboriginal communities for the Australian Institute of Aboriginal Studies (AIAS), including *Takeover* (1980) and *Collum Calling Canberra* (1984).[8]

Some form of subject collaboration may be present in nearly every documentary film, if only to the extent that the subjects have allowed themselves to be filmed, and often only doing certain things. But it has also been seen as democratising the cinema, giving film subjects a voice in a domain previously dominated by institutions and individual authors. In some films this claim may be valid enough – one thinks of Celso's role in Gary Kildea's *Celso and Cora* (1983) – but in others it may be an exaggeration or simply express the filmmakers' idealism. A filmmaker may feel uncomfortable about occupying a position of power (as a filmmaker *per se* or more broadly in society) and seek to attenuate it. In the history of advocacy films, there are many cases of ceding power to an oppressed minority, or at least attempting to do so. Two Australian examples are *My Survival as an Aboriginal* (1979), crediting its protagonist Essie Coffey as director but filmed, produced and edited by others; and *Two Laws* (1981), produced by Alessandro Cavadini and Carolyn Strachan.

In the latter film the filmmakers asked Aboriginal people in the Borroloola community to determine the film's content and style of filming. Turning to an example with which I am more familiar, *The House-Opening* (1980), made in the Aboriginal community of Aurukun, the main protagonist, Geraldine Kawanka, collaborated in determining many of the editing decisions and then provided a voice-over commentary for the film.

Next to the benefits of subject collaboration one must consider the limitations. As I mentioned earlier, any form of collaboration requires compromise, but when there is a considerable gap between the backgrounds and interests of the filmmaker and subject, the compromises may result in a kind of double negation, so that the interests of neither are properly expressed, or else remain blurred. It may be impossible to know whose perspective the film finally represents. My experience of collaborating with film subjects, which initially I embraced, has convinced me that the resulting ambiguity often constrains both parties. It may be far better to create the conditions in which each can make their own films, or failing that, construct films (such as by alternating scenes) to show two different perspectives. This stance retains and reaffirms the value of individual authorship.[9]

5. Sponsorship

A type of collaboration that in many ways appears self-evident is *sponsorship*. It is not, however, without nuances and variations. Let us say a company or institution sponsors or commissions a film. The film is meant to promote a particular idea or product, and the filmmaker is expected to make a film that does so. The collaboration in this case consists in bringing together their different resources to achieve one objective, and they may do so through a loose agreement or much closer consultation and supervision. Sometimes, as in the case of *The Song of Ceylon* (1934) by Basil Wright, this programme is not carried out quite as intended. The film was sponsored by the Empire Marketing Board on behalf of the Ceylon Tea Propaganda Board to promote the British tea industry. The sponsors had commissioned four short films on the tea industry. What the sponsors got instead was a more lengthy meditation on colonialism and the evil effects of commerce on a once pristine culture, followed only much later by the four short films. *The Song of Ceylon* received so much critical acclaim that the Empire Marketing Board might have thought it best to leave well enough alone. In the end it got its short films too, resulting in a happy outcome for all concerned.

Sometimes the sponsor merely wishes to have its name associated with a worthy subject. When the Shell Oil Company sponsored *Between the Tides* (1958), there was no doubt a felicitous link between the company's logo and a film about sea life, but the broader aim was to suggest that the company cared

7.4 Life before electrification in *Power and the Land*

about natural science. Since the film was nominated for an Oscar, one assumes the company was well satisfied. The Standard Oil Company had already trodden this ground when it sponsored Robert Flaherty's *Louisiana Story* in 1948, and Flaherty had responded with a benign vision of oil-drilling in the Louisiana bayous. This film was also nominated for an Oscar.

A more clear-cut case of sponsorship achieving its objectives was *Power and the Land* (1940), a film commissioned by the US government's Rural Electrification Administration. The aim was to demonstrate that bringing electricity to American farmers would result in social progress. The benefits would exceed the costs and would also indirectly benefit electrical appliance manufacturers. As directed by Joris Ivens, previously known as a radical filmmaker, the film did just this, creating an idealised farm family whose lives are vastly improved by the introduction of electric lighting, electric water pumps, electric milking machines and domestic appliances. At the beginning the 'Parkinsons' are shown worn out by house and farm work, spending their evenings by the dim light of kerosene lamps (figure 7.4). At the end the farm work is done with the aid of electricity, and the women are able to cook, wash and iron with it.

In making the film, Ivens' associates (who included Pare Lorentz, the editor Helen van Dongen, and writer of the narration, the poet Stephen Vincent Benét) collaborated closely with the staff of the Rural Electrification Administration with the aim of winning the approval of both rural and urban audiences. The fictional family, the Parkinsons, were carefully made to appear poor, but not too poor, and in order to heighten the before-and-after contrast, to be notably lacking a telephone, battery-powered radio, car and other possessions that even a non-electrified farm would probably have had at the time.[10]

The degree of compromise necessary between a filmmaker's and a sponsor's objectives may be minimal, and in other cases so great as to become unworkable. A large number of documentary films made for television are contracted to independent filmmakers by a commissioning editor, who oversees the result. Just occasionally the commissioning editor may adopt a hands-off approach, as is usual in commissioning a piece of music, the rationale being that the best results will be obtained by giving the filmmaker a free hand. In these instances it usually means that the filmmaker has a sufficient creative reputation to command respect. But this is a rarity in television, where commissioning editors are more likely to look upon filmmakers as generators of 'content'. One of the few filmmakers who has consistently been able to achieve such freedom is Frederick Wiseman, who for years was able to make commissioned films that had not been clearly mapped out and approved in advance.

Far more often, the commissioning editor wants to know what the film will be like before it is made and intervenes at various points of the production to make sure that it is, or that something equally acceptable is produced. The reasons for this are not only to protect the television company's investment. Television executives and commissioning editors have their managerial roles to consider. To give filmmakers too much freedom is not only to run the risk of receiving unusable material but to diminish their position as arbiters of popular taste. A commissioning editor need not have an opinion about what makes a good film, only about what makes good programming. Many have never actually made a film and have come up through the ranks of administration or advertising.

There are of course exceptions. A colleague of mine once approached a commissioning editor about a new film. When asked what it would be about, he said he didn't know. He only knew where the film would be made, a place where he had made two previous films, and he would have to see what came up when he got there. Knowing the filmmaker's track-record, the commissioning editor guaranteed a pre-sale and told him to go ahead. In most other situations filmmakers who approached a commissioning editor in this way would be expected to make a 'pitch' and be thought ridiculous if they didn't. Today one may even have to submit an assembly of 'found' footage on the film's proposed topic to give an impression of what it will be like. One notable deviation from these procedures was the BBC documentary series *Fine Cut*, the premise of which was that each film in the series would be made by a different filmmaker and represent that filmmaker's distinctive vision. What was unusual about this in television was that the focus was more on the programming of filmmakers than on the programming of topics.[11]

6. Complicity

The line between sponsorship and *complicity* is sometimes difficult to define, but I consider this a separate type of collaboration. In 1934 Adolf Hitler asked Leni Riefenstahl to make a film of the Nazi party congress to be held in Nuremberg. She had already made a short film about the 1933 party congress at Hitler's request. At first she hesitated, but later she agreed, on condition that neither Hitler nor Goebbels (with whom she was on bad terms) would see the film until it was completed. She was given funds and all the facilities she required from UFA, the national film studio. This arrangement differed from more straightforward commissions in that the content and purpose of the film were well understood on both sides but remained unstated. Riefenstahl was an ardent admirer of Hitler, and the resulting film was a paean of praise to him and a masterpiece of propaganda. That she was complicit with the regime is an understatement, although she always maintained that she was simply documenting an event. In fact she designed many of its key elements. Although she was not told what to do, the film was clearly an expression of her own ecstatic feelings.

If *Triumph of the Will* (1935) is the prototype, there are many other films that offer examples of complicity between filmmakers, individuals, governments and institutions, including several more by Riefenstahl.[12] A substantial number of those that focus on famous people are unmemorable because, predictably, they are both hagiographic and dull: films about movie stars, popular singers, religious leaders, politicians and sports heroes. They are typified by an uncritical servility towards their subjects. One would expect most films about Pope Francis, the Dalai Lama, the Beatles, Winston Churchill and Mother Teresa to fall into this category. If they are made during the subject's lifetime, the subject must agree to be filmed, and very often the result is, as Pauline Spiegel puts it, imbued with 'a sense of politeness, of reticence' (1984: 15). The more august the subject, the greater the politeness.

A case in point is *Royal Family* (1969), a documentary film about the family of Queen Elizabeth II made by Richard Cawston for the BBC and ITV. The film showed ordinary events in the day-to-day life of the family (figure 7.5). The idea came originally from William Heseltine, the Queen's press secretary, who thought it would be a good idea to present the public with a more intimate and down-to-earth view of royalty. It was broadcast to over 30 million viewers but was later withdrawn from circulation at the Queen's request, apparently because it was felt to be too intimate. While making the film, Cawston was nothing if not polite, saying later, 'there was never a question of asking for something that would have to be turned down' (Rosenthal 1971: 204).

Today it is hardly likely that a major political figure would give filmmakers the kind of access that President Kennedy and Robert Kennedy gave Robert Drew and his fellow filmmakers D. A. Pennebaker and Richard Leacock when

7.5 Family intimacy in *Royal Family*

they made *Crisis: Behind a Presidential Commitment* (1963). The film concerned the confrontation over racial integration at the University of Alabama in 1963. In the film the brothers are shown in intimate scenes telephoning each other and discussing with their advisors at the White House what to do next.

7. Symbiosis

There is finally a special type of collaboration I would term *symbiosis*. This involves a relationship between filmmaker and subject that I think differs in quality from both subject collaboration and complicity. Where it exists in a film, it gives an impression of a merging of the filmmaker's and subject's intentions, even a merging of consciousness. The making of the film creates an atmosphere of cooperation in which both filmmaker and subject are caught up. As in biological symbiosis, there is a process of exchange and interdependence between the two sides.

Over the years Les Blank made many films, such as *Spend It All* (1971), celebrating the music and food of ethnic communities in the United States, especially of the Cajuns of Louisiana and Spanish-speaking populations living along the Mexican border. These are for the most part joyous films, driven by the music and Blank's response to it. The performers seem energised by the fact that they are being filmed, and their pleasure in turn seems to energise Blank's camerawork, inspiring him to improvise lyrical poems from whatever catches his eye. They typically have to do with the preparation and enjoyment of food but also include glimpses of random but evocative details, such as chickens running across a farmyard. In the inter-subjectivity and unconscious choreography of these scenes there is something reminiscent of Rouch's interaction with his subjects in his film *Tourou et Bitti, les tambours d'avant* (1971), which consisted primarily of an extended sequence-shot following the drummers and dancers at a possession ceremony in a village in Niger. It was in relation to this film that Rouch often spoke of the experience of *ciné-transe*. And indeed, in many films in which *symbiosis* is present, it is because the filmmaker becomes entranced by the spirit of the subject.

In some films a person being filmed seems to step forward and take possession of the film, and often of the filmmaker too. This occurs in Tanya Ballentyne's *The Things I Cannot Change* (1967), in which the chief protagonist, the father of a large impoverished family, dominates nearly every scene with a barrage of non-stop talking and self-justification. Something similar happens in Shirley Clarke's *Portrait of Jason* (1967), which was intended as an extended interview. It becomes more than that as the protagonist, Jason Holliday, a black gay hustler and aspiring nightclub performer, seizes the opportunity to reinvent himself before the camera.

I have personally experienced the phenomenon of symbiosis in two films. In 1983 Judith and I began making a film about Sunny Bancroft, an Australian Aboriginal stockman and manager of a cattle station in northern New South Wales. One of Sunny's passions was horse racing, and every year he used to try out stock-horses at the picnic races that were held in his part of the state. He began buying new working horses that he thought would race well, and eventually he bought a former racehorse named King. We followed these events, which culminated in King's disappointing finish at the races and Sunny's determination to buy yet another horse.

At the beginning we envisaged the film as an observational documentary about country life. We invited Sunny to record extemporaneous lines of narration to fill in some of the narrative gaps. But Sunny was not interested in the facts; in his narration he began spinning the story into a fiction, and we soon found ourselves charmed by his enthusiasm and letting him do so. The film began to take on the qualities of a legend, and in our editing we took it further in this direction, creating what Rouch would have called a work of ethnofiction. In the end we felt that the film, *Sunny and the Dark Horse* (1986), was more true to Sunny's character and inner life than the original documentary would have been.

My second experience of symbiosis occurred while making a very different sort of film. *The Age of Reason* (filmed 1998, released 2004) was the last of the five films I made about life at a boarding school in northern India. The film was an offshoot of the more general film I was making about the boys in one of the first-year dormitories. The new film focused on Abhishek, a twelve-year-old

Nepali boy who was one of the group of new students who had just entered the school. From the start I found him remarkable, with a maturity of judgement and breadth of knowledge unusual for his age. Abhishek took an interest in the filming and engaged me in long conversations about his life and ideas. I began filming these conversations, and he took this largely as a matter of course, as by this time he had become used to my filming him and others in the dormitory. He also seemed to welcome these interactions, volunteering information about himself and his thoughts. It soon became obvious that the volume of material I was gathering about him would not fit into the film I was then making, and it was at this point that I decided to make a separate film about him. From then on it was a matter of recording my further interactions with him and significant events in his life at the school. He seemed always ready to cooperate in this project. The filming had become an extension and mediator of our friendship. In the type of collaboration I have called symbiosis, there is a tacit understanding that emerges between filmmaker and subject. This was clearly the case in my filming of Abhishek. (The making of this film is discussed in greater detail in Chapter 11.)

The viewer as collaborator

In considering collaboration it is important to remember that every film requires one further element for its completion: the collaboration of the viewer. A film is a set of fragments pulled out of the stream of life. As viewers, we fill in the gaps of time and space with our imagination, but equally we try to make sense of the film, both intellectually and emotionally. Without this, without our interest and engagement, the film remains flat on the screen. If it touches us or arouses our curiosity, this means that something we have seen in the film connects with our own desires or experiences. It may be a face, an object or a familiar predicament.

This sort of collaboration does not happen automatically: every film must create the context for its own viewing. At the start it must somehow situate itself in relation to us, providing a reason why we should continue to watch it. This not only means supplying information for us to grasp but signalling what sort of film it is likely to be. It must, in effect, establish the rules of the game for our viewing of it. Is it going to be fiction or nonfiction? Will it proceed swiftly or take its time? Does the filmmaker stand with us or stand apart? Some of these matters can be taken as given when the film clearly belongs to a particular genre, but in most cases they must be part of a process of discovery carefully structured for the viewer by the filmmaker. In the end, it is the collaboration between filmmaker and film viewer that matters most.

One may well ask what effects the various types of collaboration have on the viewers of a film. It is clear that many forms of collaboration remain invisible to the audience. Yet collaboration does influence the overall style of a film, and this partly determines the wide variety of films that are made. Films and television programmes made on the industrial model, using large crews and passing through many hands, are more likely to reflect an institutional rather than a personal voice. Similarly, films with a glossy, high finish – what Dai Vaughan described as films 'with their cellophane wrap of commentary and captions and studio presentation' (1999: 114) – tend to exude an aura of professionalism from which the viewer may feel excluded. Conversely, films resulting from collaborations of the second and third types (co-authorship and creative assistance) are more likely to express an individual point of view with which the viewer can identify.

Films involving subject collaboration, such as those by Jean Rouch, often have a playful and improvised quality in which the pleasurable or experimental nature of the collaboration is felt. In these cases the viewer may feel drawn into the game as a kind of co-conspirator. Or the collaboration may simply impart a feeling of informality. In *Celso and Cora*, when Celso confides his worries to the filmmaker, it is almost as though he is confiding them to us as well. In such films, the sense of trust and mutual regard between filmmaker and subject comes through to the viewer. One feels a similar trust and mutual regard in the conversations between Nigerian women and Éliane de Latour in *Contes et comptes de la cour* (1993), which could never have been made without the women's active collaboration.

There is another kind of documentary film in which the filmmaker no longer remains behind the scenes but is present in the film, confiding directly in the audience. In these self-reflexive films – reflecting back upon themselves as created objects – the mask of professionalism is put aside and the viewer is allowed to witness the process. In Jean Rouch and Edgar Morin's film *Chronique d'un été* (1961) we note first of all the collaboration between the two filmmakers. A second collaboration then becomes apparent between the filmmakers and the subjects, who participate in an experiment to examine their lives at a particular moment in their history, during the summer of 1960. There is finally a third collaboration. This is with the audience, for the film effectively throws open its doors to us to show what the filmmakers are trying to do. Rouch and Morin appear on screen towards the start of the film, discussing the project with Marceline, one of the participants. The framing of the film has metaphorically been moved outwards, showing not only the subjects, as in most documentary films, but also the filmmakers at work. As viewers, we feel invited into the film.

This move is not only of emotional or rhetorical significance, for it also stands as a declaration that the film is being presented not as a definitive view of its subject, a stance assumed by most traditional documentary films, but is simply a film. It has been made by specific people and is fragmentary, limited and subject to circumstance. What we see is what the filmmakers have been able to film, arranged as they have decided to show it to us. This is not always stated as explicitly as in *Chronique d'un été*, but it is the common ground of most films of *cinéma-vérité* and the observational tradition.

In the end, all films choose their form of engagement with the audience. The choices range from the strictures of genre to the personalities of the individual filmmakers. Viewers make their choices too, being drawn to some films and not others. Filmmakers need not always be consistent – the very spice of many films is to take us by surprise – but they must not promise more than they can give, nor betray the trust we place in them.

Notes

This chapter was first published in a slightly different version in the journal *Studies in Documentary Film* 16(1) (2020), copyright Taylor & Francis, http://www.tandfonline.com, DOI 10.1080/17503280.2020.1854150.

1 The convention of obscuring a film's authorship, on the other hand, was clearly challenged from 1980s onward by such self-reflexive and autobiographical documentary films as Ed Pincus's *Diaries 1971–76* (1982) and Ross McElwee's *Sherman's March* (1985), perhaps influenced by the elevation of the filmmaker as *auteur* during the French New Wave.
2 In a 1975 essay I proposed, as an alternative to ethnographic films that tended to objectify their subjects, a 'participatory cinema' that would allow for greater involvement of the subjects in the making of such films (MacDougall 1975). Since then there have been important developments in interactive and collective models for creating visual media, made possible by new digital platforms on the internet. These new forms of collaboration and co-creation are discussed by Cizek and Uricchio (2019), Dovey (2014), MacDougall (2001), Pink (2004) and Zimmermann and De Michiel (2018).
3 In 1973–74 James Blue and I collaborated on the ethnographic film *Kenya Boran*, not as filmmaker and anthropologist, but as co-authors.
4 For a description of Wiseman's working method, see Levin (1971: 313–28).
5 In the end a shorter film, *Nawi* (1970), filled this role, as it was finished first.
6 For descriptions and discussions of Flaherty's working methods see, among others, Flaherty (1950) and Ruby (2000: 67–93).
7 Criticisms of Rouch's collaboration with his African protagonists have often been raised by African critics, most famously in Ousmane Sembène's accusation that Rouch looked at Africans 'comme des insectes' (Cevoni 1965: 17). These critiques are discussed by Paul Henley in *The Adventure of the Real* (2010: 310–37).
8 From 1975 onwards, as a matter of policy, AIAS films were only made at the express request of Aboriginal communities.
9 I discuss the potential ambiguities of collaboration in MacDougall (2019: 144–7) and the multifaceted character of subject collaboration in MacDougall (1998).
10 I am indebted to Ronald R. Kline and his article 'Ideology and the New Deal "Fact Film" *Power and the Land*' for a number of the observations about this film (Kline 1997).
11 My film *Tempus de Baristas* (1993) was one of the films in the *Fine Cut* series and was co-funded by the BBC. The television version, titled *Time of the Barmen*, was 90 minutes long, with the full version running 100 minutes.
12 For the details of Riefenstahl's life, see Bach (2008).

8

Microstructures of film editing

ON the two occasions when I was editing a film with Dai Vaughan, he sometimes complained, 'This won't cut.' By which he meant that two shots wouldn't go together. Equally often, I saw no reason why they shouldn't. I gradually learned that this wasn't just perfectionism on his part but an instinct that something was out of alignment or continuity. If one put the two shots together one would be guilty of an inconsistency. Dai's resistance in these cases always indicated some deeper commitment to the unwritten compact between filmmaker and viewer. If one said one was doing one thing one shouldn't do another.

Take the example of camera positions. I have mentioned earlier that in editing *To Live with Herds* I had to throw out half the material for one scene because I had shot it from two different camera positions. To use both would have violated the premise that I was witnessing the event, and therefore I could not arbitrarily have occupied a second position or, rather, two camera positions at the same time

When Dai Vaughan and I were editing *Tempus de Baristas* (1993) there was a scene in which a similar inconsistency appeared. I had filmed Pietro and his father talking in their shepherd hut while Pietro worked at making goats' milk cheese. I had filmed Pietro from his right-hand side, with his father in the background (figure 8.1), but at a certain point I moved in front and towards his left for a close-up of his hands on the cheese-making mould (figure 8.2). Thereafter I returned to the first position (figure 8.3). Dai said, 'This won't cut.' Even to me, it was clear why this was so. I had crossed what cinematographers call the 180-degree line, the notional line that cuts through the subject from fore to aft, and I had switched sides. The reasoning behind the 180-degree line is that if you stay on one side of it, even if you move a little, there is still a consistency to your viewing position, but if you cross it, the subject's position on the screen appears reversed. For example, a person's nose will point to the right in the first image, but point to the left in the second.

Perhaps I had thought that by using an extreme close-up such a discontinuity would not matter, but Dai shook his head. 'But I'll make it work', he said. His solution was to remain on the first shot for an extra length of time, in order deliberately to make the viewers focus their attention on the cheese-mould and become slightly impatient. The extra length of time (along with the sensory

8.1 Pietro making cheese, shot 1, in *Tempus de Baristas*

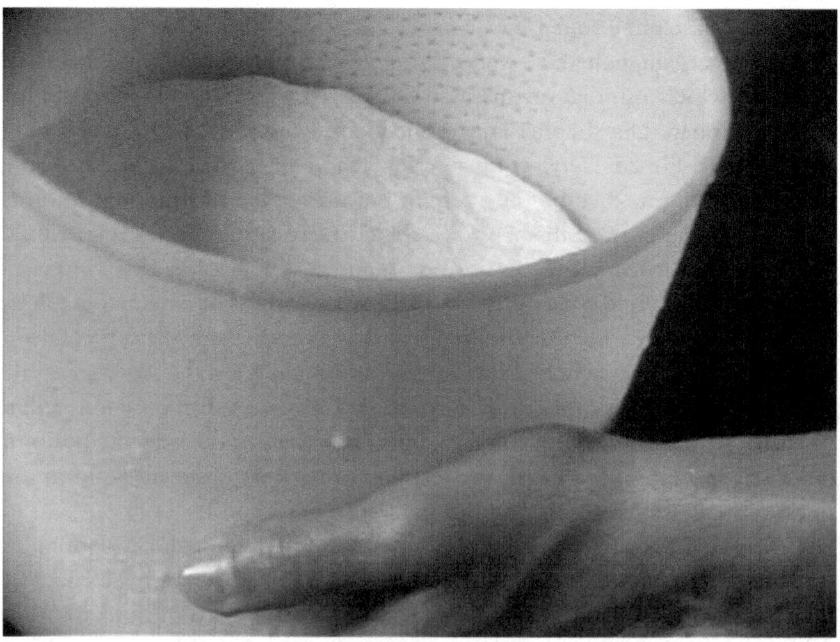

8.2 Pietro making cheese, shot 2, in *Tempus de Baristas*

8.3 Pietro making cheese, shot 3, in *Tempus de Baristas*

qualities of the cheese and the sound of dripping milk) made them ready to accept almost anything that followed. But Dai had done one further thing. He had held the shot until Pietro's hands tilted the cheese-mould a little towards himself. This small movement acted as punctuation, motivating the cut to the next shot, the close-up. He allowed a similar movement to be included at the very end of the close-up, followed by Pietro picking up a cheese rack and sweeping it in front of the camera to place it where the cheese-mould could be set down. This mimicked what film editors call a 'matched cut', in which an action in one shot is continued in the next, except that in this case it was not one action but two. In this instance at least four of the most basic microstructures of film editing were brought into play. It demonstrated to me Dai Vaughan's genius as a film editor. He was simultaneously taking account of angle, textures, sounds, pace and movement.

Cuts, links and commonalities

Film editing arranges shots in linear fashion, and wherever two shots meet there is a junction, or cut. The nature of these junctions needs examination, for they are of very different kinds. Some have the function of linking two shots together, others of creating a contrast between them. But in linking two shots there is also always some contrast (except, perhaps, in what is called a 'jump cut'), so we may consider linking junctions to have a double function, whereas contrasting junctions have but one. Eisenstein made much of the contrasting function, so that in his editing there is a pronounced emphasis on juxtapositions. Even within a scene, in which some continuity must be maintained, the juxtaposition of compositional elements stands out in his work. For example, the diagonals may run one way in the first shot and run the other way in the second, or a wide shot may be followed by an extreme close-up. Eisenstein built his theory of editing around this principle. Other filmmakers have developed different systems of editing (e.g. 'continuity' editing, or *découpage classique*) in which the linking function predominates.

It is worth taking a moment to examine what is implied by linking. When a linking function is apparent in a cut, some elements of likeness are maintained across the two shots. Some elements of the first are carried forward in the second. In narrative cinema these are most often commonalities of place, time and character. When a larger number of shots are linked together by common elements they constitute what may be called a scene, a concept familiar to us in the theatre. In both cases the audience observes the same people at a certain time and in a certain place. But other, less noticeable kinds of commonalities may also be present. Films routinely run background sounds or music over cuts, tying the shots together even more firmly. Actions begun in one shot may be continued in the second. There may be subtle continuities of colour, camera angle, mood or movement. When Dai Vaughan said 'It won't cut' he was not declaring an absolute fact, for you can always cut from one shot to another, but displaying a sensitivity to these less obvious linkages. There will always be a difference between the two linked shots, but what is similar about them overrides what is different. Commonalities and differences are therefore present in a kind of tension. Connections and contrasts seem to be the counter-balanced principles of film editing.

Except in Eisenstein's approach to editing, a cut whose function is to create a contrast rather than a link is usually used to shift from one scene to another. Even here, however, some commonalities are maintained. The same characters may be seen, although in another time and place. The purpose of the cut is to mark the change, and this kind of punctuation has become familiar to audiences. Beyond simply marking the change of scene, it brings variety to the film and produces the sort of shock that Eisenstein believed to be the underlying principle of cinema. In the hands of today's filmmakers, the juxtaposition of whole scenes rather than shots is perhaps the most important survival of Soviet montage.

Why, it may logically be asked, should there be cuts at all within a scene, if the purpose of filmmaking is to link the elements within it? Fragmentation within the scene would seem only to add to the problem of maintaining continuity. During a scene in a play there are no such interruptions. To provide a full answer we would have to consider the aesthetic and psychological effects of creating scenes out of fragments rather than single takes. A more immediate answer is an historical and technical one. Many of the first films, such as those of Edison and Lumière, were single shots extending for an entire piece of film. Film at the time was manufactured in short strips, those from the Lumière factory of about seventeen metres in length, similar to those of Edison's rolls of fifty feet. Longer films, such as Georges Méliès's *Le Voyage dans la lune* (1902), simply strung these extended shots together. Soon, varying the shots became a way of bridging the discontinuities between them. And when actions needed to be compressed in time, editing became a positive advantage, for less important parts of an action could be left out. It also became the primary means of changing the audience's point of view and suggesting the subjective experience of the characters themselves. It was many years before filmmakers began using longer takes again and, in the case of documentary films, inventing the equipment to do so.

Connections, differences and energies

Film editing is about arranging segments of film, beginning with the arrangement of individual shots into scenes and ending with the arrangement of scenes into entire films. This conforms roughly to the division of traditional plays into lines, scenes and acts. My immediate concern here is not with the longer segments but with the microstructures of editing: specifically, how one shot meets another. For even when whole scenes are juxtaposed, there is still the meeting point where important dynamic processes take place. Even when there is continuity between two shots there is also a difference. A change of camera angle or framing, however slight, makes us see something differently. We can say that one of the first principles of editing is that of surprise. Something is taken away from us but immediately replaced by something new. In this lies the potential for disappointment (what is removed or curtailed) followed by reward (something given). This repeated reversal of our feelings is what gives film editing much of its power to attract us and yet to impose its will upon us. In a sense we can say that it is the content of a shot that allows us to see, but the editing is what *makes* us see. In a film we are caught up in a struggle with the filmmaker about what we wish to see as opposed to what the filmmaker wants to show us. This can be both unsettling and exhilarating, like riding a strong-willed horse.

Except at the beginning and end of a film, every shot is framed by two others. Each shot is literally cut off at both ends in time and space, giving it the status of something specially selected, enclosed by the line of the cut. It is presented as a fragment, even as it is wedded to the whole. Furthermore, each shot acts as a foil to the one before it and the one following. It affects the next shot just as it is affected by what precedes it, casting both forwards and backwards. It may force us to re-categorise or reassess what we have seen if, for example, something that looked like a person in the distance in fact proves to be a tree. In the classic use of the reverse angle, it implies that what someone was just staring at was *this* object, *this* landscape.

Most of the effects of joining two shots together are less literal. A shot conditions our viewing of the next shot through multiple factors of subject matter, timing, texture and mood. We can best understand these effects by examining each factor involved, although all rely on the common principle of difference. What is important is the nature of the difference.

If the subject is the same in two shots, what matters to us, apart from the continuation of some action, is generally the difference of angle or distance. There are specific emotions associated with drawing closer or moving away from something, of intensification and intimacy on the one hand and relinquishment on the other. In the example described earlier of Pietro making cheese, the close-up satisfies a desire to see more clearly what he is doing. The wetness of the cheese becomes more evident, intensified by the sound of dripping water. We may identify with his hands holding the container, almost as if they were our hands. The shot combines the textures of skin, the hardness of the container, the emerging liquid and the softness of the cheese itself. These are accompanied by the kinaesthetic effect of coming suddenly closer.

It is important to understand the generation of energy that can be produced by a cut such as this. The change from one image to the next creates a moment of intensity, partly because of the demands it makes on the viewer. In a fraction of a second we must register what kind of change it is, whether it is one of angle, distance or subject matter. The shot may show the same subject from a different perspective or cut to a completely new scene. It may, despite being different visually, be part of the same scene, as when two people speak in a dialogue of alternating shots. A shift to a new scene, however, requires a major intellectual leap on the part of the viewer, whereas continuing a scene requires only recognising the use of a particular editing style. The second shot may also come as the answer to a question implied by the first, resulting in a sense of completion. This happens commonly in fiction films when the 'look' of a character is immediately followed by a shot of what he or she is looking at. Similarly, in documentary as well as fiction, a second shot may satisfy us simply by allowing us to see something in greater detail.

The comparative intensity of the shots is also important. Very often one shot will seem to taper off, without much happening, rather like a diminuendo in music, to be replaced by a more energetic shot that seems to pick up the pace. Here the differential in energy levels thrusts the film forward, re-engaging the viewer's interest. Following the same principle, the reverse may also happen. A shot that ends with a pronounced spike of emphasis may be followed by one that begins much more calmly. In this case, the response of the viewer may be of relief, welcoming a chance to rest and engage with the next part of the film at a more relaxed level. A new scene often begins with a general shot, made from quite far away, often following upon a shot of intense emotion or physical action.

Another phenomenon is perhaps best explained by the principle of *transferred* energy. This is when an action seems to be cut off prematurely, leaving the viewer unsatisfied. The viewer's expectations are then transferred to the next shot, whether or not it relates to the previous one. Sometimes it does, continuing the action in some way, but there are times when the transferred energy is a purely physical response in which a kind of mistaken logic is involved. The interest taken in the second shot replaces that lost in the first one without necessarily having anything to do with it.

Timing and rhythm

The energies involved at a cut may depend as well on further factors of rhythm, emphasis and timing. If a particular rhythm has been established in a shot or series of shots, or through sounds or a pattern of cutting, the next cut can come either in time with the rhythm or against it. If it is in time with the rhythm, then it more easily fits into the sequence, but if it is in counter-rhythm, then it takes the viewer a little by surprise. This can be done purposely to heighten awareness, or to create a sense of edginess or unpredictability. Cutting against rhythm also tends to make the first shot seem incomplete, coming, as it were, before the beat.

Cutting in or out of rhythm can be considered a kind of punctuation, since it reinforces or subtly alters the flow of a film. Sometimes, however, a sense of rhythm is created not by the pattern of previous cuts, or even by a rhythmic activity within a scene, but by something foreign to it. Extraneous sounds can be one such foreign element. A cut will very often come immediately after a click or other noise on the soundtrack, produced by something unrelated to the subject. It is as though the sound cues the cut. Film editors often exploit this possibility, although its basis is in many ways hard to explain. A possible explanation is that when a shot seems to have exhausted its potential to reveal anything more, and the viewer is anticipating the next shot, the sound gives licence to make the cut, as though allowing the film to move on. The cut tends to come about one heartbeat after the sound, an interval that editors commonly call a 'beat'.

A related tactic available to an editor is to delay a cut. This is sometimes done to emphasise the importance of a particular shot. In *Tempus de Baristas* (1993) there is a scene in which Pietro accompanies his sister to a neighbouring town to change his secondary school course from the field of the hospitality industry to agriculture. As they are driving back to their village, Pietro says, 'Anyway, waiting on people or serving at a bar … I haven't the patience for it.' The shot is purposely left longer than normal to emphasise what he says, as it marks a crucial turning point in the film. An extended shot of this sort is often the last shot of a scene. Its purpose is to anticipate the shift to the new scene. It allows the present scene to slow down and lose its intensity, somewhat like the final cadence in a passage of music. It may also help to motivate the shift by creating a sense of impatience. When the cut to the new scene comes it is welcomed as relief from a shot that has seemingly gone on a little too long.

A series of shots may be cut to a particular rhythm for a variety of reasons. It sometimes produces a quality of formal abstraction, either in concert with rhythms in the shots themselves or independently of them. In the latter case one is very aware of the filmmaker's hand imposing a pattern on the editing. One of the scenes I filmed for *Doon School Chronicles* (2000) was about a physical training exhibition put on by the whole school. Each of the school's five houses competed with the others in coordinated gymnastics, dressed in their house colours of red, blue, green and yellow. The display already had a mechanical, abstract quality that I intensified in the way I shot and edited it. I did so by cutting to specific rhythms and using a mixture of still and moving shots. Although the scene is more formal than others in the film, it expresses one of its most important themes. Within the regimentation of the event one sees the struggle of individuals to keep up.

Imposing a rhythm can produce an atmosphere of forward activity, hurrying the viewer along. In films based primarily on poetic associations, it provides much of the organising structure, inviting one to make connections in disparate material and giving the film a sense of regularity, like the ground bass of a musical composition. Jean Vigo's *À propos de Nice* (1930) is cut to very regular rhythms and is rounded off at the end by repeating images used at the beginning. If a film has a musical soundtrack, the cutting is very often determined by it, as in innumerable music videos and Jean Mitry's *Pacific 231* (1949), based on a piece by Arthur Honegger. At a particularly dramatic moment in Michel Deville's *Eaux profoundes* (1981), in which the protagonist prepares to drown one of his wife's lovers, the shots are brilliantly cut to a passage from a harpsichord concerto by Manuel de Falla.

Camera movement or movements of the actors may also motivate many editing decisions. Editing so that one move begins as another ends gives a choreographed fluidity to a film. This can be seen in feature films such as Jacques Becker's *Touchez pas au grisbi* (1954) and Jean-Pierre Melville's *Le Doulos* (1962). In both films editing on movement imparts an unexpected poetic quality to French gangster life. This style of camerawork and editing, linking shot to shot, also conveys a sense of relentlessness. In the latter film an entire scene unfolds as one actor, Jean Desailly, circles a room for almost eight minutes. By contrast, if a movement is purposely interrupted by a cut, the move somehow feels violated. Used repeatedly, this kind of cutting can create an edgy unpredictability in the film, creating anxiety in the viewer. The sequences have an unhinged, unnerving quality. This perhaps explains why the technique is a standby of horror films such as Hitchcock's *Psycho* (1960) and *The Birds* (1963).

In documentary films, movements of the camera often express the filmmaker's thought processes and feelings. A shift from one frame to another reflects a shift in attention or a connection being made between one person or object and another. When filming is done in long, unbroken shots, as has become common in documentary, these meanings are even more apparent. Use of a zoom lens can provide yet another kind of movement, from telephoto to wide-angle, or the reverse. An almost imperceptible move closer to a person's face creates an increased sense of intimacy. Filmmakers often plan to cut out many of the zooms within a shot in the editing, but those that remain express a way of looking. Similar connections can of course be conveyed by cutting from one shot to another, but if the cinematographer's moves are left intact they preserve a record of his or her intentions in time and space.

Preparation, variations and progressions

Dai Vaughan often used to speak of the potential of one scene to 'kill' the next. By this he meant that if the second of two scenes was too similar in mood or pace or subject matter to the first, it would feel like a repetition and the audience would lose interest in it. The first scene would have 'killed' the second. But very often if the same scene were placed at another point in the film it would come alive. This suggests that an important principle in editing is to create variations between scenes, so that each scene starts off in a new direction and produces a fresh stimulus of interest. An impression of repetition may occur for any one of a number of reasons, overshadowing other differences. Sometimes it is something as simple as the same rhythm being picked up in the second scene, or the same faces appearing framed in roughly the same way, or the sound also being similar, or the light. Editing often becomes like arranging the beads on a string, so that no two neighbouring beads are too similar in colour or size. One of the great pleasures of film editing is finding that a shot or scene that is creating problems in one part of the film can, when moved, solve a problem in another.

Placing two similar scenes or shots together doesn't necessarily weaken the second, and there are many occasions when it can make the second stronger, more acceptable or more comprehensible. Just showing something happening may seem incidental and unimportant if no reason for it is given. It may even pass by unnoticed. To give it weight, another shot or scene may have to be placed before it to explain it. A typical case is when there is a conversation about a topic that has not previously been mentioned by the speakers. Without knowing the context, the audience is likely to find it boring or confusing. Another scene must therefore be found to precede it, in which the topic is shown or discussed. Keeping this in mind, the filmmaker may even have to shoot such a scene later.

Another case is when the second shot or scene is clear enough, but another is needed to prepare for it properly. An obvious example in fiction filmmaking is to build suspense. Thus in Hitchcock's *The Birds*, a group of schoolchildren run down a road, pursued by attacking crows. But prior to this Hitchcock has shown us a shot of the crows gathering in the playground, seemingly getting ready for action.

A different kind of preparation may be required in other situations. In *Tempus de Baristas* there is a shot of Pietro helping his uncle to slaughter a young goat (described in Chapter 2). The throat is cut and the blood pours out. It is a shocking sight, and Pietro's distress is registered on his face. During the editing we felt this scene needed some kind of introduction, otherwise it came too abruptly, as if introduced merely for its own shocking effect rather than its effect on Pietro. At the same time, Pietro's attitude towards the goats needed amplification. The shot placed just before it is therefore one of Pietro looking at a group of young goats with obvious affection as he lets them out of their night-time shelter. In a sense this makes the scene even more shocking, but it also deepens our understanding that young shepherds must learn to get used to killing their livestock. The scene resonates with an earlier scene of Miminu showing off his goats with obvious affection and a later scene in which Pietro's father discusses with several other shepherds the distress they feel at killing their animals.

I encountered a similar situation when editing *The New Boys* (2003), the fourth film about the experiences of young boys in their first year at Doon School. One boy is continually homesick and we see him in a sad state during a visit by his parents. Afterwards, when they have left, we see him crying. It was important to show what led up to this – his parents' visit, and the desolation it left behind – but it was also important not to leave the scene hanging on such a raw and seemingly unfeeling note. The scene immediately following it is therefore one of the boy in a more cheerful mood, discussing homesickness with a group of his friends. The experience of homesickness becomes generalised, as most of the boys have felt it one way or another. One could say that the second scene relieves the previous one and in retrospect somehow justifies it.

Often within a scene the very purpose of combining shots is to underline the continuities between them, not their differences. But equally, if there is not a significant progression between shots – a sense that each shot is adding something new – the viewer will feel a slackness in the film. What we commonly see in a badly edited film is that one shot more or less repeats what we have seen in the previous one, adding nothing new to our understanding. The filmmaker has been unwilling to give up any of the material, however repetitious. This is often justified by the mistaken idea that to lose a part of something is to impair its fidelity to the truth.

It has often been argued that there is a psychologically logical way of organising the shots in a scene. The scene should begin with a general or 'establishing' shot and then proceed to its details or the main action. The reasoning is that the audience should be given the context within which the scene unfolds, otherwise they will be confused. This thinking is based in part on the model of academic prose, in which the facts are usually set out before any conclusions are drawn. But it misses an important principle of cinema. A film audience is expected to play a part in constructing the film, interpreting the fragments out of which it is constructed. An astute filmmaker, instead of telling us everything at the beginning, selects and arranges shots so as to draw us into the film. Providing the context is not a necessary preliminary, it can be distributed throughout the film. As a tactic, withholding information until it is needed is far more effective than providing it before anyone wants to know it.

Examples of this tactic can be found in the films of Robert Flaherty, who, contrary to the didactic approach of informational films, often starts a scene with a close-up, leading us to question where we are and the significance of what we are seeing. Not only does this immediately involve us in the protagonists' intimate experience of the material world but it singles out certain objects and their possible thematic significance. Entire films are often started off this way. It's a common enough way of provoking the question: why are we seeing this? Robert Gardner starts his film *Dead Birds* (1963) with a bird flying and *Forest of Bliss* (1985) with a dog trotting along the sand, and Rahul Roy starts *The City Beautiful* (2003) with fingers and feet working a loom. *Tempus de Baristas* begins with a close-up of an alarm clock and *Doon School Chronicles* with shots of laundry drying in the sun. If every film is in the end a work of progressively revealing something, it must necessarily start from something more limited.

Style and meaning

Until now I have been discussing the dynamics of cutting between two shots, but there are other microstructures of film editing that have a different basis. Some are useful at specific points while others are capable of ranging across entire films.

A film's atmosphere is partly determined by its visual style. Some films are made with an obvious concern for the formal qualities of the image, others less so. Some see the film frame as enclosed, excluding most of what is around it, while others convey a sense of the frame as permeable, with the world extending on either side. A film may tend towards using close or long shots, telephoto shots or more wide-angle ones. A preference in any of these directions will affect the film's general ambience. Emphasising closer shots draws attention to physical details and often indicates a close engagement with people, whereas using wider shots tends to project a cooler, more disengaged attitude. In some films, close-ups highlight the significance of specific objects, such as the keys in Hitchcock's *Dial M for Murder* (1954) or the sight of money or food in many other films. A repeated emphasis indicates a film's underlying themes and the particular preoccupations of its maker. From the audience's point of view, closer shots may bring its sensory qualities to the fore and produce feelings of intimacy. Wider shots, apart from giving a sense of spaciousness, often serve as a kind of punctuation, providing 'intervals' between major segments. Film editors will often use these shots to vary the pace and intensity of a film that would otherwise become too uniform in tone.

While editing, Dai Vaughan used to keep aside certain shots that he called 'specials'. He never expressed it to me in so many words, but I came to understand that these were shots for which he had an affection but for which he saw no immediate use, or in which he saw some quality that he found hard to define. Every so often he would find a place for one of the 'specials' in the film he was editing. These were very often used to provide the kind of intervals I have just described. At other times they contained something about a person in the film – some fleeting expression or posture – that went to the quick of who they were. Such shots were more difficult to place.

Occasionally whole scenes fulfil a similar purpose. When shooting *Tempus de Baristas* I filmed an exchange between Pietro and Miminu that struck me as particularly revealing. At the time Pietro was seventeen years old. For the first time I saw him speaking forcefully to an older person as if he were the older adult. There was a new spark of confidence in his eyes and manner. The fact that he and Miminu were discussing the habits of wild boars was almost irrelevant, as the subject was of little importance to the film. What was important was the way in which Pietro was speaking. I included the scene in the film for that purpose alone. Some viewers may have wondered why it was there, but for others I hoped it would reveal a significant maturing of Pietro's character.

Certain shots in a film can assume a special meaning if they resonate with shots elsewhere in the film. A network of associations is created that has a cumulative weight. In *Doon School Chronicles* there are persistent references to measurement and numbers, a legacy of the school's origins in the scientific rationalism of its founders. The shots concerning numbers not only refer to particular events but to a larger constellation of meanings, as do shots that allude to clothing and several other apparently ordinary objects. Normally these allusions emerge during the filming, but it is one of the functions of editing to bring them out and, at times, to discover new connections between them.

Sometimes shots contain material that can be used as recurring motifs, but this must be done sparingly. Otherwise they lose their literal meaning and end up as little more than symbolic markers. A symbol carries the most weight when it is almost not a symbol. I have used such devices in *Link-Up Diary* (1987) and *Gandhi's Children* (2008), but always with some hesitation. In the first film it was passing trains. In the second it was sewage spewing from huge pipes next to the shelter-cum-juvenile detention centre where the children lived. Shots of the pipes and the sewage appear a number of times, punctuating the film and serving as reminders of the harsh urban environment in which the film is set. They also refer specifically to the poor quarter around the shelter, whose waste has nowhere to go but to be pumped into adjacent fields. In a sense there is a connection with the children themselves, who have been abandoned by society.

Shown too often, such shots simply become an annoyance to the audience. Symbolism of any kind always risks displacing the materiality of life. Films have some advantage over literature in this regard, in that they are so firmly grounded in physical objects. In a shot one can often see that a specific parallel is drawn without it necessarily relinquishing its ties to a particular time and place. In *Tempus de Baristas* I included a shot of Miminu carrying a large piece of timber up a hill. Here it referred both to the difficulties of building shepherds' camps high in the hills and more generally to the other burdens Miminu had to bear. Occasionally, simple shots can take on unexpected meanings that can be turned to the film's advantage. In making *Doon School Chronicles* I happened to film a bird flying around an empty classroom and landing on the blade of a ceiling fan, which was slowly rotating in a draught from the window. I eventually placed it in the film at a point where I thought it would suggest not only the feeling of being alone in an empty classroom but the way students often feel alone and trapped in a large institution. Fortuitous symbols like this sometimes become the most expressive.

One of the absurdities one frequently sees in television interviews is a cut to the hands of the interviewee. It is essentially a meaningless device, the nervous tic of a bad editor. One supposes such shots were once meant to express something about the subject's life, as seen in their hands. Almost always, though, it is simply used to bridge a gap in the interview. Although this is a particularly irritating example, it is nonetheless a kind of cutaway, one of the staples of the film editor's repertoire.

Here it is important to distinguish between cutaways and parallel actions. Two actions are often established in a scene as occurring simultaneously, cutting back and forth between them. An example might be someone cooking a meal while speaking to another person standing nearby. This is a convention with which most cinema-goers are familiar. The two actions occurring may be of equal importance, or one less so. Perhaps here the cooking is less important than the conversation, in which case it is simply a parallel action, like a piece of stage 'business' in a play, but it is nevertheless integral to the scene. A 'cutaway', referred to disparagingly, is an action that is presented as parallel in time but that seems irrelevant and arbitrary. It lacks the importance to be considered a parallel action. An old Hollywood joke was, 'When in doubt, cut to a seagull.'

Normally for a cutaway to be convincing, it has to enlarge one's sense of the scene, not simply be introduced for the editor's convenience. The reasons for developing parallel actions in films are at least twofold. On the one hand, they round out a scene, giving it greater depth and verisimilitude, since very often in life many things go on simultaneously. It allows one to see around the subject, as it were, to learn more about the setting. On the other hand, a parallel action allows the editor to condense the time scale of a scene, concentrating upon its most important elements. There is a doubling or layering effect as well, since the two actions give the scene greater complexity. When cutting to a parallel action, the experience of many editors is that it is more effective to use two or three shots rather than one. The act of cutting away is thus justified by the comparative attention devoted to the second action, since the second action develops sufficient complexity to merit the diversion. If we compare this with the alternative of filming the scene in a single shot, there are both gains and losses. By accepting the convention of parallel actions, we lose a sense of actually being present, witnessing the event from a single perspective, in favour of a more omniscient and abstract construction of it. We lose fidelity to chronological time but we may also lose some of the tedium of waiting while little of interest is happening. The success of films made in unbroken takes is often dependent on choosing only those takes that avoid the longueurs of inaction or are choreographed to avoid them.

Punctuation

We come finally to those familiar devices of editing that act as punctuation – fades, dissolves, titles and other devices less familiar but fulfilling similar functions. The practice in many recent documentary and fiction films is to do away with most of the standard transitions, while the practice in some others, such as music videos and television commercials, is to embrace and exaggerate them. The use of dissolves or fades between scenes, also used to avoid jump cuts (i.e. cutting directly between nearly identical frames, as in interviews), was once considered essential in cinema but was discarded by New Wave directors such as Jean-Luc Godard as unnecessary artifice, even as these same directors reached back to silent cinema to reintroduce intertitles, which often served a similar purpose. And yet these editing conventions are not just whims of fashion. Simply removing them creates some of the same problems that arise when removing commas, capital letters and quotation marks from writing. The gain in simplicity or purity of form may be at the expense of intelligibility.

Nonetheless, in my own filmmaking I have dropped nearly all these devices except fades, which I feel mimic natural changes in light and such effects as changes of volume in music. I feel a dissolve, however, is an optical effect unrelated to the way we see, as is also the use of the zoom lens in cinematography. Jump cuts simply acknowledge that something has been cut out, and the jumps they produce can be a salutary reminder of that fact, underlining the materiality of the film process. Softening the cut with a dissolve or a quick fade-out/fade-in simply introduces a new artefact which adds nothing to our understanding. Where I find fades useful is in closing down one scene and opening up another, where a direct cut would give less sense of shape to the film. A fade underlines a shift in time, and often of place. Using fades between scenes also allows direct cuts elsewhere in a film to be more forceful, especially when they involve sharp juxtapositions. Titles provide yet another way of framing sections of a film and guiding the audience's interpretation of it.

Technical devices such as fades, dissolves, jump cuts and freeze frames have kinaesthetic effects distinct from the meanings conventionally assigned to them. A fade-out marks the formal closing of a scene, but it is also a literal dimming of the light. It resembles the coming of night, or a cloud passing over the sun. In fades we may experience feelings of loss, or an inescapable change of state. We associate a fade-out with separation or, more directly, with a departure, whereas a fade-in produces feelings of arrival as the light increases. In its own way, each type of fade tells us to prepare for something new – a new scene or, less often, the film coming to an end.

While making *Doon School Chronicles* I began introducing still frames. At first I used the video camera's capacity to make stills when I was not actually filming live action. The stills caught ephemeral moments – sometimes fleeting facial expressions, sometimes postures or gestures. They seemed to fix the materiality of objects as immutable, beyond human control. During the editing of the film I let the stills interrupt the action, as if to say to the viewer, stop for a moment and reflect. They halted the flow of events, allowing one to step back and see the lives of others from a different perspective, situating the film and its actors in a wider historical frame. They also seemed to emphasise the position of the viewer as an outsider. As I became more familiar with these effects, I began freezing individual video frames during the editing and using them in a similar way. In some respects the use of stills is not so different from interjecting titles in a film, stopping the action and abruptly changing registers. Freeze-frames had, of course, been used in films such as *The 400 Blows* (1959) as an ending. They allowed the audience to draw back from the story, but also signalled that at any arbitrary point the future is unknown.

Beneath the film

Film editing employs both strategies and tactics, except that here the tactics are not merely devices for linking the substantive material of a film but are highly expressive in themselves. These microstructures, as I have called them, are capable of conveying fundamental modes of feeling and intent. They are the means by which a film announces its themes and creates patterns more complex than any linear description of the film would suggest. They control its textures, energy levels and pace. They are the chief evidence of the filmmaker's hand as it guides the viewer in what to see and how to see it.

In *Portrait of an Invisible Man*, Dai Vaughan's book about the film editor Stewart McAllister, he wrote that style is not secondary to a film's meaning but fundamental to it (1983: 4). As a documentary film editor himself, he saw style as an expression of thought and feeling, and in the end, something more: a moral stance in relating the film to reality. It was not for nothing that he wrote that in his own experience 'very real ethical problems … presented themselves with every choice of camera angle, with each cut, with each decision to put something in or leave something out' (1999: 15). For those at the coalface of film production, the microstructures of editing mattered. 'It is we, not the audience', he concluded, 'who must take responsibility if dubious conclusions about the real world are based upon the false premises of our errors' (1999: 23).

While recognising the constructed nature of documentary films, Dai Vaughan maintained that because they were imprinted by things in the real world – and departed in that respect from most other arts – film editors should resist giving them the attributes of fiction. To some degree they should leave untouched the variegated, arbitrary nature of life even while trying to impose some order or meaning on it. This was why, for him, uncut rushes were often more telling than the films eventually made from them, with their carefully controlled disclosures and superficial polish. His call, as a film editor, was always to keep in mind the troubled existence of living creatures underlying the coherence that a film presents to the world. To write about a horse, he said, you need only pen and paper; to make a sculpture of one you need only stone or clay; to paint one you need only paint and brushes; but to make a film about a horse, you need a horse (1983: 27). In a curious sense, then, Vaughan felt documentary films had an obligation to undo the order they had created. Even with all their faults, they allowed us to glimpse something in the world that a filmmaker had cared enough to film. Beneath the film, he wanted us to see the horse.

Part III

9

Films and feelings

FILMS are born out of ideas and hard work, but also out of the energies and emotional lives of their makers. In writing about this I am not primarily concerned with the feelings that films engender in their viewers, nor with the feelings of people who have been filmed, although this enters into the discussion. My main concern here is the experience of filmmakers themselves.

For many documentary filmmakers, film is not just a way of representing the world but a way of entering into it and, in some cases, coming to terms with it. At the same time, it involves an almost endless preoccupation with filmmaking as a craft, its technicalities and the practical and human problems that go with it. Even for a filmmaker as apparently nonchalant as Jean Rouch, there must have been times when he worried about whether he had enough film left, or how to frame a shot, or if anyone would show up the next day.

If it were not for the moments of pleasure in filmmaking, many of its frustrations would hardly seem worth the effort. Some pleasures occur during the filming, some when it nears completion and others when one sees it with an audience. Still others come much later, when seeing the film again allows one to re-encounter the people and places one has filmed. Many filmmakers feel a particular fondness for some of their films and the people in them. Some they may hardly care to see again.

Moments of grace

Filmmakers sometimes remark on particular moments they remember while filming, when everything was falling into place and a sense of grace seemed to irradiate the world. Such moments occur only rarely, and only when it seems there is a fortuitous conjunction of elements. Robert Gardner has described one such experience when filming *Forest of Bliss* (1985), his film about the rituals surrounding death in Benares (now Varanasi) in India. One of the recurrent images in the film is of paper kites in the sky, flown by children. The kites take on a special significance, reflecting a soaring of the spirit in contrast to death and the cycle of childhood and old age. Another image, of boats on the Ganges, is also omnipresent in the film, bringing firewood for funeral pyres at the ghats along the river. Most bodies are burned there and the ashes committed to the

9.1 River burial and falling kite in *Forest of Bliss*

sacred water, but the bodies of children, or people too poor to afford a funeral pyre, are often simply tipped into it.

Gardner had hoped to film a kite falling into the river, when the breaking of its string released it from its flight, but he had not succeeded. One evening, just as he was filming men in a boat putting a child's body into the river, a kite began falling behind it and ended up in the water (figure 9.1). Describing this later, Gardner said:

> As the body is put in, the kite joins it. The whole thing seems to get said in one quite simple symbolic passage that is, at the same time, powerfully actual. This was great luck, and someday we should ask ourselves what proportion of nonfiction film proceeds from luck. (Gardner and Östör 2001: 110)

On another occasion he was filming the Dom Raja, the mafia-like boss of the funeral pyre business, who was drifting off to sleep holding a lighted cigarette in his fingers (figure 9.2). 'There certainly would have been no way for me to stop the camera once I saw what was happening through the lens', Gardner said later.

> These are relatively rare experiences, at least for me, and they are very trancelike when they happen. It's impossible to resist the urgency of the experience.... You're at the height of your power, at the height of your ecstasy as a filmmaker. (Gardner and Östör 2001: 36–7)

A similar elation has been described by John Marshall:

9.2 The Dom Raja falls asleep in *Forest of Bliss*

> When you're on, when you're with it, you have this feeling, 'I'm on; I'm on.' You know, 'I'm getting it. It's happening; it's happening. I'm in the right place at the right time.' (Marshall 1993: 144)

Jean Rouch also felt moments of 'grace' like these, as if presented with a precious gift (2003: 150). In this connection he often referred to the experience of *cine-transe*, in which he felt himself possessed by the spirit of his subject, moving unconsciously in concert with it (183). Other filmmakers have described a similar trance-like state. I can remember several of these: once, of being drawn along by the rhythms of ritual dancing when I was filming Gisu initiation ceremonies in Uganda in 1968.[1] I felt unable to stop filming as the dancers moved up and down the mountain paths. A similar experience occurred as I was filming a physical training exhibition at Doon School for *Doon School Chronicles*. As the performers went through their exercises to the sound of shouted orders, I found myself filming almost involuntarily, weaving together arms and legs and different colours in what later became the most abstract sequence in the film. On this occasion, however, I am sure my trance-like state was enhanced by the fact that I was suffering from viral fever.

Filmmakers are sometimes filled with wonder at simply being present at a certain place and time. Basil Wright described making his film *The Song of Ceylon* (1934) as a religious experience, a feeling he never recaptured when making other films (Levin 1971: 53). Towards the end of filming *To Live with Herds* in 1968, I felt a similar elation. We had left the dust and poverty of the permanent Jie homesteads behind and had gone to a cattle camp in the west where there was abundant grass and water. I watched entranced through the

9.3 At the cattle camp in *To Live with Herds*

viewfinder as men and cattle walked along the edge of a lake, tracing their silhouettes against the water. It seemed like a restorative moment for the Jie, when for a brief spell all seemed well in their lives (figure 9.3).

There have been other such times but, at least for me, they have occurred rarely and unexpectedly. Almost always this happens when I have been filming for months and have full confidence in my abilities. It has also depended on being present at the right moment. This happened during the final days of filming *The Wedding Camels* (1977), after the long-drawn-out marriage negotiations and the conclusion of the ceremonies, when all the wedding guests had departed. We came upon Lorang, the father of the bride, sitting with his closest friend, Ngimare (figure 9.4). He seemed exhausted. They began discussing the meaning and consequences of all that had happened. We were astonished that such a conversation was taking place before our eyes, for providentially it seemed to tie up all the loose ends of the film.

I remember a more fleeting experience when one day at dawn I was filming monkeys playing along the rooftops of an Indian village. The ancient palace of the region loomed overhead in the background. The film focused on the life of the village in contrast to the remoteness of the palace (now a luxury hotel), and it seemed a miraculous beginning for the film I was then making.[2] But not all such experiences occur at times of quiet reflection. They may take place in the midst of intense activity, or during some quite ordinary event when a person does or says something that takes you completely by surprise. At those moments you feel amazed to be there with a camera.

9.4 Lorang and Ngimare after the wedding in *The Wedding Camels*

Worries and frustrations

The price paid for such gifts is the time and effort that go into the ordinary routines of filmmaking. Much of one's time over days and weeks is spent waiting and observing people in their daily lives. Typically a filmmaker will turn the camera on for only a few minutes out of the many hours spent with the film subjects. This is not time wasted. Every hour offers opportunities to learn more about them, reinforcing one's commitment to them and to the purposes of the film. Every hour also increases the subjects' familiarity with one's presence. Occasionally too, something unpredictable happens that turns out to be crucial, moving the film in a new direction and rewarding the filmmaker for all the time spent.

Waiting requires patience and is usually accompanied by both major and minor frustrations. What you hoped to film very often never happens, or it turns out to have happened yesterday. Something starts to happen but breaks off for no apparent reason, or is interrupted. You miss the beginning of a conversation, so it remains incomprehensible. Or the topic is understood implicitly by everyone present but is never actually mentioned.

Some of these frustrations can be put down to chance, but it is also easy to be frustrated by your own mistakes, whether real or only imagined. Often you find yourself in a place just as you realise that what you wanted to film is happening elsewhere, or two key things start happening simultaneously in different places. Other frustrations occur during the filming itself, when you feel that a scene is going nowhere or, if it happens to be going well, you are filming it badly. As with playing a sport or a musical instrument, there are days when you feel in command of your skills and other days when you feel inept and out of practice. You are in the wrong position, or you make an awkward move, or you turn the camera off at just the wrong moment. There is nothing more discouraging than feeling you have made a mess of a good opportunity.

Then there are technical difficulties. These may depend on what equipment is being used, whether film or video. Most of the practical and aesthetic skills required when working with film apply to video, but the process is different. With video you see immediately what you are recording, whereas with film it may be days or weeks before you see the film developed and printed. With film you often have to hope the exposure is correct; with video you can be sure of it. Film must be loaded into magazines, with a roll typically lasting no more than twelve minutes. There is always the worry of running out as something crucial is happening. Towards the end of a roll you may have to decide whether to continue filming or hold some film in reserve.

Video poses its own problems. Many cameras have hundreds of settings, some of which can be adjusted only through a menu. Consumer cameras, many of which produce excellent images, have limited manual controls. The more controls that are automatic, the greater is the potential for error, contrary to what one might think. Automatic focus or exposure may respond to the wrong cues, causing the image to go dark or out of focus. It may not be possible for the filmmaker to control the exposure and focus at the same time. Sound recording poses its own problems. The advent of digital video has allowed filmmakers to work alone, but there is no longer a second person to monitor the sound. It may be difficult to do so while trying to concentrate on the images. Microphones mounted directly on the camera may have a restricted range, and so on. Video, despite its obvious advantages, is not a panacea for the filmmaker.

Despite the many technical pitfalls that exist, most of the anxieties filmmakers experience are of a more personal nature. There comes a time in almost every film project when the filmmaker feels indecisive or discouraged. After the initial excitement and optimism, a period of doubt sets in. The interest people may have had in being filmed has worn off. A great deal of material may have been filmed, but it feels scattered and disconnected. In this situation, prior experience counts for a lot, for filmmakers come to understand that such a hiatus is to be expected, and with time and effort it will be overcome.

Pleasures of creation

Among the attractions of filmmaking, apart from its rare moments of catharsis and revelation, are the pleasures of practising the art itself. These are both physical and aesthetic. Filming is as much a physical skill as an intellectual and creative one. When one is filming well, the camera feels like a part of one's body, not merely an extension of one's vision. Filmmakers learn to respond to the slightest signs, such as a glance from one person to another. One of the greatest pleasures of filming is thus the sensation of responding to the responses of others, implicit in Rouch's concept of *ciné-transe*. One feels in perfect accord with them, even to the point of sharing their consciousness.

Another of the skills necessary is the ability to anticipate what others will do, sensing it in their expressions and the dynamics of the situation. It means being prepared to start filming at any moment, attuned to both verbal and non-verbal cues. A shot may be triggered by something said, or by a slight shift in a relationship or simply by familiarity with previous occasions and social rituals. Control of one's own responses goes hand-in-hand with control of the camera, the two as closely linked as a painter with a brush or a skilled worker operating a crane. Some filmmakers develop strong feelings of affection for their cameras. The satisfaction of filming comes both from such skills and from achieving a film's broader objectives.

Part of the pleasure lies in selecting and framing one's material. Many filmmakers habitually keep both eyes open, one fixed on the frame, the other on what is occurring outside it, so that the world and its representation are in constant dialogue. Selecting what to show is a complex process, combining feelings of acquisition with those of bestowing, or at least acknowledging, value. The choices are also influenced by convention, for most decisions about framing have antecedents in painting, architectural forms and still photography. In one sense, framing a scene involves reshaping reality, putting a personal stamp on it, but at the same time the image continually reasserts its own independent existence.

Framing a shot necessarily negates as much as it includes, for if not, everything would be deemed of equal value. Framing rules out the peripheral to varying degrees. Some kinds of framing imply that the rest of the world is to be ignored; others acknowledge the importance of the image's connections with it. A so-called 'closed' frame asserts that everything of importance can be found within it, whereas an 'open' frame is permeable, with objects extending and moving beyond it. Filmmakers like Orson Welles have been ostentatious about exerting control over their framing whereas others, such as Jean Renoir and Roberto Rossellini, always seemed to be saying that the world is as one finds it, and a film can only view a part of it. Within some documentary traditions, such as in the 1930s and 1940s, the formality of the framing was felt to signify the status of documentary as an art form. In later times, in Free Cinema in the 1950s and Direct Cinema and *cinéma-vérité* in the 1960s, the formality of the image gave way in importance to filming the singularity of events as they occurred.

When filming rapidly evolving situations, the formal properties of the image are often the farthest from one's mind, but this does not mean they are absent.

With greater experience they become integrated into a more comprehensive process. One's immediate concerns may be whether a shot reveals something new or is logically connected to the other shots around it. Some of the formal properties of shots result from necessity. If one is close to two people, it may be necessary to film them obliquely, keeping one in the foreground and one behind. Filmmakers instinctively take up such strategic positions, which at the same time impose a particular tone or aesthetic framework on what they are recording. The view may be strategic, but it also expresses the filmmaker's beliefs about how one should represent reality, and this also implies a moral framework. Any aesthetic rewards are concomitant with finding the right frame for the purpose and, moreover, one appropriate to the subject.

Some filmmakers seem born with a sense of space and proportion. In others it must be learned – how, for example, not to cut off the top of someone's head but leave some headroom; or how to provide some space in the frame on the side that someone is facing. Choices like these typically belong to a realist tradition that avoids drawing attention to the frame, reducing distractions and downplaying the filmmaking process.

The decisions governing framing are closely linked to constructing scenes from successions of shots. Some of the bitterest frustrations come from being in the wrong position to do so, or having misjudged a situation by failing to anticipate a shift in the position of others. Conversely, when the filming is going well, everything seems to fall into place. There is a sense of losing oneself in the event. Filmmakers often become oblivious to things happening around them, losing any sense of fear in dangerous situations. They cling to the images, prepared to follow wherever they lead.

Apart from these matters of aesthetics and technique, filmmakers are likely to develop emotional ties to the people they are filming. Close personal relationships sometimes result from this, as well as a broader concern for the subjects' welfare. How the film will affect them can be a major consideration in this kind of filmmaking. At the same time, one of its main attractions can be the sense of risk and the open-ended nature of the undertaking. As a film progresses, it may lead to new levels of understanding for, unlike most fiction films, a documentary film is always in flux. 'The camera is for me', said Jean Rouch, 'what lets me go anywhere, what permits me to follow someone. It is something with which one can live or do things that one couldn't do if one didn't have the camera' (2003: 154). If documentary films began as a way of presenting existing bodies of knowledge, they later became ways of exploring the unknown.

Filming also provides the simple pleasure of looking at the world: the expressions on a face, the way light falls on a hillside or the textures of ordinary objects. A filmmaker's interests may be contemplative, aesthetic or have a more practical basis, but running through them is the way filming intensifies ordinary experience through its attention to details, the tactility of its vision and its sense of giving permanency to what it sees.

In editing a film, as in shooting it, there are anxieties and risks. Starting to edit a film is a little like facing a blank page – the same hesitation to take the first step, the fear that there may be no going back, the doubt about where to begin. Unlike a writer, however, a filmmaker at least starts with a concrete body of material to work with. Decisions may also appear less weighty today with the advent of computer editing. Blocks of material can be moved around with ease, and the re-editing of a scene, which used to require manually taking all the film splices apart, can now be done with a few swift moves of a cursor.

Editing tends to become more enjoyable as a film takes shape and material that initially seemed unwieldy falls into place. There is the further satisfaction of refining it through small improvements, making it flow more smoothly. Some of the most satisfying moments come from finding solutions to seemingly intractable problems, which usually means abandoning one tenaciously held approach and trying another. Sometimes two problems are solved at one stroke simply by moving a scene from one place in the film to another.

Finally, there are the mixed pleasures of screening a film in public. Apart from sitting with an audience to gauge their responses, there are sometimes more personal responses. Members of an audience may speak to you, although others may think it unnecessary, assuming filmmakers already receive sufficient praise and criticism. A film may win a prize, but this can be less than satisfying if it is for the wrong reasons. Reviews in books, journals and newspapers may provide a further response, if there are any. They often provide the only considered judgements a film will ever receive. Personally written responses are perhaps rarer: occasional letters to the filmmaker, testimonials given, jury statements at festivals and (only twice in my experience) new works inspired by viewing the film.[3]

The camera as passport

The world of fiction filmmaking is a world of its own, composed of studios and scripts, actors and screenwriters and the varied locations where the films are shot. For documentary filmmakers the experience is usually very different. The camera can become a passport, allowing them to cross the borders into other cultures and enter profoundly different social environments. The extent of all this, of course, depends on the time that filmmakers devote to a project, their choice of subject, their individual personalities and whether they make their films alone or in company with others. Ethnographic filmmakers are likely to experience the most radical shifts for, like anthropologists, they tend to spend extended periods of time in the communities they film.

Making ethnographic films, for me, has involved much more than observing and recording the lives of people in other societies. It has allowed me to exchange my own familiar surroundings for very different experiences of life. It has often resulted in disorientation and doubt, but I have generally accepted this as a positive aspect of the process. It has introduced me to cattle herders in Africa, mountain shepherds in Sardinia and Australian Indigenous communities, as well as a variety of communities in India. A long-term study of institutions for children has led me to re-examine the very nature of childhood – not my own remembered childhood but the childhoods of others, seen at very close range.

One of the benefits of these dislocations is that they produce a kind of continuity at another level. They allow the filmmaker to see more clearly those elements that cut across cultures and that, in the end, provide a degree of connectedness among all human beings. Each new film tests their ability to live among strangers. While this can make the filmmaker feel exposed and vulnerable, it also opens up new ways of sensing, thinking and acting. The boundaries crossed are, most obviously, those of culture and language, but they may also be those of social class, gender, age and radically different patterns of living. More often than not, ethnographic filmmakers have to deal with several of these differences at once.

Filmmakers have responded in various ways to filming outside their own societies. For some, like Jean Rouch, it has been an adventure undertaken with the conviviality of friends. For others, like John Marshall, who as a teenager began filming in remote !Kung communities in south-west Africa, the attraction was almost certainly to escape into a life very different from his own. In Ian Dunlop's case, it was to discover, with a sense of wonder and reverence, the extensiveness and majesty of an unfamiliar culture. For Robert Gardner it seems to have been a quest to find a sense of poetic order and universality. My own response has involved an admiration for certain human qualities: for the skills, gravity and eloquence of African pastoralists, the hieratic imagination of Indigenous Australians, the austerity and generosity of Sardinian shepherds, and the resourcefulness, autonomy and instinctive fairness of children. I came to respect the judgement of certain children as much as that of any adults I have known, and I remember many others with affection. But such statements become banalities on the printed page. To gain any real sense of a filmmaker's thoughts and feelings one must turn to the films themselves.

Friends and collaborators

Part of the attraction of filming in another society lies in finding a new time and place to think for oneself. The experience may also produce new friendships, often with people who stand a little apart from the people one is filming. Friends like these can be indispensable at times when the filmmaker feels most alone. They frequently take an interest in the film project, recognising the challenges it presents to the filmmaker.

Relationships with local assistants and translators are by their nature different. On the one hand, a degree of intimacy often develops when an assistant works side by side with the filmmaker, but there is also always a certain distance, as between employer and employee. Many of my assistants on films have been secondary school students or recent school graduates. Some have committed themselves enthusiastically to the project. Others have become distracted with the passing of time, when they felt, as I often did, that the project was making slow progress.

Some assistants become much more active collaborators. In making *Tempus de Baristas* (1993) in Sardinia, it seemed essential to have a Sardinian sound recordist. My assistant, Dante Olianas, had already worked as an ethnomusicologist recording traditional Sardinian music. He worked with me for much of the filming and became the chief interlocutor in our exchanges with the shepherds. His own father had been a shepherd and he had a deep commitment to shepherd culture. He was also committed to the approach and aims of the film. Because of his background, he soon earned the trust of those we filmed, in part because he came from a different part of Sardinia and had no local loyalties or other attachments to complicate the relationship.

I was also fortunate in the assistant I had when making *Gandhi's Children* (2008). On this occasion I used video and recorded the sound myself, but I needed someone who spoke several north Indian languages. Siddhartha Kumar had just completed his work for an MPhil degree in sociology at the Delhi School of Economics. He had several months to spare while awaiting the results. He was a lover of cinema and I found him eager to work on the project. It was to be a study of the Prayas Children's Home for Boys, a juvenile detention centre and shelter for orphans and homeless boys on the outskirts of New Delhi.

Siddhartha's interests and background recommended him for the job, but several other qualities proved even more important. He had great sympathy for the boys at the home and did whatever he could to make their lives less difficult. He never condescended to them and listened seriously to what they had to say. Many were from poor villages in Bihar. Because Siddhartha was also from Bihar he understood their dialects. During the filming he was never intrusive, understanding the need to concentrate on the boys' experiences and what they could tell us about their lives.

At times our filming was overtaken by more urgent concerns. One boy began to demand our special attention. I first encountered him in the middle of the night when I awoke to hear him crying. I found him huddled on one of the galleries that surrounded the inner courtyard of the building. He appeared to be about eight years old. I could understand little of what he was saying, but I remained with him for several hours, doing what I could to comfort him. He stopped crying when he became exhausted and finally fell sleep. The next morning Siddhartha arrived, and we learned something of his story. He had been enticed away from his village by a man who promised to take him to his brother in New Delhi. What the man's purpose was we never learned. Soon after coming to the city they became separated and the boy wandered the streets until he was picked up by the police. He had not told his parents he was leaving, and he realised they had no idea what had happened to him. He feared he might never go home again, and this was the main reason for his distress. Over the next few days and weeks we counselled him as best we could and encouraged the staff to make enquiries on his behalf. His village was eventually located, and as we were completing the filming he was about to be taken home. Many other boys faced similar problems, and during the filming our lives often became enmeshed in this way with theirs.

A split personality

However involved filmmakers become with the people they film, part of their consciousness always remains at a distance from them. There is a sense of double vision, of being both present and apart. The split between one's subjects and the practicalities of the film creates a disturbing undertone in one's emotions.

Some of a filmmaker's preoccupations are purely technical. Many times while filming I have wondered whether the light was sufficient, or if the sound quality would be good enough. Other concerns are tactical and strategic, such as whether to change camera position, or how to approach a difficult situation, or whether to film something today or tomorrow. Filming usually requires anticipating and working around the moods and desires of one's subjects. This means that one's personal instincts in relating to them are always to some degree compromised by the making of the film.

At times the film must come second to other demands, even when these are fairly minor. A car breaks down or someone needs a ride to get somewhere. Once when I was filming *Gandhi's Children* a fight broke out between two boys, and I had to separate them. Other incidents can be more serious, as when I had to seek medical attention for boys who became ill or take one to hospital. Interventions like these are rarely shown in the films themselves, but they are part of almost every film project in which human relations are involved.

Certain situations that one encounters in filming can have broader ramifications. Judith and I stopped making a film about a local artist in Indonesia when we realised it would put him at risk. He was using motifs in his paintings that could have made him liable to lawsuits under international copyright law. Although we felt it was a case of fair usage, a film about him would have increased the danger. Recent precedents of appropriation in art would have offered him little protection. After completing the filming for *Three Horsemen* (1982), we learned that one of the three protagonists, a boy of thirteen, had died unexpectedly of an illness. We put the film aside for several years and completed it only at the request of his family.

The dilemmas of filmmakers sometimes have one further dimension. They may feel overcome by the sensation of seeing someone they are filming twice: that is, both as a living person and as the ghostly copy of themselves that they are recording. It is like looking ahead, seeing the person both as they are now and as they will appear on the screen. The person has somehow become embalmed, even as their life is playing out. One can experience this curious sensation in reverse when viewing old photographs, seeing in them an instant seemingly in the present that actually took place many years ago.

A similar sensation is likely to be felt during the editing of a film. As filmmakers view the same images again and again, they come to know the faces, mannerisms and voices of the people they have filmed in exhaustive detail. Their images remain locked in the film, even as they have gone on living their lives elsewhere, the film now behind them. The deceptive familiarity of the images to the filmmaker can lead to a profound sense of loss. If the filmmaker should someday meet a person they have filmed, the images of them may remain burned in their memory, but any feelings of intimacy they have felt are unlikely to be reciprocated.

Regarding the work

However much their personal feelings are involved, filmmakers are constantly stepping aside to examine their work more objectively. This begins early in a project, in trying to envisage the look and focus of the future film. Films take shape largely around the people in them. Sometimes they are known well in advance, as in the case of films about prominent public figures, but more often the filmmaker ends up choosing among several likely contenders.

Deciding which persons to film is partly intuitive. The filmmaker may look for subjects who possess certain personal characteristics or occupy certain positions in life, but others seem to emerge out of nowhere, even contrary to one's expectations. This happened to us in 1973–74 when we were preparing to make *The Wedding Camels* (1977), about the Turkana of north-west Kenya. We spent the first nine months without filming at all but meeting the main families in our area.[4] As the film was to focus on marriage customs, learning which people might possibly marry was a crucial first step. The need for such intelligence might have come straight out of a Victorian novel.

Here fate took a hand. Among the five or six large families in the area was one we knew almost nothing about. Its people remained aloof, and we later learned that the patriarch of the family had told them to avoid us. It was only after we had become familiar with all the other neighbouring families that we finally made an effort to meet him, perhaps feeling a little piqued at his indifference to us. He was a lean, patrician figure named Lorang, and in the end it was with his family that we finally made the film and two others, with Lorang prominent in all of them. In the end, it was as much our curiosity about Lorang, and Lorang's about us, that brought us together. Once we met, we found we had many interests in common. Lorang had travelled widely and brought an acute intelligence to his understanding of Turkana society. After our first conversations he overcame his distrust of us and became a friend, taking an active interest in the making of the films.

This case was perhaps unusual, for more often a filmmaker begins to notice certain individuals quite soon who stand out for their character, appearance or social position. They are identified as possible protagonists, even though it may be hard to predict how they will appear in the film. This is perhaps why fiction film directors have traditionally scheduled screen tests of new actors, for someone who appears interesting in life may turn out to be less so on film. Conversely, others who at first glance appear unremarkable and retiring occasionally emerge as forceful and expressive characters, drawing one's attention whenever they appear on the screen. Whether it is some hidden quality of the individual or the peculiar vision of the camera that creates this disparity is hard to know. Even though the subjects of documentary films are rarely subjected to screen tests, they are often selected, however unconsciously, as surely as actors in fiction films. The selection is influenced as well by the filmmaker's own more obvious aims and personal interests. The filmmaker may feel that someone exemplifies some fundamental aspect of the situation being filmed. Or it may be that having encountered someone remarkable, the filmmaker simply wants others to know them too.

These factors, both subjective and calculated, all played a part when in 1992 I was preparing to make *Tempus de Baristas* (1993) in Sardinia. One of the purposes of the film was to look at the changing historical and economic status of shepherds in Sardinian society. I began by searching for three shepherds from different generations within a single family, reasoning that presenting their different life experiences would be a way of tracing recent changes in social and economic history. I found several such families in which a grandfather, father and son were all shepherds, but none seemed quite right for the film. Either their interest in the project seemed half-hearted or I failed to warm to them as individuals.

Someone suggested I meet a shepherd named Franchiscu, who, he claimed, believed strongly in the shepherds' way of life. I found him late one afternoon at his *cuile*, or shepherd's hut, far from his village. As I explained the purposes of the film, the idea of it seemed to interest him. He also impressed me at once as intelligent and articulate, and I liked his gravity and sense of humour. His son, Pietro, soon appeared, a boy of about sixteen. He listened intently as Franchiscu spoke to me. He had an alert expression and seemed to share his father's views of shepherd life. His youthful face contrasted strongly with

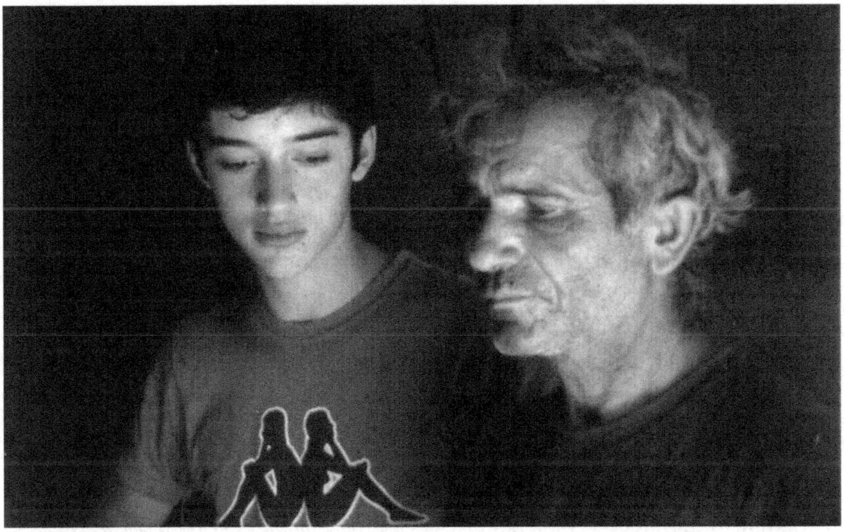

9.5 Pietro with his father Franchiscu at their *cuile*

his father's rough-hewn one (figure 9.5). As they stood side by side, I sensed immediately that this father and son would be ideal for the film, and I had an inner conviction that I would soon be filming them. Not long after, I met Miminu, a friend of theirs, also a shepherd, intermediate in age between Franchiscu and Pietro. In this way I assembled the trio I had been looking for.

For documentary filmmakers there tends to be a strong desire for a film's larger meanings to be found in existing people and situations, rather than being imposed on the film abstractly or didactically. This is related to the belief that there are certain aspects of social life that can be expressed properly only through the experiences of individuals. To be understood, they must be shown *in situ*. These meanings are often elusive and may be revealed only in fleeting moments – as expressions on faces, postures or gestures, or the ways people handle familiar objects in their lives.

As this applies to individuals, so it applies to the larger circumstances of their lives. Filmmakers ideally want their films to have a minimum of external explanation. Simply to show a person's actions may reveal little about their significance or motivations. Preparing the context within which particular scenes appear is therefore crucial. One may raise questions early in the film that are answered by scenes that appear later. Another approach is to surround a scene with subordinate scenes that help it to be understood. This may require filming them long after the primary scene has been shot. Films achieve their greatest power through this kind of organic contextualisation, for it mirrors the complexity already present in life. In preserving multiple connections, filmmakers are able to look more deeply into the heart of their subject.

Achieving this sort of density is not without risks. There comes a time in the making of a film, particularly towards the completion of the editing, when it is in grave danger. In filming others, filmmakers reveal something of themselves, and in the end they may retreat from this, feeling vulnerable and exposed. They may be tempted to soften the film's edges or its depiction of reality. Another hazard is overfamiliarity with the material, leading them to think it is too obvious or lacks interest for others. All too often at this stage filmmakers moderate the creative gambles they have taken, the very things that make the film distinctive. The film becomes weakened through retractions or excessive pruning, or a desire to make it more polished, acceptable and conventional. Resisting these impulses is not easy, especially for a novice filmmaker. It is a time for courage.

Notes

1 The film finally produced from this material was *Imbalu: Ritual of Manhood of the Bagisu of Uganda* (1988), directed by Richard Hawkins and Suzette Heald.
2 *Under the Palace Wall* (2014).
3 An instance of this is a suite of seven poems by Siddhartha Menon, written after viewing *Gandhi's Children*. It appears in his collection *Writing Again* (2008).
4 The project resulted in the *Turkana Conversations* trilogy, comprising *Lorang's Way* (1979), *A Wife among Wives* (1981) and *The Wedding Camels* (1977).

10

The life of others

To the casual observer, another person is often little more than a shifting set of images. Even if we know someone well, observing them can be like viewing them through a prism, seeing one aspect through one facet and a different aspect through another. When we try to convey our impressions to others, the language we use interposes its own meanings, narrows others and alters familiar perceptions. In the end, how much of the person survives its transmission through this process?

Documentary films that focus on specific people are akin to biographies, in that they attempt to convey something of the person's character and actions. Films made after the subject's death can cover a lifetime, as evidenced by the numerous television programmes about famous artists, sports stars and politicians. These retrospective films typically rely on reminiscences, interviews and previously recorded archival footage, bolstered by additional material about the period in which the person lived. There is a sense of regret that goes unstated in many of these films: 'If only we had managed to film them earlier, when they were still alive!'

Films about living people are a wholly different matter. Here there is usually some form of direct contact between filmmaker and subject, the extent and nature of which are revealed to varying degrees in the films themselves. Rather than viewing the person as a subject out of the past, these films allow us to observe moments in their present lives. The periods treated often vary considerably. One film I made took only three days to film, whereas another took over a year.[1] Films stretch out the time frame in different ways. Nicolas Philibert's *Être et avoir* (2002) follows a teacher through an entire school year, noting the changing of the seasons. John Marshall's *N!ai, The Story of a !Kung Woman* (1980), although it focuses on its subject as an adult, incorporates footage of her as a little girl that Marshall had filmed many years earlier.

Written biographies are typically based on family records, letters and diaries, as well as the subject's published works, accounts by friends and associates, and personal acquaintanceship (if this occurred) – most famously in Boswell's life of Dr Johnson. Autobiographies and memoirs dwell more on childhood memories, the thoughts and opinions of the author, critical events in their lives and witty or revealing anecdotes. Films, in contrast to these forms, tend to engage more in portraiture, based on more limited glimpses of their subjects' lives.

In her essay 'Telling Stories, Screening Lives: Notes Towards an Anthropological Biography', Anna Grimshaw (2020) explores the topic of life-writing in anthropology, surveying its various genres, from early transcriptions of oral histories such as Paul Radin's *Autobiography of a Winnebago Indian* (1920), to person-centred ethnographies such as Marjorie Shostak's *Nisa* (1981), to dialogic encounters, including Vincent Crapanzano's *Tuhami* (1980) and Ruth Behar's *Translated Woman* (1993). She contends that film offers anthropology an opportunity to expand the written forms in new directions, presenting a person to our senses with greater immediacy than is possible in a text. One of her points is that biographies classically explore character, and film has a special potential to reveal character through encounters with people embedded 'in a web of relationships that open out to include the anthropologist and others' (2020: 180). This marks a decided shift away from the traditional anthropological preoccupation with individuals viewed primarily in terms of their representativeness.

Most films about living people try to build up a composite image of their subjects in varied situations. In D. A. Pennebaker's *Don't Look Back* (1967) we see Bob Dylan joking with friends, belittling a naïve reporter, preparing for concerts and performing live. Wolf Koenig and Roman Kroiter's *Stravinsky* (1966) shows the composer conducting one of his works at a recording session, being polite to an importunate admirer and in intimate conversation with one of his oldest friends. Some portraits rely extensively on interviews. Several, such as Shirley Clarke's *Portrait of Jason* (1967) and Errol Morris's *The Fog of War* (2003), are based almost entirely on interviews with one person.

In making films about others, one difficulty lies in understanding the complexity of our relations with them. Part of our knowledge of them comes from everyday contacts but much of the rest through the filming process itself. Making a film produces its own intensity, its own forms of perception and creates its own unique circumstances. Films may be instruments through which filmmakers mediate between the subject and the viewer, but they are also instruments in which they are deeply involved. The means by which they perceive the people they film must to a large extent also be those they use to portray them for others.

Appearance

Physical appearance is one of the most basic means by which we know and recognise others. In many ways a person's identity resides for us in their appearance. Their thoughts and feelings, on the other hand, may be accessible only through what they tell us or, secondarily, by interpreting their moods and expressions. It is the physical likeness that photography primarily arrests. This may be as short as a microsecond (in a photograph) or as long as material gathered over a year (in a film). That likeness survives the changes that will eventually overtake them. Filmmakers often have the disturbing sense that they are already constructing images of others as they were in the past.

In filming another person we are first of all conscious of their facial expressions, distinctive features and body movements. How we respond to these often influences how we continue to film them, based on our predispositions and cultural background. We may be drawn to a person, be repelled or remain indifferent. A film creates a circuit capable of conducting the aesthetic, kinetic, idiosyncratic and erotic potential of another human being, and this produces films that range from admiration to obsession to antipathy. Typically, filmmakers look for moments that express characteristic aspects of their subjects' lives. Some of these moments show events of major importance while others attest to little more than the person's continuing existence.

Filmmakers are attuned to faces, and the cinema is pre-eminently a play of facial expressions, registering the subjects' moods and character. Facial expressions become signs in a visual language that varies from person to person. It may be a language with which we are familiar or which we are still learning. Faces are often taken to register a person's previous life, and we tend to read their history in them. Yet some people we remember as a composite of multiple images and others only in the context of specific situations. Films mirror this inconsistency, for as much as they convey general characteristics, they also record highly specific details. These may be as slight as a way of smiling, a movement of the eyes or an expression of pleasure or distaste.

We are used to assessing character from gestures and fleeting expressions. Within a foot of film containing twenty-four frames (or the equivalent in video), a person's facial expressions can change radically. There are often quite noticeable changes between one frame and the next. During the editing of a film, the filmmaker is privileged to have access to expression at this level of detail, but psychologists tell us that even slight shifts in expression are noticed by others and have real consequences in everyday life. How a smile is delivered or how a gesture is made can thus have a subtle effect on the overall reception of a film.

Some actors are known for specific mannerisms that are repeated in film after film. Humphrey Bogart's characteristic way of rubbing his lip was so well known that it was copied by Jean-Paul Belmondo in Jean-Luc Godard's *Breathless* (1960). Jean Gabin reputedly refused to sign a movie contract unless the script included one of his famous explosions of anger (Bazin 1971: 177). Seemingly involuntary acts such as these were taken to testify to the actor's (or character's) authenticity. In documentary films, distinctive mannerisms play a similar part in identifying individuals, and the filmmaker may consciously or unconsciously choose scenes in which they appear. This helps make the individual more recognisable, but used in excess it can lead to an oversimplification of character.

Appearance is often measured against a set of stereotypes. Many societies create such human typologies. In Europe, before the rise of the realist novel, the characters of literature were more often ascribed to generic categories than treated as individuals. In the seventeenth century Charles Le Brun equated human faces with those of animals. This fascination with physiognomy was revived in the nineteenth century, influencing the way novelists described their characters – as foxy or reptilian, for example. Facial features, despite much evidence to the contrary, were believed to indicate a person's inner nature. This belief remains engrained in society today, reinforced by popular culture. Facial features, size, skin colour and posture are perceived as carrying implications of intelligence or stupidity, industriousness or sloth, competence or incompetence. From the beginning, Hollywood cinema presented a parade of human types, with its Laurels and Hardys, its dumb blondes, its men of low cunning and its variegated gangs of children, including the obligatory fat boy with glasses. In addition to the stereotypes presented in cartoons, books and films are those we create ourselves, often based on quite arbitrary encounters.

Stereotypes are sometimes advantageous to filmmakers, providing shortcuts in the task of characterisation. In fiction and documentary films people are often 'cast' by appearance, particularly in genre films. In documentary films this poses a problem if someone's character does not conform to a stereotype. Audiences may wrongly assign someone to a particular category even when this runs counter to what the filmmaker observed or intended.

This created a problem for us in *To Live with Herds* (1972), a film we made in post-Independence Uganda. The film includes a scene with an assistant district commissioner, who proceeds to harangue a group of local elders about government policies. These policies are clearly much resented, and the official comes off in the film as insensitive to their culture and needs. For viewers he fits the predictable role he occupies in the film, as the representative of an oppressive bureaucracy. In private, however, we knew him to be more thoughtful than he appeared on the screen, coming, as it happened, from a pastoralist culture very similar to that of the people he was haranguing. In a sense he was thus both right and wrong for the part he played in the film. Many documentary films undoubtedly contain similar instances of unresolved conflicts between appearance and reality.

Films vary in the extent to which they allow for a range of interpretations. Viewers' responses depend partly on the film's complexity but also on the discernment that the viewer brings to them. In her article on anthropological biography, Grimshaw notes that many critics have found the portrayal of Allakariallak in Flaherty's *Nanook of the North* (1922) 'narrow and stereotypical of Western ideas of the simple, childlike Eskimo'. In contesting this, she reminds us that, unlike most written texts, films address us on multiple levels, so that 'Nanook exceeds whatever interpretive frame is placed around him – including the filmmaker's' (2020: 174). Allakariallak is there in his own being, separate from the constructed figure of Nanook. As films age and their ideas and cultural contexts become outdated, discrepancies like this tend to become more obvious.

Film viewers are assumed to be inexpert at telling people apart in societies different from their own, where similarities of appearance and dress may outweigh differences of character. This poses a particular problem for ethnographic filmmakers, often forcing them to over-compensate in identifying the people they present. One method has been to superimpose people's names over them in titles when they first appear. But this labelling can objectify them still further, and in any case may prove ineffective. Viewers simply forget the names, just as they tend to forget or ignore the dates given in films. Even if they remember the names, they may still be confused by changes in dress. The potential for this kind of misapprehension became apparent when we were making the film *The House-Opening* (1980). A group of sisters decided in a light-hearted moment to have T-shirts made with their names printed on them. At first we welcomed this, as we thought it would help viewers tell them apart. Then they started wearing one another's T-shirts.

Voice and speech

Allied to physical appearance is the human voice, for voices, like faces, have unique and evocative qualities. A phrase spoken in a certain way is sometimes what we most clearly remember from a film, rather than a visual image. Certain screen actors become closely identified with their voices, such as Marlene Dietrich's famed huskiness or Sean Connery's distinctive Edinburgh accent. In a technical sense, a voice is a more direct and intimate emanation of a person than an image, for it is produced by them, whereas an image is simply a record of the light reflected from their bodies. The addition of sound to films has produced an effect more powerful than the mere realism of spoken dialogue. Its verisimilitude reaches into our imaginations and releases a flood of other impressions, among which one of the most vivid is the sense of touch. The tactile immediacy of a person's voice can be as expressive as their words, and from sounds we seem to be able to feel the textures of objects.

Nonetheless, language provides the primary means by which we learn about the thoughts and feelings of others. A person's spoken words can carry the weight of experience and the urgency of thought itself. Until the advent of sound, speech in films was confined to printed titles. But even with the coming of sound, the voices in documentary films were rarely those of the people we saw. The words were produced by a writer and read out by a professional narrator, who remained anonymous. The result was that people in documentary films remained mute, and their personalities were similarly muted. They tended to be reduced to human types even if their faces varied. The face was a mask, and it was nearly impossible to guess what went on behind it. The heroic labourer's face might conceal a mind thinking about its dinner, or worrying about a sick child.

Documentary filmmakers have tried in various ways to go behind the mask. Some early documentary films, including *Nanook of the North*, created narratives of their subjects' lives, as well as rendering their speech in intertitles. Another method was to dramatise their lives. Robert Siodmak and Edgar G. Ulmer's silent film *People on Sunday* (1930) showed the carefree leisure activities of a group of diverse Berliners, and Harry Watt's *North Sea* (1938) included scenes of the shoreside life of a fisherman on a deep-sea trawler. Images from nature were also sometimes employed to express the protagonist's subjective experience, as in Flaherty's *Louisiana Story* (1948). Here swamp water and floating debris seem to mirror the perceptions of a boy brought up in the Louisiana bayous, blurring the boundaries between his inner and outer worlds (figure 10.1). Jean Rouch employed the method of asking his protagonists to record voice-over soundtracks for the films *Moi, un Noir* (1960) and *Jaguar* (1968), giving an insight into their imaginary and emotional lives. Jorge Prelorán combined the oral histories of his protagonists with images of their daily routines, creating what he called 'ethnobiographies'.

The coming of synchronous sound to documentaries provided the immediacy of speech, but it had further consequences, for it immediately drew

10.1 The swamp environment of *Louisiana Story*

attention to the personalities of the speakers. Film subjects could no longer be conveniently classed as representative types. With each word they revealed a mind at work with its own distinctive thoughts and feelings. There had been early attempts to use synchronous sound in documentary films, as in the British film *Housing Problems* (1935), but the technology at the time was too cumbersome to be practical. The film remained an anomaly, presaging things to come. The transformation began in the late 1950s in such Canadian *cinéma direct* films as *Les Raquetteurs* (1958) and *The Days Before Christmas* (1958). In the 1960s a flood of films appeared in which people spoke informally to one another and to the camera. Some films focused on celebrities, such as D. A. Pennebaker's *Jane* (1962), about the actress Jane Fonda, and Wolf Koenig and Roman Kroiter's *Lonely Boy* (1962), a portrait of the popular singer Paul Anka. Others focused on the lives of ordinary people, including Tanya Ballantyne's *The Things I Cannot Change* (1967), about a poor family in Montreal. Several explored the psychology of their subjects, as in Jean Rouch and Edgar Morin's *Chronique d'un été* (1961), followed by Shirley Clarke's *Portrait of Jason* (1967) and the Maysles brothers' *Salesman* (1969). Films that formerly would have presented general critiques of institutions such as prisons now focused on specific ones, notably *Titicut Follies* (1967) and *Attica* (1974).

Synchronous sound not only gave access to people's thoughts and opinions but revealed the subtler aspects of their emotional lives. In *Lonely Boy* Paul Anka speaks in a formal interview about his ambitions, but in a more spontaneous scene we see him ingratiating himself to a nightclub owner. In the final scene we see him, with his manager and entourage, driving to yet another gig somewhere in the American South. One of them complains, 'What am I doing down here?' Anka, looking worn out, says, 'You *know* what *you're* doing.' We suddenly see a different side of him, a celebrity who has lost his way (figure 10.2).

Perhaps unexpectedly it was television that pioneered some of the most important innovations in documentary, beginning in 1960 with the film *Primary*, about the American primary election in Wisconsin. Mobile synchronous sound cameras were crucial to this development and were used extensively in several British multi-part series, *The Space between Words* (1972), *The Family* (1974) and *Police* (1982), as well as in the American twelve-part series *An American Family* (1973). In 1974 the film editor and writer Dai Vaughan noted that synchronous sound had forced documentary films, including those made for television, to change their approach. Instead of presenting general impressions of 'types' of events, as they had in the past, they now had to identify specific ones (see Vaughan 1999: 12). Synchronous sound began to be used in ethnographic films for television as well, most notably in such series as Granada Television's *Disappearing World* (1970–93) and Melissa Llewelyn-Davies' multi-part series for the BBC *Diary of a Maasai Village* (1984).

10.2 Paul Anka on the road in *Lonely Boy*

Interactions between film subjects

In daily life we judge the character of people through their interactions both with others and with ourselves. We exercise a similar kind of judgement when viewing the interactions of film subjects. In many films the subjects address the filmmaker directly, either in formal interviews and conversations or more spontaneously. In these cases the filmmaker becomes a kind of surrogate for ourselves, so that when someone speaks to the filmmaker, we share the filmmaker's position. There is nevertheless a partial separation, for we perceive the filmmaker's presence and actions independently of ourselves, just as we view the independent presence of the film subjects. We thus assess 'character' through several different cinematic registers. Films can shift rapidly between these, even within a single shot.

An example of this occurs in a scene I filmed at Doon School in India.[2] A group of boys were talking about ghosts. One told the others strange stories he had heard. Another suddenly turned to me as I was filming him and asked, 'Sir, have you seen a ghost?' Before I could reply, he immediately began asking the others the same question. A general discussion then began about how one could make a ghost appear. One boy said he knew how to do it, and then addressed me directly, describing the use of a kind of Ouija board. A second boy chimed in, explaining this to me again. A third described a method involving a coin.

And so it went on, sometimes including me in the conversation, sometimes not. Viewers of this scene thus have the sensation of being pulled back and forth between several different perspectives.

Grimshaw has described the written anthropological portrait, in contrast to the life history, as having 'no temporal extension' but as being 'primarily a representation of an encounter between anthropologist and subject. At its core is a dynamic forging of subjectivities' involving 'the creation of a hybrid narrative generated at a particular moment in time' (2020: 179). In ethnographic films there is a similar intersubjective quality to the encounter. These films often take the form of an extended give-and-take between filmmaker and subject.

Something of this kind can be seen in one of the films of the *Turkana Conversations* trilogy, mentioned in the previous chapter. Lorang, the subject of *Lorang's Way* (1979), initially wanted to have nothing to do with foreigners, having experienced the effects of colonial oppression as a young man. Eventually we got to meet him, and from then on the relationship between us changed rapidly. We were impressed by Lorang as a thoughtful and dignified figure, and he appeared to enjoy talking to us. We learned about his unique perspective on Turkana society, which he revealed during a number of long conversations. Encountering thoughtful and eloquent individuals was not unusual in Turkana, for discussing fundamental questions of life was a Turkana cultural tradition. But in Lorang we felt we had met a Turkana intellectual, someone who had travelled widely, reflected on his own situation and developed his own distinctive view of life. The resulting film depended on a reciprocal relationship between us. He was interested in our life and ideas, and we in his. In this sense the film constitutes the kind of 'hybrid narrative' described by Grimshaw as a 'dynamic forging of subjectivities' (2020: 179).

Film portraits tend to reveal a subject's character on a variety of levels. Some of their interactions are dramatic and occur in the public sphere while others are more transient and private. Still others are so ephemeral that one has to look closely to notice them at all. Many occur around work, disputes, formal events and social rituals. In Koenig and Kroiter's *Lonely Boy*, as we have seen, they revolve around Anka's interactions with his manager, co-workers and fans. In *Stravinsky* (1966) they include a recording session, Stravinsky's travels and a conversation with one of his oldest friends. Some filmmakers have based their films entirely on the interactions of two subjects. A notable example is Edward Owles' *The Auction House* (2014), about two brothers who have vied for years over the directorship of a family business in Calcutta. In one of the more public scenes in *Lorang's Way*, Lorang demands repayment of a bull from another man. At one moment he is imperious, at another reasonable and firm and at a third quietly menacing. The man who owes him the bull is submissive and tries to ingratiate himself. Lorang responds impassively, secure in his position as a respected elder. The shifts in his behaviour reveal the different sides of his character: his understated power, his rational thinking, his sense of propriety.

10.3 The boy helps his father in *Three Domestics*

John Marshall's films about the Pittsburgh police department, shot in the 1960s, present a series of incidents in which the police interact with the public. The series was made to show law students instances in which the police have to make decisions and respond on the basis of limited information.[3] In *Three Domestics* (1971) the police are called to deal with a series of domestic arguments. In one episode they decide to take an abusive and drunken man away from his family to spend the night at the police station. To film this, Marshall had to position himself strategically to show not only the interactions of the police with the family, but also those among the family members, and where each was located physically in the apartment. While the man's wife and older son sit angrily at a table in the kitchen, the younger son persuades his father to go with the police. He helps him dress, put on his shoes and find his wallet (figure 10.3). The boy's distress is evident, but also his determination to care for his father. The insights we thus gain into a broken family are worthy of Balzac or Zola.

Filmed scenes of social interaction do not usually have this intensity, but their cumulative effect can be to reveal both deep variations and continuities of character. More often films show people meeting socially or performing routine tasks. Many scenes contain the sorts of minor exchanges that regulate the flow of everyday life: the greetings and casual remarks that express little more than mutual recognition. Not all the interactions observed involve speech. How people move and position themselves often reveals as much about them as what they say.

I realised this when filming a scene for *Tempus de Baristas* (1993) in Sardinia. I was filming Franchiscu and his son Pietro one morning at their *cuile*, or shepherds' hut. They were both in a bad mood. Pietro had been cooking something in a pot, and Franchiscu told him to put it to one side. When he put it in the wrong place, Franchiscu said irritably, 'No! By the box.' Pietro reacted equally irritably, saying 'I know! I was about to!' Then he sat down on the bed, his head hanging, saying: 'Do it yourself!' It was an unexpectedly rude remark for a Sardinian boy to make to his father. But instead of reprimanding him, Franchiscu turned and said gently, 'If you get so easily annoyed about things now when you're young, what will you be like at my age?' Mollified, Pietro gave a half smile and said, 'I'm sure I won't get annoyed at your age.' 'You'll be starting a new life, then?' Franchiscu asked. 'Certainly,' Pietro replied.

I was aware while I filmed this how much the small details of their speech and manner revealed about their personalities and respective positions in life. On the one hand it was a typical scene of teenage rebellion, but it was tempered by a deeper understanding between them about how far Pietro could go. Pietro's outburst appeared half serious, almost as if parodying the situation, and Franchiscu's response the opposite of what might have been expected, turning the incident into good-humoured badinage. It also revealed larger aspects of the situation they were in, in which traditional shepherding was changing and young people might well have to find new paths in life.

In another scene I filmed Pietro drinking beer in a village bar with a group of his age-mates. It was partly significant for showing him with other young shepherds rather than his school friends, but equally for showing how he remained a little outside the group. During the scene one of the boys speaks animatedly about his goats while the rest ask him questions. Pietro looks on nervously and says little. He spends most of his time pouring beer for the others.

Much may also be learned from an absence of a response. In 1972 James Blue and I filmed *Kenya Boran* (1974), a study of cattle-herding people in north-east Kenya. One of our concerns was how schooling altered the outlook of the younger generation. While giving them literacy and new aspirations, it lessened their access to traditional sources of knowledge. Peter Boru had dreams of becoming a doctor or provincial commissioner. During his school holidays we filmed him when he returned to his village. What was revealing was that he seemed disaffected, with nothing to do and little connection to others. He played with a rolled-up magazine, juggled some stones and chased some small children around. Finally he disappeared into a house. His disconnection from village life was clear. Later he told us of the shame he would feel if his education finally led to nothing.

Filmmakers need to be constantly attuned to such nuances of behaviour, and more generally to its awkwardness or flow. What someone does in one situation can provide a point of comparison for what they do in others. These variations also reveal basic aspects of personality: how tolerant a person is, their openness, sense of humour (or lack of it) and whether they respond thoughtfully or impulsively to those around them.

Other interactions

Two other kinds of interactions may also play a part. One of these is how the film subjects relate to the material world. *Onórino il fabbro!* (1993), a film by Lorenzo Brutti, is a portrait of a blacksmith. Although we hear him on the soundtrack commenting on his life and work, we learn far more from his actions. As he works at the forge, every move, every tap of the hammer, seems choreographed. His evident skill is reinforced by his air of total confidence. Blacksmith, tools and metal seem joined together by years of work and intimacy.

When I filmed at Doon School I encountered similar demonstrations of embodied knowledge. One day a member of the kitchen staff was distributing stainless steel plates on the dining hall tables. He did it at high speed and with an artist's finesse. The plates landed exactly at each place, accompanied by the musical sounds they made as they hit the tables. Even the slight correction he made to one plate underscored his years of experience. I later included this scene in *Doon School Chronicles*.

Students sometimes exhibited comparable skills, or the lack of them. I filmed two Sikh boys tying their turbans. One always tied his neatly. The other's was always a mess. On one occasion I filmed a boy making his bed. As he did so it became clear that the scene revealed more about his personality than about school routine. He spent endless time over the task, constantly adjusting the bedcover to make it perfect. Here was a boy who was not only obsessive about detail but, one felt, trying desperately to deal with the stresses of living in a frightening new environment.

Films also sometimes reveal skills in the making. The *mridangam* is a double-ended drum of South India. Filming at a school in Andhra Pradesh, I watched two students trying to learn to play this instrument. The teacher's skill was obvious, and at one point he gave an impressive display of it. The two students were trying to memorise the fingering patterns he was using. Their lips were moving, following the special language used to describe these patterns. As the teacher continued to play, I noticed the hands of one of the students starting to move on the mat in front of him. His fingers were automatically following those of the instructor. He was learning to play through his whole body. I felt I was filming not merely a lesson but the process of learning itself.[4]

Another relationship often revealed in films is that between the subject and the filmmaker. As documentary films changed in the 1960s, filmmakers increasingly put aside conventions of authorial invisibility and acknowledged more about this relationship. This emerged particularly in the course of interviews. The styles of interview varied greatly, some consisting of studied questions while others verged on intimate conversations. Some interviews were one-sided, in which we heard only what the subject said, while others included the voice of the filmmaker. Some seemed to develop according to a plan, while others grew more organically. The quality of the interaction clearly influenced the kind of information produced. Formal interviews generally focused on what the subject knew or had witnessed, while less formal ones focused more on their character.

Interviews can be used in a variety of ways, from exploring the psychology of an individual, as in the interviews with participants in *Chronique d'un été* (1961), to eliciting reflections on public policy in Errol Morris's *The Fog of War* (2003). Some interviews reveal an interdependency between filmmaker and subject. In Toni de Bromhead's *My Eyes as a Stranger* (1984) we see a subject increasingly drawn to the filmmaker and the opportunities the film affords to express himself. Occasionally this goes further, when the subject seizes the initiative to speak, as happens throughout much of Gary Kildea's film *Celso and Cora* (1983).

Relationships between filmmakers and their subjects are likely to evolve over time. Sometimes this shift is at the heart of a film, as in Doug Block's *The Kids Grow Up* (2009) and my own *The Age of Reason* (2004). Films also offer opportunities for people to speak of things they would never mention in other circumstances. Jean Rouch maintained that people were infinitely more sincere when being filmed than when they were not (Blue 1967: 84). The scene in *Chronique d'un été* in which Marceline speaks pensively of her return from a concentration camp is often cited as an example of this, and of the catalytic power of cinema. In this instance, the filmmakers went to the Place de la Concorde, where they hoped to find another film crew making a film about the Occupation, thinking this might provoke Marceline's memories. In the event, this proved unnecessary. As she carried a tape recorder alone across the Place, the idea was sufficient to start her speaking to herself of the experience.

Some films create an atmosphere of intimacy in which the subject feels free to confide in the filmmaker. This may occur even with the knowledge that the film will later be shown in public. In Bob Connolly and Robin Anderson's *Rats in the Ranks* (1996), a film about a local Australian politician, Larry Hand, there is a moment when Hand asks his secretary to leave the room so that he can speak to the filmmakers in private. Cases like this raise questions about the power of filmmakers to exploit such situations. Had they induced Larry to say more than he meant to? Or was Larry Hand conning the filmmakers? At what point do the interests of the film displace those of the subjects? There can be no easy answers to this, for each situation has its own mix of competing motivations and imperatives. Documentary filmmakers are constantly presented with such moral dilemmas and are finally responsible for the decisions they make.

Films that contain such scenes tend to place the viewer in a new position as well, standing figuratively alongside the filmmaker. As viewers we share the filmmaker's enquiry, so that when the subject speaks it is almost as if they were speaking to us. We become conscious of the filmmaker's role, and the film appears as an altogether more fragile and contingent enterprise, for we sense how subject it is to personal whim and circumstance. We may even wonder why it was made. The subject's position too appears more precarious, for it depends crucially on the filmmaker's choices and skill. In some films the subject seems caught, as it were, in the filmmaker's headlights.

As filmmakers have become more prominent in their films, more films have turned towards autobiography. In *Sherman's March* (1986) Ross McElwee sets out on a journey through the American South after a breakup with his girlfriend, whom we never see. Instead, McElwee meets a series of other women and reflects on love, his personal life, the American Civil War and war in general. The unwieldy subtitle of the film is *A Meditation on the Possibility of Romantic Love in the South During an Era of Nuclear Weapons Proliferation*. Other films that focus on the filmmaker's interactions with family or lovers include Doug Block's *51 Birch Street* (2005) and Tomer Heymann's *I Shot My Love* (2009).

With the proliferation of documentary forms, filmmakers can no longer be seen as quite so detached from their films as they once were. The ambiguity and subjectivity of the process has placed an increased emphasis on the interior lives of both filmmakers and their subjects. Still, there are questions. How close can a film come to revealing the interior life of another person? How much can a film tell us about the filmmaker? Even in the most amicable filming situations, what kinds of complicity underlie the filmmaking encounter? Some film subjects seem constantly aware of being filmed. Others seem hardly to care, or appear indifferent to it for extended periods of time. Yet in the end, every image of a film subject is of someone under the camera's eye, in the unusual situation of being filmed. Can films ever escape from this, or should they even try? The interactional nature of filmmaking brings all these questions to the fore.

Intangibles

Although film and video appear to show us people much as we see them in daily life, filmmakers have long been aware of the special qualities that certain people seem to possess when viewed on a screen. It has long been a matter of debate whether the abstract qualities of photography are responsible for this difference, or the intimacy of the close-up, or the psychological effect upon the subject of being filmed. A certain mythology has grown up around the topic, such that even critics have been reluctant to examine it too closely.

And yet some aspects of the phenomenon are clear. Films bring us physically closer to people than is usual in daily life. They allow us to watch without being seen. This is not only a matter of including close-ups, which permit us to see the expressions on a face in greater detail. Even in wider shots a film frames its subjects for inspection, making us more aware of their gestures and postures, how they present themselves and to some extent how they may be seen by others. The phenomenon could even be due to the limitations that a film imposes on our ways of seeing. In daily life we are used to seeing others casually, and as we like. Rarely do we look at them as deliberately and narrowly as we do in films.

For the most part filmmakers choose whom they wish to film, and it is not surprising that they choose people whose manner and expressions communicate something essential about their interior life. They also tend to film them at particularly revealing moments. This concentrates the signs that we receive as viewers and, combined with the proximity that film allows, greatly intensifies the impression they have on us. Someone whom we might give scarcely a glance in everyday life becomes, in a film, a distillation of qualities.

In responding to others we are often struck by some distinctive feature they possess. It may be a way of speaking, or moving, or the timbre of a voice. This singularity is not unlike the *punctum* that Roland Barthes describes when viewing still photographs: that trait or pointed detail that attracts our attention. In photographs these *puncta* may differ widely for different viewers, but in films there is usually some consensus, something noticed by many viewers on repeated occasions. The trait comes to stand for the person as a sign.

There may also be more elusive factors. The philosopher Gernot Böhme has written of the distinctive 'atmosphere' that seems to belong to certain places, buildings and works of art (Böhme 2016). We may sense it in a landscape, a village square or a house we have known since childhood. It may be specific to a painting or a piece of music. It is a quality that cannot easily be attributed to any of the elements that make up the object, and yet it is unique to it. Böhme calls such atmospheres 'intermediate phenomena' located somewhere between subject and object, but intangible.

We might extend Böhme's observation to people. Certain people appear to possess a unique 'atmosphere' or personal quality that resides in their manner and is immediately recognisable. It cannot be linked to a particular trait or idiosyncrasy but seems to be a more pervasive aspect of their being, an attribute which could belong to no one else. In films we become aware of this as a physical presence. It is as though the person is present with us, even years after the film was made. Barthes describes this quality as inarticulable and literally meaningless, since it appears to escape from conventional systems of signification (1977: 56–65). It is simply there, 'obtuse', extending beyond verisimilitude and meaning. Either consciously or unconsciously, filmmakers clearly take this elusive quality into account in their filming of others.

There is another effect commonly experienced by filmmakers, and perhaps shared as well by biographers and portrait painters. It is produced by watching someone repeatedly and intensively over a long period of time, and it results in a preternatural familiarity with the details of their manner and appearance. This occurs most frequently towards the end of editing a film, when the filmmaker begins to feel they know the person better than even their friends and relatives, possibly even better than they know themselves. In terms of physical appearance, this may be literally true, for filmmaking has the effect holding a magnifying glass up to everything in its presence. This unrelenting exposure can also give rise to a strange sense of the inevitable, as in scene after scene the person seems to perform precisely to their nature. This may help to explain the affection and even sense of ownership that some filmmakers come to feel for their subjects, while holding them in such intimacy, as well as their need to show them to others. To have caught the essence of another person, however imperfectly, is to suggest their potential value to any of us.

Mixed feelings

If the biographer's aim is to bring a person's life before us, the filmmaker's is to bring us the person. In the varied ways that films convey their depictions of individuals, translation and condensation play a fundamental part. The shorthand of cinema squeezes its observations into a frame that is both more confined and more focused than what the eye sees. In an hour or two a film sews together a series of images made under different conditions, some of the filmmaker's choosing and some quite accidental. The result is a selection from an almost infinite range of possibilities, loosely or more tightly directed by the filmmaker's interests. It is a process that can produce mixed feelings in the filmmaker, for as much as a film may be valued as a creation, it also represents a radical reduction of its subject. For viewers, on the other hand, it is more likely to evoke an existence much larger than what they actually see. Filmmakers are aware of this disparity, but they have limited means of dealing with it, and they may well view the more convenient cinematic methods for doing so with distrust.

A filmmaker's resources lie largely in the analogues of direct observation that they command. A close-up is analogous to the scrutiny that we give the faces of others, often in private glances of which the subject is unaware. The sifting and assembling of film editing resembles an accumulation of memories. If film lacks some of our most common senses, such as tactile sensitivity to textures, it can evoke them in its choice of lighting, camera angle and perspective. Sound heightens these impressions with scrapings, breathing, footsteps and the brushing of one surface against another. The selectivity of the camera allows filmmakers to isolate details that would be lost to more casual ways of looking. It simulates what we do in everyday life when we single something out, declaring an interest it. The significance it gives to details may be aesthetic, symbolic or part of the chain of events that the film is following. This singling out may say anything from 'this attracts me' to simply 'this is what happened next'. Employing repetition in a film also conditions the way we interpret its contents. The repeating of certain traits in a person shapes our idea of them, much as we sometimes define others in our minds as a collection of familiar images. In these and other ways films mimic some of the processes of human perception and thought.

There is a secrecy in human relations to which film gives added powers, among which is the power to watch without being seen. Filmmakers and film viewers are accustomed to watching others in ways that in daily life are more socially constrained. In films we regularly observe aspects of people of which they are largely unaware. Films thus afford a less inhibited expression of otherwise ordinary behaviour. As a consequence, if someone looks unexpectedly at the camera, we are a little shocked. It is a reminder that, but for the anonymity of cinema, they might be looking directly at us, and we have the sensation of being discovered. Despite this, films only simulate the forms of intimacy we have with others in daily life. Normally when we exchange looks with someone, they look back with understanding, creating a charged atmosphere between us. In films we experience this only vicariously, through the relationship the filmmaker has established with the subject. Although the result may be powerful, the situation is different, for we remain isolated from the encounter, as though watching from behind a screen.

Filmmakers, like biographers, have varied reasons for being interested in other people. If a film is a narrative of events, the reason may be to examine the forces surrounding the person's life. Alternatively, it may be to show how their character changes over time, or the effects of their own actions, or how their life fits into larger patterns of history. The way a film ends can tell us a great deal about how the filmmaker regards human agency – whether the person's future remains open, or is satisfactorily resolved, or is predetermined by external forces. When a film avoids strict chronology, we may suppose that the filmmaker's interest lies less in events and more in customs and ideas, or personal experience, or the relations between individuals. None of these interests, however, fully explains what attracts a filmmaker to a specific person, for this may spring from a number of different circumstances and desires. In nearly all cases the framing of a particular life assumes that it has significance, however ordinary it may seem.

If, as Grimshaw (2020: 179) has suggested, a film portrait is in some sense a dialogue between filmmaker and subject, certain traces of the filmmaker's character should be evident in it, including some indication of the motivations for making the film. How evident this becomes depends on the style of the film and the filmmaker's intentions. Some filmmakers are primarily concerned with controlling the effect the film has on the audience, and they are uninterested in offering us anything about their own role in it. For others, portraying another person is closely linked to the experience of encountering them, which to a greater or lesser degree is expressed in the images. One must assume it is even more directly expressed when the filmmaker is also the cinematographer.

How much of the filmmaker's experience is actually communicated to an audience is difficult to gauge. To a large extent filmmakers work in a vacuum. Viewers' accounts of their viewing experiences are rare, and even if given may be misleading or contradictory. Even when viewers are willing to describe their impressions they may have difficulty doing so, for this may require putting intuitive responses into words. Viewers may also respond in highly personal and idiosyncratic ways, perhaps disliking a protagonist because they have disliked someone similar in the past. Then there are the culturally and historically conditioned responses. Despite a filmmaker's best efforts, audiences may automatically consign a person to a particular generic category – coloniser–colonised, manager–worker, bureaucrat–citizen – with all the favour or opprobrium that goes with it.

Apart from written reviews, filmmakers tend to receive the majority of responses to their work in person. Some responses to my films have been quite wide of the mark. One viewer professed that a film showed deep sympathy for a protagonist whom I never knew at all well. A viewer's predispositions may also override what is shown objectively on the screen. Several American viewers, after viewing *Gandhi's Children* (2008), which showed the neglect and bad management of a shelter for homeless children in New Delhi, thought the shelter was doing an excellent job. Indian viewers were less impressed. A critic writing about another film assumed a scene in it had been set up when it was quite spontaneous, perhaps assuming that all scenes which appear spontaneous have been set up. When looking for reliable ways of assessing an audience's response, one of the best ways is to view the film with them. One key indicator is how well they respond to its humour.

As Grimshaw has pointed out, written biographies give us the thoughts, actions and emotional ups and downs of a person's life. Films give us something else: an intimation of a person's living presence. Looking into the mirror of a film, film subjects may catch glimpses of themselves as others see them, but this experience is almost always tinged with a degree of disbelief. For most of us there is an implausibility about seeing our own images, which bear so little resemblance to what we know ourselves to be. Most portrait films, I would submit, also have this provisional quality, suggesting a work in progress rather than the finality of a written account. For in them we see the subjects still testing themselves, stopping briefly on the way to what they will become. Such films can have no real ending.

Notes

1 The first was *Arnav at Six* (2012), about a precocious six-year-old in India. The other material was shot for *Sunny and the Dark Horse* (1986), a film portrait of an Australian Aboriginal stockman, Sunny Bancroft.

2 *The New Boys* (2003).

3 The Pittsburgh Police series was shot in 1968–69 and was produced for the Lemberg Center for the Study of Violence at Brandeis University.

4 The scene appears in *Awareness* (2010).

11

The strangers within us

We are made up of fragments of others, in body and spirit. We inherit the genetic characteristics of our ancestors. We learn to speak a language from our parents and childhood friends. In food and drink, we absorb the properties of the material things around us. If, as they say, we are what we eat, it is not surprising that we also become what we see, and form ourselves in our connections with others.

This principle has been supported by neuroscientists, who have found that seeing the actions or expressed emotions of another person activates some of the same responses in ourselves, if only subliminally.[1] It suggests that human societies are not made up of dispersed individuals but are in some ways more like groups of social animals such as bees, ants and corals. Those of us who as artists, actors, writers or filmmakers observe others closely sometimes have the disconcerting sense of being suffused by their presence. It is as if for a time we put our own consciousness aside and become intermixed with theirs. Later we may discover ourselves using a gesture or turn of phrase that is not our own. This can haunt us for days until we identify where and when we first encountered it.

An impression of being both outside and inside another human being is a common experience for filmmakers, especially those making biographical or portrait films.[2] Over weeks and even months the filmmaker is 'exposed' to the person and registers their qualities like the film in a camera. Filmmakers learn to move with the subject and anticipate their actions and responses. They become acutely aware of the subject's mannerisms, how they move, their facial expressions, specific details of their appearance, the timbre of their voice and their characteristic ways of speaking. It is not surprising that under these circumstances the subject's living presence enters increasingly into their imagination. A filmmaker may even feel a partial loss of his or her own personal identity. How these displacements of being are possible can perhaps be grasped from the way that, as onlookers at a tennis match or other sports event, we move unconsciously with the body movements of the players and share emotionally in their successes and disappointments.

Such a sympathetic relationship is not always the case, however. In the making of portrait films the relations between filmmakers and their subjects vary greatly, from the mutual antagonism between Nick Broomfield and Eugène Terre'Blanche in *The Leader, His Driver and the Driver's Wife* (1991), to D. A.

Pennebaker's somewhat offhand curiosity about Bob Dylan in *Don't Look Back* (1967), to the intensity of Johan van der Keuken's depiction of the girl in his film *Beppie* (1965). The length of exposure may be crucial. Some portrait films take years to complete while others are made in a few days. In films about celebrities and public figures there may be no contact at all between filmmaker and subject, whereas many other films involve close personal relationships. Some film subjects contribute little to the project; others collaborate extensively. In a few further cases a close but tacit understanding develops between subject and filmmaker, a form of collaboration that I have termed 'symbiosis' (see chapter 7).

For many makers of portrait films there is a strong underlying desire for a film somehow to embody its subject, by capturing not only the person's physical appearance but also a sense of their living presence. This comes partly from having observed the subject closely over a period of time and partly from having sensed the potential for such immediacy in other films. It is not uncommon when watching a film to feel someone vividly present even when they are now long gone. In film after film, actors like Humphrey Bogart, Simone Signoret, Ingrid Bergman and Jean Gabin continue to convey their distinctive personalities to us, projected across the gulf of time, geography and an imperfect technology. In documentary films as well, we may feel we have had an almost physical brush with a living person, an experience that perhaps goes back to Nanook in 1922. Nor need the person necessarily be central to the film: occasionally someone stands out vividly in the background, glimpsed briefly but never forgotten.

Every maker of a portrait film faces the question of how the film can possibly present its subject in any complete way. It is clear that, like a photograph, it can present a person's physical appearance, including details that might escape notice in everyday life. Films have an advantage over photographs, however, in being able to show the person repeatedly and in varied situations, engaged in a range of activities. This leads to a more rounded view and creates a strong impression of reality, yet even in the best films there is often a sense of absence and of something monumental and unreachable about the person seen on the screen. There may also be a disconcerting inevitability about the person's appearance and behaviour, for the subject of a film can no more look other than how he or she looks than act fundamentally differently from how he or she is.

The problem of how to present a person's inner life and experience of the world is more complex than presenting their physical appearance. It can be approached in part through their own words and at another level through the tell-tale signs of their thoughts and feelings. A person in a film may, if they choose, reveal through speech a great deal about their ideas, feelings and what they have witnessed in their lives, but this is always subject to their powers of expression. Often there is a great deal they are unable to put into words and other matters that lie at the very margins of their understanding. There are still other matters that they are likely to misrepresent, both to themselves and to others.

Portrait films are full of interviews and, less often, informal exchanges more like conversations with the filmmaker. Even if a person's words are not spoken directly on screen they are often used in a voice-over commentary. This technique has been adopted very effectively in portrait films, an early example being Roman Kroiter's *Paul Tomkowicz: Street-Railway Switchman* (1954), about a Polish immigrant in Canada who, during the night, sweeps the freezing snow and mud from Winnipeg's streetcar tracks. Here the very limitations of the subject's utterances and command of English become powerful metaphors for his life.

Apart from using speech, filmmakers can chart their subjects' emotional lives by observing their responses to the events and people around them. These responses may include both explicit expressions of feeling and the more general play of their emotions when engaging with others or with the filmmaker. How viewers interpret these signs depends on their acuity and background, but also on how familiar they have become with the subject's culture and personality through the film. As a film progresses, viewers become increasingly attuned to the meanings underlying the subject's reactions. At first they may interpret this behaviour according to some general typology, but with familiarity more subtleties begin to emerge. A smile given in one situation possibly indicates amusement or friendship but in another merely politeness or ironic forbearance. Identifying these responses correctly tends to deepen the viewer's identification and sense of complicity with the person filmed.

Jean Rouch often claimed that people are more likely to speak honestly when they are being recorded than when they are not.[3] One can understand that this might be true from the subject wanting to satisfy the filmmaker's wishes, or because the filming brings forth a desire to set the historical record straight. There is also often a confessional quality to interviews, as if the subject were stimulated by the occasion to say things they had been unable to express before. Being filmed seems to allow their minds to roam freely and explore thoughts not yet fully articulated. At other times the filmmaker's evident interest in them seems to stimulate their powers of analysis as they strive to explain some complex aspect of their personal life or social circumstances. There is something both confessional and analytical in the words spoken quietly by Maasai women to Melissa Llewelyn-Davies in her film *The Women's Olamal* (1984). Although these are matters that Maasai women might well discuss among themselves privately, the situation is altered by the presence of a sympathetic outsider intent on finding out how their society works. The women clearly respond to this both as an intellectual challenge and as a sign of friendship.

Filming of this kind can also provide an avenue for complaint. Sometimes the complaint is motivated by self-justification or the hope that it will effect a change. At other times it seems more to be a means of putting problems at an objective distance, to better understand them and perhaps be reconciled to them. A person's sense of powerlessness or confusion may be alleviated in a symbolic way by the power of words. The surge of autobiographical films made since the 1980s, such as Ross McElwee's *Sherman's March* (1985) and Tomer Heymann's *I Shot My Love* (2009), can often be ascribed to filmmakers using their films to confront and contend with problems in their own lives.

When we observe a person on film speaking confidentially to the filmmaker and then interacting with others, we often have an uncanny sense of being both inside and outside them: outside their social life but with privileged access to their feelings. We have the impression of sharing their consciousness, much like what we feel when we read the experiences of fictional characters in novels. In this way films bring together two of the primary channels through which they address us, the public and the private, forcing us to reconcile what we see of a person's behaviour with what we feel we have come to know about them.

At another level a film can reveal something about a person through the filmmaker's own responses to them. These are encoded both in the types of scenes that are filmed and in how the camera is used to film them – whether there is a sense of intimacy, attraction, aversion or sympathy. The filmmaker, as intermediary, passes on these responses to the viewer, either consciously or unconsciously. Viewers interpret the way the camera frames the subject, how close it comes, what details it chooses, how it moves between subjects, where it lingers and so on. In this way the person's existence becomes embodied in the film partly by way of the filmmaker's own body. One demonstration of this can be found in the filmmaker's original decision to make the film. What drew the filmmaker to the subject? How is the subject positioned in the film? A complex set of attitudes emerges through the relationship that develops between them. In a film that touches us, we are drawn to the filmmaker's sensibility, and we participate in the filmmaker's interests, discoveries and pleasures.

Filmmakers sometimes feel overwhelmed by the sheer scale of the person they are filming, amplified by the knowledge that this is but one person out of millions, each of whom possesses a similar depth and complexity. They may, at the same time, feel a proprietorial pride and excitement at being able to bring the person to others. Some have compared this emotional state to spirit possession, or to being put in a trance, or even to falling in love.[4] The writer James Agee described it as a yearning to put the 'cruel radiance of what is' into words.[5] And yet, for all the exhilaration it may bring, filmmakers often experience a sobering sense of inadequacy in trying to make a few scenes stand for the immensity of a life.

The making of a portrait film

I have experienced a number of these feelings when making films, but perhaps never more than when trying to portray children on film. Why this should be so is unclear, but it may be a response to the openness of children's personalities or the memory of having been a child myself. I suspect it also has to do with being in the presence of minds and bodies still in formation, as children try out new thoughts and new ways of being. The urgency of their searching reaches out to the filmmaker, and often to the viewer. Some of their attempts clearly reflect their immediate culture and surroundings, but others have often struck me as more exploratory and, indeed, pre-cultural. This openness has tended to influence my own thoughts and feelings at the time of filming. In my encounters with children I have often felt changed into a more stripped-down version of myself, less structured and more receptive.

This state of mind became familiar to me while making a series of films at Doon School in India (as described in previous chapters). The project had been suggested to me by an anthropologist who had studied three elite schools in northern India and was in the process of writing his PhD thesis about them.[6] Among the schools he had studied was Doon School, perhaps the best-known and most prestigious boys' boarding school in the whole country, with a tradition oddly combining the aspirations of India's Independence leaders with the rigid conventions of a British public school.[7]

Within the first few months of arriving at the school I began work on a film about its ideology, rituals and structure. Not long after, I started another film on the experiences of boys in their first year at the school. This focused on thirty twelve-year-old boys in Foot House, one of the school's 'holding' houses for newcomers, named after Doon School's first headmaster, A. E. Foot. The life of students in Foot House subsequently became a major focus of the project.

I quickly found myself filming children both in the mass and as individuals. This double focus never posed a particular problem for me, although it did produce different filming strategies and different kinds of filmed material. What I most recall of the boys *en masse* was the impact of their physical presence: the chorus of their voices, the jostling, the thicket of arms and legs, the smell of skin and hair, the roughness of school uniforms – sensations familiar to anyone who has worked with similar groups of children. Other impressions included the sounds of running, doors opening and closing, names and imprecations shouted out and the tap-tapping of table tennis being played on the veranda. What I recall of the boys as individuals, however, was very different and was closely allied to the challenges of conveying their distinctive personalities on film.

I began as an observer, immersed in the midst of activities in the house, my presence tolerated but equally often ignored. After their initial curiosity, the boys began to regard me less as a filmmaker and more as another adult, although one who, as an outsider, had less influence over their lives than the school staff. I never directed them to do anything for the film nor interfered with their activities, and they soon lost interest in the filming. What might have intrigued adults about what I was doing was of far less interest to them than their immediate social needs and concerns. Because I was almost constantly present with the camera, they seemed to regard my filming as more or less neutral, emphasising no one thing more than any other. Several of them told me later that they remembered me clearly but couldn't remember actually being filmed.

I sensed this general indifference when filming group activities, but when I was filming just one or two boys a different dynamic often took over. Boys would address me directly, or show me things. Although I was an outsider, I was one with whom they could share certain activities: eating a meal, appreciating a joke, observing how other boys behaved. My curiosity was not in fact so different from their own curiosity about each other and the situation in which they found themselves.

For me their foreignness as individuals and as members of Indian society was a constant source of interest and wonder. The great differences in their personalities also soon became apparent. I tried to imagine their lives with their families, an upbringing so different from my own. I wondered how it felt to live in a child's body, which I remembered only vaguely. Above all, what was it like to be a new person in the world, trying to understand its divisions of power and purpose?

While I observed the children and filmed them, they looked back at me with varying degrees of interest. Some made efforts to be friendly; others couldn't have cared less about me. How in the end my presence affected them was hard to gauge. For my part, however, these experiences were both vivid and unsettling. I sensed everything with a heightened intensity, and in this sensory overload there was both pain and pleasure. It was exhilarating to feel connected to their lives but frustrating when I felt clumsy and out of step with them.

The scope of my filming at Doon School gradually narrowed, moving from the first general film to films about two successive groups of boys in Foot House and then to one final film, a portrait of a single boy in the second group. I first noticed him as I filmed his cohort arriving on their first day at the school. Most were accompanied by their parents, who were helping them carry their trunks and suitcases into the dormitories. I filmed the boys' faces as they inspected the new world where they would now be living. One face caught my attention. It belonged to a small boy, quite neat in appearance, with carefully combed hair and watchful eyes (figure 11.1). What struck me most was his calmness, despite his obvious wonder at being in a new place. He did not have the stunned look of the other boys, who were glancing around anxiously. His was a more studied curiosity as he assessed his surroundings. Later I learned two facts that helped explain this. The first was that he was not from India but from Nepal. The second was that, unlike most of the other boys, he was already familiar with boarding schools, having been in one since the age of six.

He also had another quality, a special alertness or acuity that made him stand out. While looking at old photographs, my wife and I used to play a game as we viewed those of school groups. As we scanned the rows of faces

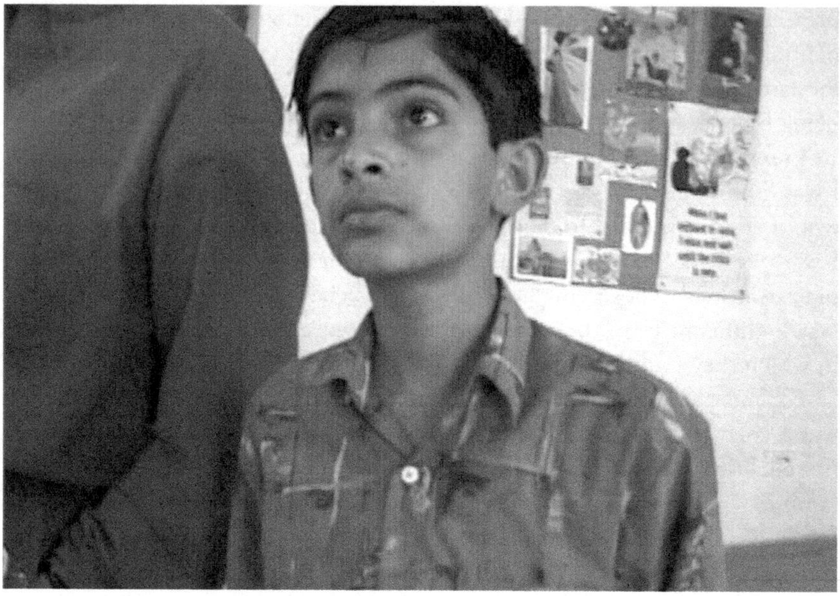

11.1 Abhishek upon arrival at Doon School in *The Age of Reason*

we would often ask each other which among them we would ideally choose as our own child. Invariably we picked the same one. In such a photograph I would probably have picked this boy.

As the group settled into the house and I began filming them I learned that the boy's name was Abhishek. On the first evening they lined up to receive their towels and school uniforms for the next day. As Abhishek's turn came, he turned slightly and looked back at me, at once acknowledging the filming (the others seemed largely oblivious of it) and with a slight smile suggesting he found the whole proceedings amusing. His look seemed to say, 'We two are outsiders observing all this'. During the following days his interest in the filming continued, along with his slightly ironic view of school life. Most of the time he accepted being filmed along with the others, but there were other times when he looked directly into the camera and made a joke about it or some further sign to me.

For the next four days, because it was a mid-term break, the entire school went on a series of expeditions. The new boys from Foot House went to stay at an old Forestry Department rest house at Lachhiwalla, where they were able to swim in a river and walk in the forest. I accompanied them on this trip and could see several friendships forming immediately as boys looked to one another for reassurance and companionship. Other boys, including Abhishek, joined in the general activities but kept more to themselves. I noticed, however, that he had a playful sense of humour, suddenly breaking into unexpected laughter at some joke or minor incident. I noted in my journal: 'He is rather solitary, often preferring his own company to that of the other boys, and yet he is not unsociable with them, nor does anyone seem to dislike him. But he is more intellectual and better educated than the others and tends to gravitate to adults.'[8]

One afternoon most of us were resting on mats on the lawn outside the Forestry Department bungalow. Abhishek, who knew me a little by now, put his mat down beside me. For the next hour he talked about books he had read, films he had seen, and how he had attended a Jesuit boarding school in Kathmandu. He had definite ideas about knowledge and education. Later I noted: 'It's not only that he is precocious that makes him attractive – that could as easily produce a stuck-up bore – but that he has such cheerfulness and such a sense of wondering discovery.' Thereafter he continued to seek me out. Once I found him alone and asked him what he was doing. He said: 'Oh, I am just sitting here thinking of so many things, sir.'[9]

Back at Doon School, academic life took over again and I filmed the boys preparing for their classes. As I filmed these activities I would often discover Abhishek following me about. He enjoyed talking and joking with me. At one point he made me turn my camera in a full circle as he described what he thought it was seeing. For several weeks I filmed him and the others in Foot House intensively.

I was busy during this period trying to film the group as a whole and identify some of the individuals within it. I wanted to show how they were adapting to their new environment and how they were learning, in a very short time, the things they would have to know about the school. There were many episodes of confusion and awkwardness as the boys got to know one another. There were fights. There was homesickness. One boy began to be bullied. Abhishek always stood a little apart, although he got on well with the others. He joked with them when he felt like it, but without feeling obliged to join in. He seemed to prefer talking to the adults around him, which included me, the housemaster, the housemaster's wife (the house mistress) and a woman who served as the house tutor and counsellor.[10]

One day, as it was a holiday, there were no classes. The dormitory was quiet and I found Abhishek lying on his bed. I sat on the bed next to his and left the camera running, wondering what he would say to me. He began talking casually, and in this conversation, which I recorded in full, he seemed relaxed and even slightly drowsy. At intervals he would sit up and then lie down again, cease speaking, or speak reflectively as different thoughts came to him (figure 11.2). It took only an occasional remark on my part to keep the conversation going. He spoke of wanting to be a scientist, of his success at academic subjects and of writing letters to his family and friends. This led him to speak of the dangers of going to the post office in Kathmandu, especially for children, whom

11.2 Abhishek talks to the author in *The Age of Reason*

he referred to as 'small people'. In an offhand way he remarked that children could easily be kidnapped for ransom or to harvest their kidneys, which could then be used for transplants, leaving the child half dead. There was something so shocking and coolly adult about these observations that I was left with a new impression of him. Here was a breadth of understanding I had not seen before, and a highly individual intelligence.

In the coming weeks I got to know more of Abhishek's nature. He could be sociable, but also at times dismissive of those he thought less intellectual or knowledgeable than himself. He read books more difficult than those read by his classmates. He found many things amusing, and when he was struck by some quirk or absurdity his laughter was infectious. Once I found him playing pranks on an older student, apparently in the hope of gaining his attention. He was interested in history, even though he proclaimed it his worst subject, and he spoke of the advanced technology of the Indus Valley civilisation and Nepal's resistance to British colonialism, while at the same time deploring the country's lack of economic development. He was interested in language and the meaning of words, and he quickly improved his grasp of Hindi, which had been quite limited when he arrived. He was sensitive to the beauty of the school's campus, or professed to be. He could think quite analytically, perhaps influenced by his Jesuit teachers, and he was able to draw out general principles from his personal experience. He believed people should learn things for themselves rather than accepting the views of others. He spoke of the importance of family life and the need to recognise the feelings and situations of other people, especially those less fortunate than himself. Sometimes it seemed that he was repeating things he had heard before, but for the most part he appeared to be formulating his own ideas and exploring his own thoughts as they came to him.

It was these conversations with Abhishek that gradually led me to think of making a film about him. Until now I had planned only to include him as one of the boys in the general film about Foot House. I realised, however, that the conversations I had filmed with him would not fit well into it, for they were much too long and complex, and to use only brief fragments of them would be both awkward and fail to do justice to Abhishek himself. I nevertheless continued my filming of him for its own sake, for I felt there were few extended records of how children actually thought and spoke. Material like this might help to counter the often prevalent belief that children lack the perceptual and intellectual skills of adults.

In this way I slowly began putting together a film portrait of Abhishek. It eventually emerged as *The Age of Reason* (2004), its title referring indirectly to British Enlightenment views on childhood and to the age at which I believe children are capable of serious reflection and judgement. As well as recording further conversations with Abhishek, I filmed everyday events in his life and his gradual adaptation to the school, which was not always smooth. He spent some time in the school hospital with viral fever. One boy taunted him for his Nepali accent. With great effort he taught himself how to swim in the school pool. Throughout the first term he continued to be something of an outsider and to take refuge in his relationships with adults, especially with me and the house counsellor. It was only towards the end of the term that he began to distance himself from us. I felt this as a personal loss, for I had grown fond of him, but I also believed it was a necessary step for him to take. In this way the film also came to an end.

Over the next few years I maintained some contact with Abhishek. I saw him on my occasional visits to the school. Four years after the filming, I asked him to view the material I had shot of him, and whether he thought I should try to make a film out of it. He agreed, and a year later, when he was seventeen, I showed him the edited film, which he accepted with his usual humour and good grace. After that I saw him only a few times as he progressed through university and graduate work overseas, studying English, Irish and American literature. We exchanged letters every now and then. His were always cordial and detailed, describing his work, his thoughts and his current situation. As he completed his doctoral thesis he asked me to read drafts of it, which I did. I made very few suggestions, for here was Abhishek, meticulous to the last, exploring his subject with far more logic and precision than I could ever muster. Eventually he returned to India to teach at a new university. Somehow, for all that had changed, the connection between us held.

In retrospect

The experience of making the portrait of Abhishek brought home to me the level of personal engagement required when trying to convey the being of another person, especially someone very different from oneself. As filmmakers draw closer to their subject a certain tension often develops, and perhaps on both sides a recognition that there is a boundary not to be crossed. In my filming of Abhishek I was conscious of taking a risk, for to do so was to commit myself to a process with unpredictable consequences. Despite the apparent rapport between us, there were also formidable differences of age, culture, experience and social convention. How close could I come to presenting him in his own existence and singular view of the world? What would the process be like for me, and how might it affect him? There was also a suggestion of danger, for I was unsure how this interest in a child who was not my own might be interpreted by others. And yet to bridge the gap between us might be possible on some level. There was also the attraction of Abhishek himself and my wish to convey to others just what he was like. It was an opportunity I felt I should not let go out of fear or expediency.

In a portrait film the relation between the maker and subject requires an interest on both their parts. The maker perceives something of value in the subject and tries to preserve it in the film. The subject responds to the maker's interest but also tends to look to them for reassurance. They may wonder what it is in themselves that deserves such attention. The filming may merely arouse their curiosity or it may create an atmosphere of complicity. There is often a kind of bargain struck, the subject giving something of themselves in exchange for the attention they receive. But this opening of the self, this vulnerability, is also reciprocated, for the maker too gives up something by acknowledging a dependence on the subject. The portrait is shaped by the relationship that develops between them. It is not a definitive drawing, but more often a series of impressions, propositions and tentative forays into the mystery of another human being (figure 11.3).

At Doon School I was a foreigner, not of that place. There is something both inviting and unsettling about being in such a liminal position, disconnected from one's normal life but with one's perceptions and senses preternaturally alive. By voluntarily choosing such a state one performs an act of self-dislocation, relinquishing a degree of security. It is the same in one's contacts with the people one meets. Their very difference, with its unknown potential, becomes part of the attraction and part of the risk. Things may go well or badly.

One small incident brought home to me the distance between Abhishek and me, despite the things that had brought us together. I had just filmed him having his hair cut by the school barber, a taciturn man who made the rounds from house to house, cutting the hair of all the boys who needed it. The barber whisked away the cloth from around Abhishek's neck and Abhishek stood up.

11.3 Abhishek plays a game with the author in *The Age of Reason*

Quite automatically, without looking at the barber, he held out his hand, and the barber proceeded to trim his nails with a sharp knife. This unconscious gesture, with its innocent expectation that another would perform the task, pierced me with a sense of Abhishek's other life. For a moment he seemed alien and unreachable.

I was a foreigner at the school, with all the uncertainty and dissociation that came with it. Abhishek was one too, so we had that much in common. It was perhaps natural that he should gravitate towards those in a position like his own. One of his few school friends was a boy from Bhutan. But for all the times that he seemed self-assured and even overconfident, there were also those when he seemed unsure and out of place. At one point in the film he wanders alone through the school's natural history museum, inspecting a skeleton, a snake, a human brain and a human foetus in a jar. Mixed with my absorption in filming this was also the question of what we were both doing there, which perhaps he wondered as well. It seemed as if we were on the edge of some precipice. Towards the end of the film he plays with a still camera I have lent him and takes a photograph of me. We face each other in an uncomfortable void, where time seems to have stopped. There is a sense that we have now seen altogether too much of each other.

Notes

1 See Ramachandran (2010) and Molenberghs et al. (2012), for example, on mirror neurons.
2 My own acquaintance with making portrait films was as follows. As a student I had made a short film, *J. Lee Thompson: Director* (1967), a study of the British film director; and later, with Judith MacDougall, *Lorang's Way* (1979), a portrait of a Turkana elder in East Africa. Two other films could be described as 'triple' portraits, *Three Horsemen* (1982), also co-directed with Judith, about Australian Aboriginal stockmen in Cape York, and *Tempus de Baristas* (1993), about mountain shepherds in Sardinia.
3 In conversation, but also see Blue (1967: 84).
4 In describing his state of mind when filming an initiation ritual among the Sorko people of Niger, Jean Rouch writes: 'I myself was in a sort of trance that I call a ciné-trance, the creative state, which allowed me to follow very closely the person who was being initiated' (2003: 183). When making *Los niños abandonados* (1975), about Colombian street children, Danny Lyon said he 'fell in love' with his subjects.
5 Agee expressed the purpose of his and Walker Evans's book *Now Let Us Praise Famous Men* as an 'effort to perceive simply the cruel radiance of what is' (1960: 11).
6 This was Sanjay Srivastava and resulted in his book *Constructing Post-colonial India: National Character and the Doon School* (1998).
7 I have written in detail about the school's origins and distinctive culture in chapters 5 and 6 of *The Corporeal Image* (MacDougall 2006).
8 Journal entry, 3–7 April 1998.
9 Journal entry, 3–7 April 1998.
10 The Foot House tutor and counsellor was Minakshi Basu. She appears in a number of the Doon School films.

12

How children see

FROM 2011 to 2016, two colleagues and I conducted a series of video workshops with school children in different parts of India.[1] Our overall aim was to gain new knowledge about how these children perceived and interpreted their surroundings, and what their perceptions could teach us about contemporary Indian society. We also hoped the children would benefit from the experience of looking at familiar things in a new way. In all, we conducted six workshops, of which I conducted four, while the two others were conducted by PhD student volunteers. All but one workshop also employed a local assistant. The project made use of relatively inexpensive video cameras – high-definition consumer models of the sort that were then growing increasingly available throughout the world. The children came from a variety of social and economic classes and geographical backgrounds. The workshops were held in both urban and rural settings, ranging from Andhra Pradesh in the south to Ladakh in the north, and from Kolkata in the east to Rajasthan in the west.

How can one understand how others see, and what they choose to look at? One obvious approach is to equip them with instruments through which to look at the world. This was the approach we adopted. We were aware that video projects had often been conducted for quite different reasons. Over the years there had been numerous projects involving children using both video and still cameras, and many of these projects appeared to have a therapeutic purpose. One of the prevailing assumptions seemed to be that if you gave cameras to disadvantaged or troubled youth it would somehow solve their social problems. I immediately rejected this idea, on several grounds. I was not convinced that fostering self-expression by itself had the benefit often claimed for it. Nor did I feel that simply giving young people access to camera equipment would be productive without creating a structure in which they felt they were using it for some purpose. All too often video and photographic projects with children appeared shallow and condescending, some motivated by rescue fantasies or the assumption that such projects would automatically be worthwhile. This attitude could only reinforce existing power structures and mistrust between adults and children. Children, I believed, ultimately sensed the condescension and felt diminished by it.

I took the view that because children see society from a unique position, they understand many things about it that adults do not, and there is much that we, as adults, can learn from them. It was important, too, that the children in the workshops understood that they had something to contribute and were engaged in creating new knowledge. The workshops were therefore organised as research projects. The children first chose topics they considered important or relevant to their own families and communities. After being given some basic instruction in using the cameras, they began using them to explore their chosen topic. The project offered them a chance to investigate subjects that were often not well known, or were known only from an adult perspective. For the most part they took this remit seriously and embraced it with enthusiasm (figure 12.1). In the end they constructed films or video reports on their topics based on a selection of the material they had shot.

The children were aged from ten to thirteen. The workshops lasted from six to twelve weeks. For practical reasons each workshop could include no more than ten or twelve children, and most contained fewer than that. For some of the children the workshops seemed like an experiment, but I regarded the entire project as an experiment, for to my knowledge nothing quite like it had been tried before. For this reason I was prepared to see it change and evolve. The biggest change occurred early, in the selection of topics and in selecting the children who would participate in the project. In the first workshop, at Rishi Valley School in Andhra Pradesh, I proposed that the children decide on a single topic as a group, after which they would each contribute something to it, whether individually or in sub-groups.

It was necessary first, however, to assemble the workshop group. I held meetings with all the students in the seventh class, aged from twelve to thirteen.

12.1 Video workshop group (Mayank, mentioned in chapter 7, is second from left)

I explained the project as best I could, answered questions about it and then announced that I would post a paper on a notice board on which any students who were interested in the workshop could put their names. I planned to speak to those interested and then select the participants. There were fifty-one students in the class. The following day I discovered that all fifty-one had signed up. True to my word, I interviewed them all during the next few days and finally selected a dozen. I wanted a varied group, not necessarily the star students but rather a mixture of those who had interesting ideas and seemed interesting as individuals. Half of those I selected were boys and half girls. I included one or two students who seemed difficult or eccentric but with whom I thought it was worth taking a chance. The group of twelve began meeting, and after several days and much argument they finally decided on a topic.

At the conclusion of this first workshop I decided that the process of selecting participants and topics needed to change. I believed the workshop had been enjoyable for the students. At least it had provided some variety and challenges for them. But I felt the choice of a single topic had been too restrictive. It allowed too little space for them to pursue their own specific interests, and it was often difficult for the group to come to any kind of agreement. I resolved in the next workshop to ask the children to propose individual topics in advance. I would then select the group from those who proposed promising topics and seemed most interested in pursuing them. This undoubtedly involved some subjectivity on my part, but perhaps no more than in the previous selection method, which had relied on an assessment of individual character. The new approach became standard in the next five workshops and I believe led to more diverse and rewarding results. From then on each workshop produced several films, made either by individuals or small groups.

Because the workshops varied widely geographically and in the backgrounds of the children who took part, I believe it would be unwise to try to draw any general conclusions about how Indian children see their society, or even about their perceptual processes as children. One can, however, point to some interesting differences and unexpected results. Overall, we were constantly surprised by the children's choices and inventiveness. We had been careful not to dictate any particular style of filmmaking, since one of the aims of the project was to see how the children used the means available to them and the extent to which their exposure to public media played a part in their creative decisions. The initial video training was meant only to teach them how to hold the camera steady and get reasonably focused and viewable images.

One of the surprises was the sheer variety in the ways the children used the camera. I had expected that with their limited familiarity with visual media, consisting largely of television and Bollywood cinema, they would be likely to imitate the models they found there. But perhaps because we were asking them to do something quite outside their usual experience – to film their own surroundings, and to use the camera as an exploratory tool – they did nothing of the kind. I was constantly struck by the originality of their approach, and their departures from conventional cinema and television formulas. In a sense they seemed to be reinventing filmmaking as they went along, and each film reflected the personality of the child who made it.

This was made particularly clear in the films from the Delhi workshop. The children were from generally unprivileged backgrounds and attended a government-funded school.[2] The workshop produced only four films, ranging in length from fifteen to twenty-nine minutes, but they couldn't have been more varied in style and content. One, by a boy, was about the workings of a small, neighbourhood general store – the kind one finds on almost any street in any Indian city. Another was by a girl who wanted to explore the oppression of girls, and the privileges extended to boys, in the families she knew in her area. Another, by a boy, is difficult to categorise, but I will attempt to describe it below. Still another was by a girl who framed her film around the question: what do children do at home when no adults are present?

All four filmmakers were eleven years old. Apart from the obvious range of topics, the style of each film was distinctive. The film on the general store seemed to have been made by a born ethnographer, for Ravi Shivhare wanted to learn and document everything he could about the store: who ran it, who were the customers, what they purchased, their relations with the owners, how the stock was replenished, how the money was handled and so on (figure 12.2). Anshu Singh, the girl interested in the lives of girls, was the child in the group who seemed most influenced by television. She conducted a form of investigative journalism, interviewing different girls about their experiences and showing them doing piecework and household chores while their brothers were

12.2 Ravi choosing scenes for his film *My Lovely General Store*

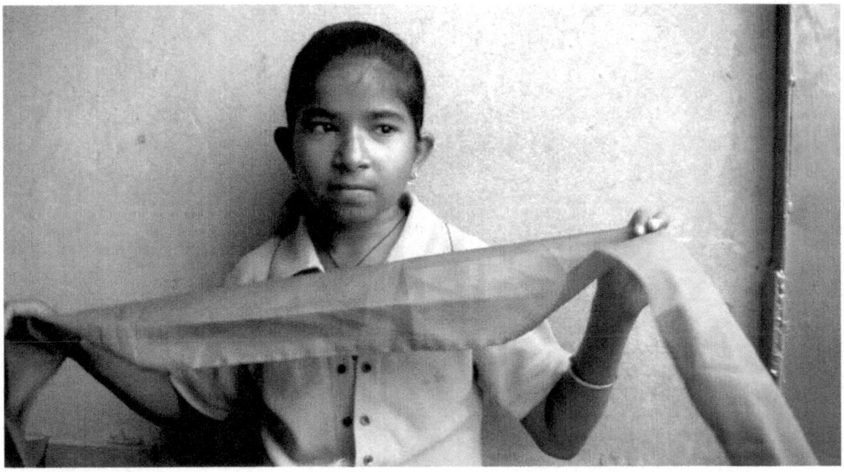

12.3 A young pieceworker in *Why Not a Girl?*

allowed to go to school and play freely outside (figure 12.3). Her film, *Why Not a Girl?*, closes with her making a heartfelt address to the camera, filming herself at dusk on her rooftop, asking why girls can't be given the respect afforded to boys. Shikha Kumar Dalsus, the second girl, made a calm, quietly perceptive film focusing on her younger brother and older sister, with simple scenes such them getting up in the morning, playing with the family dog, doing their homework and their occasional interactions with adults.

The fourth film, *My Funny Film*, made by a boy, Aniket Kumar Kashyap, is for me the most remarkable, successfully combining in a kaleidoscopic, almost anarchic manner aspects of daily life, performance, media technology, erotic attraction and touches of surrealism. More than the other films, it feels nothing like an adult's film; it is a film that could only have been made by a child. I know of no adult filmmaker, for example, who would think of singing while he filmed, but Aniket does. He sings to a dog, to other children and in a lengthy shot by himself in which he appears to be half asleep. What is also striking in the film is that about two-thirds of the way through it a girl aged about sixteen years comes into the family as a new bride (figure 12.4). From then on Aniket becomes fascinated by her, filming her in romantic images reminiscent of Bollywood and, indeed, singing to her.

It would be possible to describe further features of the twenty-four films produced in the project, which vary greatly in topic and style, but here I shall merely make several general observations about the experience of working with children in such diverse geographical, cultural and economic settings.

The project asked these children to undertake two key unfamiliar tasks: first of all, to examine their own immediate experience and surroundings, which

12.4 The new bride in *My Funny Film*

few had been asked to do before; and second, to analyse a specific topic, both visually and intellectually. Filming of this kind is in fact a process of analysis, since in conveying events and situations the filmmaker must select certain salient points through the framing and selection of shots. Most of the workshops were conducted in cooperation with schools, and children from poorer areas and in government-funded schools often found it difficult to identify topics or decide how to film them. They had rarely been asked to think independently, and their initial ideas for topics were often those they believed adults would want them to choose. This initial response was widespread, for even middle-class children tended at first to suggest topics they thought adults would approve, such as problems of overcrowding or environmental pollution. Yet unexpectedly, one or two of the most analytical films were made by children from schools in which rote learning was dominant.

I had imagined that in the age range of ten to thirteen the older children would make the more enterprising and sophisticated films. What I discovered was the reverse. The films that delved most deeply into their subjects, and that seemed to take the most care in observing the physical world, were made by some of the youngest and physically smallest children, aged ten or eleven years. Two that come to mind were both made by ten-year-olds: a film by a girl about her goat-keeping family and another, *Mayank's Family* (2014), by a boy about his father, showing him at home and in his daily work as a village barber. Whereas both these films were inventive and multifaceted, films made by children approaching adolescence seemed more circumspect and less experimental in their approach.

The actual physical size of the filmmakers also played a part in the impressions conveyed by the films. The films literally represent a 'perspective from below', for children see the world at a different level from adults. In their films physical objects seem to crowd in on one more closely and one gains a vivid sense of the enclosed spaces in which Indian families live – more consistently so than in most films made by adults.

Differences in the social class of the children also revealed some significant contrasts. Before undertaking this project, I had conducted several preliminary video workshops in other schools and institutions. One was at a shelter for orphaned and homeless children in Delhi.[3] The young filmmakers there were quite fearless in filming the most intimate aspects of their lives, including dressing and bathing, for which that institution offered little privacy. They simply filmed the sights they saw every day. By contrast, middle-class children in several of the other workshops had more inhibitions about what they felt should and should not be filmed. Anything related to the body or sexuality was immediately off-limits, despite – or possibly because – they were experiencing or were on the verge of adolescence. In one case a fairly innocuous scene of a boy not wearing a shirt was considered by the others too intimate to be included in the finished film. It seemed that these children, whatever their behaviour in private, were highly conscious of what they wanted adults to see. They lacked the bravado of the children in the Delhi shelter, who would have been astonished at the reserve and seeming lack of independence of these middle-class children. Those in the shelter also tended to show more tolerance towards one another, and there was less bullying than in the traditional, upper middle-class boys' school where I had conducted another preliminary workshop.

I have mentioned only a few of the observations that emerged from the workshop project. More will undoubtedly come to light upon further reflection and study of the films themselves. Most of our initial observations have been about differences rather than continuities, but I will end by noting one phenomenon that did seem universal. Children in the video workshops became inordinately attached to their cameras. The project had four camera kits, which were used in each successive workshop. The children took good care of them, but even so I was amazed that the cameras survived six workshops without significant damage and with the loss of only one cable and one lens cap. It was a sad moment when, towards the end of a workshop, it was necessary to take back and pack up the cameras. The children often resisted, begging to be allowed to film for a few more days. Something else also began happening. In several cases the children began treating the cameras as living things, speaking to them as they were filming, sometimes in a half-serious, half-joking way, as though to a friend or intimate companion. Below is part of what one boy said to his camera while filming himself walking alone along a grassy path as the workshop was coming to an end. It tells us that although the children's films have taught us a lot, for at least some of the children the experience of participating in the workshops went deeper than we realised at the time.

> Dear camera, we had amazing moments together, and now is the day we have to leave, disjoined, as you go to another owner and I take a new step in my second part of life. You are a great friend of mine, and shall always remain. And we together have learnt something of each other. Farewell, my old friend. Shall you live a happy and good life. The same with me.

Notes

This article was first published in a somewhat different version in *Journal of the Krishnamurti Schools* 22 (2018): 50–5.

Commentaries on the four films of the Delhi workshop by eight different scholars have been published in TAPJA, *The Asia Pacific Journal of Anthropology* 15(5) (2014): 453–79.

1 The workshops were part of a five-year project entitled 'Childhood and Modernity: Indian Children's Perspectives', based at the Australian National University and funded by the Australian Research Council.
2 Although entirely government-funded, the school had loose links to the Department of Education at the University of Delhi, which helped facilitate the project.
3 This institution was the Prayas Children's Home for Boys, as described in earlier chapters. See also MacDougall (2019: 53–60).

Part IV

13

An encounter with Robert Gardner

This encounter with Robert Gardner took place at Harvard University at 3.15 p.m. on 30 March 2010. This account of it was written on the same evening.

I had arranged with Gardner to meet a group of my students just after viewing his film *Forest of Bliss* (1985).[1] We sat around a group of tables we had pushed together. Gardner came into the room. It was a cavernous room with rows of red chairs, made for lectures and film screenings and dimly lit at the end where we were sitting. Gardner asked if this was the right place and the right time. I assured him it was, and that we seemed to have called him out on the worst of all possible days. It was raining heavily outside. He had on a short outdoor coat, which he deposited on a chair. When he came to the table he said, 'This looks pretty formal.'

I said I thought it was better to sit around a table than address a row of chairs. He nodded agreement.

Now well into his eighties, he was still a long, rangy, big-boned man. He took the chair at the head of the table that I had set out for him. The students looked at him shyly and expectantly. He was making no concessions to the occasion and looked as if he had just walked in off the street. He wore a loose shirt-like jacket and appeared not to have shaved that morning. Gardner's face is large and elongated like his body, with a long upper lip and a crown of rather untidy white hair that an earlier generation would have called leonine. Today he could have been taken for an orchestra director or musician on his day off. He looked at us and waited.

It was up to me to start. I told him we had just seen a beautiful print of *Forest of Bliss*. He asked how many of us had seen it before. Only I and my colleague, Jeff, put up our hands. I said I had seen the film four or five times. Jeff said his number of viewings was into the teens.[2]

I thought I should ask the opening question, but as it turned out I didn't have to. A student jumped in and asked him what had started him making films. What had attracted him to this kind of filmmaking? He considered this and folded his hands. His voice was surprisingly quiet and gentle, and I wondered if the students at the other end of the table could hear him.

'I was trained as an anthropologist,' he began, 'and I use the word "trained" advisedly because I had done anthropology as an undergraduate and was a graduate student completing a PhD. I had even done my orals a second time, because I had failed the first time.' With this bit of self-deprecation he settled himself further into his chair. 'I might have made a perfectly good anthropologist, I don't know. I could have written articles and ethnographies. But I didn't see myself as an academic. I couldn't see myself counting pigs.'

I asked him what films he had been seeing as a graduate student. Was there any particular film that had pushed him over the line?

'Actually, I had been seeing films for a long time before that. I think the films that meant most to me were the Italian Neorealist films made soon after the war. Rossellini. *The Bicycle Thief. Città aperta*.' He pronounced the Italian words with gusto.

We waited for him to continue.

'There was a humanity and innocence about those films. And they used non-actors. Documentary films use non-actors too. We don't direct them, of course, but they are also non-actors. Actually I don't like the term "documentary" much so you won't hear me using it very often. I prefer to say fiction and nonfiction films.'

The student across from me said that *Forest of Bliss* had seemed very modern and fresh to him in the way it was edited. It was like many films people were making today. Did he find that was true?

Gardner leaned back in his chair and for a moment seemed at a loss.

'I don't in fact see so many films these days, partly because my eyesight isn't as good as it used to be.' He stroked his face with one hand. 'I don't know.'

A student at the end of the table asked how he had decided to make *Forest of Bliss*. How much preparation had he done? This was clearly a question he had answered many times before.

'I had been to Benares – now Varanasi – about four times, so by the time I began filming I had certain motifs already in mind. Wood, fire, water....' He seemed uncertain whether we were aware of the symbolic elements of the film, and was rather hesitant to bring them up himself. It was clear he wasn't sure of the background of the students who faced him. Then, under the pressure of silence, he elaborated.

'I had in mind the things I wanted to film. I didn't actually shoot a lot of film because when you are using film there is the cost. It's not like video today, where people think they can go out and use the camera like a vacuum cleaner and suck everything up and then try to make something out of it. So I didn't shoot a lot. And the editing was surprisingly easy. The film took only five or six months to edit, whereas *Dead Birds* took several years. I don't know, I suppose I just felt less constrained. I just went ahead with it.'

Someone asked if he planned out his filming in advance with drawings or story-boards.

'There's certainly no script, and I can't draw, so I don't try to draw anything. But I do write a lot. I write a great deal in my journals when I'm filming.' His mind jumped to another idea. 'I think every filmmaker should be up with the dawn. Anyone who lies around in bed is wasting the most important part of the day, because the best light is from sunrise until about ten in the morning. After that the light is no good until the evening.'

I wondered how you could then film things that happened at mid-day, or film how things looked in the high, hard light of noon, but I didn't ask. Instead I said: 'So do you write in the morning or in the evening?'

'In the evening. I find it useful to write, and also perhaps for the future, in case anyone might want to read it or publish it someday. I wrote a lot during the making of *Forest of Bliss*. Have I told you this? I used to have a little airplane that I flew myself, and I would go from city to city. It was amphibious: it could land on the land or on water. One time I put my leather briefcase with all my journals from *Forest of Bliss* on the pontoon as I was climbing in. I took off and then I remembered the briefcase. When I landed all that was left was the tattered leather strap of the briefcase. So all those journals were lost.'

I asked him if he learned anything new through the process of filming, if the process had changed or added to the ideas he started out with. He gave that a few moments' thought, clenching and unclenching his fingers.

'I'm not sure.'

'The sand, maybe?'

'Yes,' he said, 'maybe the sand. I hadn't really thought about the sand before.'

He was referring to the barges laden with sand that appear in the film, destined to be unloaded for the construction of new buildings in Varanasi. He said he had also discovered something by going to the opposite bank of the Ganges.

'When I looked across towards the city it was clouded in this extraordinary mist, and boats were passing in the mist and I filmed that.'

What was it that he wanted to express in the film, one of the students asked, getting down to brass tacks.

'I suppose it was my training in anthropology, but it has shown me that all human beings are essentially alike. We have the same problems of living, of getting on with others, of hating our enemies, of finding enough to eat, even if this is expressed in different ways in different cultures. I was interested in using film to express aspects of our common humanity.'

He suddenly seemed energised.

'For example, in New Guinea the only thing the men wear are these extraordinary things called penis sheaths that stick up.' He made the appropriate gestures. 'It is something so strange, it seems so savage, and you wonder how they even keep them on. I thought that if you could get the audience over this obstacle of accepting penis sheaths, you were more than half way towards them recognising our common humanity.'

'But it's difficult,' he went on. 'Film can't show other people's experiences. It can bring you close, but it can't get inside. Film stops at the skin.'

It seemed like a phrase he had used before. He paused after that.

Someone asked about the relation of film to literature. Why choose film? Because wasn't it possible to express those same things in writing?

'Yes, of course, if you are a good enough writer. I was lucky to be around poets in my family, and I learned a lot from them. Poetry, I suppose, is the apex of human expression. Film is still not valued very highly in the arts.'

'Nor in the academic world,' I added. 'We still struggle with that.'

He nodded and went on.

'But with film you can perhaps be poetic. And I found it was a way out of the swamp called words. I took the epigraph for the film from the Indian scriptures, from the Upanishads as translated, or perhaps I should say written, by Yeats. "Everything in the world is eater or eaten, the seed is food and the fire is eater." I forget the exact words. And that was really what the whole film was about.'

'It's not just the cycle from one dawn until the next,' he continued, 'which is what the film shows. It's the constant cycle of birth and death and renewal. But I used the Yeats quotation because I wanted the film to have an English voice. I could never pretend to be an Indian, and in a way the Yeats quotation told you that, and it got me off the hook. A film has a voice, and the film has an English voice.'

We understood by that that he included himself as an American.

A Malaysian student asked how he felt entering other peoples' private lives with such intimacy, at a time of death. Would he be able to do the same in his own country? It was the first question with an edge to it.

'I had a colleague, a sort of guide, who was able to take me all over Benares and show me many things I wanted to see. And if there were problems, he could explain to people what I was doing. So I never really felt out of place. Also there is the Indian concept of *darshan*, which in religious contexts has to do with the importance of seeing and being seen. So this helped make the filming appropriate. But certainly there were problems, because if you have a camera everyone is interested.' I could imagine the children following him, calling out 'Shooting! Shooting!' He made gestures, as if surrounded. 'I had to keep the camera in a black plastic bag or everyone would crowd around. Of course, it wasn't a hidden camera. But I would keep the camera in the bag and then take it out when I wanted to shoot.'

A student said that for her it was hard to watch the scene of the dead animals being dragged down the steps, especially after she realised one was a cat.

'Yes,' said Gardner, 'and perhaps for others it would be a dog. You remember there is the scene of the very sick dog trying to climb slowly up the steps. I wanted that to have a significance, a meaning beyond what you see, the difficulty and struggle of life. I wanted it to suggest that.'

'You know,' he went on, 'the film is difficult, and there are many things I didn't show. I had the privilege once to be with Luis Buñuel and to get to know him a little. I asked him about *Terre sans pain*, where a donkey is killed by a swarm of bees.[3] And he said to me, "This is not the best of all possible worlds." Well, this is *not* the best of all possible worlds. I wanted the film to suggest that, but not necessarily directly. There are things that are only suggested, that are ambiguous. Like the dog that is eating something, and you hear the sound of its jaws tearing into the meat, but you don't know whether it's a buffalo or a donkey or perhaps a person. Ambiguity is very important in films. It's important that things aren't always spelled out.'

I said that I thought it was important philosophically too, to acknowledge that we can't know everything. And that things have multiple meanings.

'For those reasons too,' Gardner agreed.

I asked about the role of luck in his filmmaking, the way in which on some days everything seems to be going badly and then on another day everything seems to be magically falling into place in front of the camera. Rouch had spoken about the 'grace' or the 'gift' when everything seems to be falling in your lap. Could he tell us, for example, about the scene where the body of the child is put into the water and at the same time a kite floats down into the water? The film has by then prepared us for the meaning of kites.

It was too long a question and contained too much that was of interest to me or that I already knew, but he was ready for it.

'Well, I've tried to write a whole book about that, called *Intention, Circumstance and Chance in Nonfiction Film*.[4] Because those are the three things that shape a film. The circumstances under which you make it, your intentions, and then what happens by chance. They're all important.' Then, turning to the scene, 'I wasn't sure if people would see that, because the kite is very small in the sky. And there's something more about it that I learned but that isn't in the film. The child whose body is being put into the water died by falling off a high building.'

I expect many of us wondered if the child had been flying a kite, but none of us asked.

'What about the scene of the girls playing hopscotch?' someone said. 'Why is it in slow motion?'

'I'm glad you noticed that. A lot of people have asked me about it, and I've received a lot of criticism for it too. You know, I met someone who was interested in games and especially games that he called cosmological games. Certain games are about the cosmos, like Parcheesi, where you go around step by step at the roll of dice and then climb a ladder to the infinite. Chess is another cosmological game. I felt that hopscotch was also in some sense cosmological, where you throw down an object into squares, and I felt by filming it in slow motion I could perhaps suggest that spiritual quality.'

I said that we had been talking a lot about images, but I knew one student had a question about sound. Two chairs away from me she took up the question.

'A lot of the sound seemed to me to be enhanced, perhaps because there were no subtitles or anything, and so I paid more attention to it. Like the scene of the flowers, picking the marigolds, the sound of that.' The question was left hanging.

Gardner nodded and laughed.

'Yes, if I were re-editing the film I think I would do that scene differently. But I'm certainly not going to re-edit it.' He paused to consider. 'There is a lot of enhancement of sound in the film, you're right. Somehow you want certain sounds to stand out from everything, from the … what? The ambience, the background. So I enhanced certain sounds, but always with natural sounds, not sound effects. For example, the wood. There is a lot about the wood being dropped, and so on. And I wanted the sound of that, to give the quality of wood.'

I asked if he had learned this from the Italian Neorealist films, because they always post-dubbed the sound effects, and these stood out bell-like against the transparency of the background.

'It's true,' he said. 'All the Italian films were post-dubbed, all the dialogue too. And they still are. Yes, maybe that was an influence. I hadn't thought of that.'

I glanced at the clock and saw that he had been talking for well over an hour.

Someone down the table asked how he found his subjects. Why would he need to find them in foreign places rather than down the street, in his own country? This also had an edge to it and he took his time answering. He was tiring and I could see his hands trembling a little with the effort.

'I think I am attracted to places where I can think more clearly, where I can escape the "white noise" of my own culture. You know, the "white noise", everything around you that is familiar to you. Certain things then stand out that are common to us all, but that are expressed differently. But mostly I follow my nose.' He touched his nose. 'Sometimes your attention is just caught by something that you hear about, like Highland New Guinea. I knew immediately that I wanted to go there. It's partly a matter of chance, of circumstance, what you happen to hear about.'

There was a hiatus and it seemed a good time to stop. Apparently Gardner thought so too, for he looked around at everyone and thanked us for inviting him. We all stood up. 'I hear you've been in Cuba,' I said. 'Yes, they asked me for a week. They have a film school down there and there is an extraordinary interest in documentary. You should go there.'

I told him I'd like to.

Some of the students were moving the tables back to the sides of the room where they belonged. Others were leaving. Gardner touched me on the shoulder and in an undertone said, 'See you, man.' He went and got his coat off a chair at the back of the room. When I looked around next he was gone.

I looked at Jeff and he looked at me. 'He's mellowed a lot,' Jeff said.

Notes

1 Gardner's film about Hindu rituals of death in Varanasi (formerly Benares).

2 Jeff Daniel Silva was the teaching assistant for the seminar course 'Reading Ethnographic Film' that I was then teaching as a visiting lecturer in the Department of Visual and Environmental Studies.

3 Gardner was referring here to Luis Buñuel's film *Las Hurdes* (1933), known in English as *Land without Bread.*

4 Co-authored by Ákos Östör. The full title is *Making* Forest of Bliss*: Intention, Circumstance, and Chance in Nonfiction Film.* Cambridge, MA: Harvard Film Archive, 2001.

14

The percentage of disaster

It would be satisfying to be able to make a documentary film casually, just by picking up a camera, and once in a while this is possible. More often a film must be planned carefully, much like a military campaign, for the potential for disaster is very great. Hardly any film is completed without some kind of disaster, but the trick is to keep the percentage to a minimum.

It is easier to make a film now than it used to be. The arrival of digital video has made equipment easier to use and more reliable, and it has reduced the cost, lessening the financial risk if something goes wrong. Despite this, good planning remains important, for the risks in making any film have as much to do with human relationships as with finance. How one goes about getting permission to film, how one establishes rapport with one's subjects, and how one manages to be in the right place at the right time – these are the really crucial things in making any film.

Planning is not everything, and over-planning can produce its own problems. There have been times when I have had such a clear idea of what I wanted to film that when something different happened I neglected to film it. Later I deeply regretted the lapse, realising how important the material was. Such incidents are salutary, for they make us realise that documentary filmmaking is not about reproducing preconceived ideas but exploring the world as it exists, however unexpected it may turn out to be. To be able to change direction, to follow a subject wherever it leads: this is the sign of a genuinely interested filmmaker.

A film is ultimately the result of what one hoped to do, what one discovered along the way and what one was able to film. It is therefore in some ways a salvage process, less like chipping away marble towards some ideal form than assembling the remains of documents after a fire. This is perhaps an overstatement, for the filmmaker has some agency in directing the process and seeking out the fragments that will make up the whole. But the principle is clear, that a film can only be a sampling of what the filmmaker saw, providing pieces of evidence and making some kind of analysis. The gaps must be filled in by the viewer's imagination. At the centre stands the filmmaker, like a police officer directing the traffic.

What seems like a disaster to a filmmaker is often of no consequence to anyone else. In this sense the term is disproportionate, reflecting the intensity and self-absorbed nature of the filmmaking process, in which filmmakers tend to see themselves at the centre of events. For famously narcissistic artists like Werner Herzog or Salvador Dali this may be a boon, allowing them to exploit the chaos they encounter and sometimes create. But for others it is more important to keep their problems in some sort of perspective, and not be overcome by them.

Typically there are two main sorts of disaster that occur in filmmaking. One results from a failure of intelligence, causing one to be absent or in the wrong place at crucial times. The filmmaker has either misunderstood the situation or been given misinformation. It may also stem from making false assumptions or failing to communicate properly with others. Or it may simply be caused by bad luck and the general unpredictability of life. The second kind of disaster is technical, caused by a breakdown in some part of the complex physical chain that is required to make a film. This is probably the most vulnerable point in filmmaking, for the breakdown may be very small and yet bring everything to a halt. It reminds us of the old proverb, 'for the want of a horseshoe nail, a kingdom was lost'. Disasters of this kind can be caused by something as simple as a broken electrical connector or (as I shall describe later) misshapen perforations in the film itself.

Then there are the more amorphous disasters. I was a witness to one of these, which felt like a disaster in slow motion. One of my postgraduate professors made a documentary film for which I did most of the cinematography. A more kindly and generous man would be hard to find, but he had great difficulty in making decisions. This created its own complications while we were filming, but the main problem occurred a long time later. It took him twenty years to edit the film, by which time the film laboratory he had used had closed down and all the original negative had disappeared. He managed eventually to complete the film, but only by copying the much-scratched and faded workprint to video. It ended up much the worse for wear.[1]

One famous disaster in filmmaking was largely self-inflicted, but we are fortunate to have a detailed account of it. Les Blank's film *Burden of Dreams* (1982) catalogues the troubles that occurred during the making of Werner Herzog's film *Fitzcarraldo* (1982), many of them brought on by the obsessive drive of Herzog himself. Not content to use a model of a steamship, he had a real one hauled by hand over a muddy hill between one river and another in the Amazon jungle. Not surprisingly the local Aguaruna people, who were hired as extras to do this, nearly mutinied. Later they burned down the film set. There were several deaths and multiple injuries. Two of Herzog's main actors quit during the production, the first because of dysentery and the second, one may suppose, out of disgust. The lead actor was replaced with Klaus Kinski, with whom Herzog fought constantly.

Some disasters may make a film better, and perhaps *Fitzcarraldo* is a case in point. Herzog's woes seem to have given the film added energy, and certainly a lot of welcome publicity. The difficulties and delays that filmmakers encounter may also force them to rethink what they are doing or lead them to discover new material. Thus for all that is lost, something may be gained.

I believe this was true for our film *Photo Wallahs* (1991), despite the many frustrations Judith and I experienced along the way. The problem was that our troubles were for a long time inexplicable. Our intention in making the film was to explore the various kinds of photography practised in a small hill town in India, as a way of uncovering the different conceptions and uses of photography there. Each day we would start off to film a photographer at work or some other scene in which photography was a key element. After a few minutes, and usually as something interesting was getting under way, the film would jam in the camera. I would have to remove the film magazine from the camera body, reset the film loop and remount the magazine. We would film for another few minutes and very often the film would jam again. When this happened we would have to abandon the filming for that morning or afternoon. Most frustrating of all was that this happened irregularly, so that we never knew whether our plans would be upset or not.

Back at Fairview, the house we rented during our stay, we tried to determine the cause of the problem. It was wrecking many scenes and causing us to miss many others. Sometimes the film would run smoothly through the camera, but at other times it would capriciously jam up again. We could never be sure if we could continue, and as much of the film relied on spontaneous events there was little chance we could film them again.

At first we suspected that some of the film magazines were defective, but we could identify none specifically related to the problem. Could it be the camera then? Fortunately we had a second camera with us and now began to use it, but the film jammed in that camera too. We finally began to suspect the film stock we were using, which included several different production batches. Could certain batches be at fault? We ran tests and sent them off for analysis, a lengthy procedure involving shipping the film to New Delhi and then to the laboratory in Australia, making sure that customs officers did not open the cans upon export, a constant worry. After several weeks the reports came back from the laboratory. They could find nothing wrong with the film stock.

After eight months we had managed to film a reasonable number of scenes successfully, be we had missed or been forced to abandon many others. Returning to Australia, we ran further tests on the cameras and the film stock, all of which produced negative results. The local office of the Eastman Kodak Company assured us that the film stock was not the culprit. Finally, however, we persuaded them to send samples to their laboratory in Colorado for further testing. The answer came back that the stock was indeed defective, but not consistently so. It contained, according to the test report, 'random oversized perforations'.

Under its guarantees, the Eastman Kodak Company replaced the defective rolls of film with new ones but would not compensate us for any of the production costs or the many months of wasted time and opportunities. By now the film should have been finished, as we were well past the end date of the agreement under which we were making it.[2] But as yet we had no film. Fortunately, we had taken out production insurance, a practice which, while not always followed by independent filmmakers, had been required under the terms of the production agreement. Having received the report on the film stock, and after more months of delay, the insurance company agreed on a settlement that allowed us to return to India for a further three months of filming.

Not all our time had been wasted, however, for during the delays our ideas for the film had evolved and deepened. Moreover, when we returned to India we were able to film many scenes that had not been possible during the first period of filming. Thus it was that the film, which had suffered much from the disaster, had in other ways matured and become more interesting. It was finally completed some four years after we first proposed it.

In some respects *Photo Wallahs* was a rather abstract film, in that it developed ideas about photography and was constructed from scenes that often had no chronological or physical connection with each other. *The Wedding Camels* (1977), on the other hand, a film made some years earlier, was much more vulnerable to technical problems because in it we followed a series of connected events. Any interruptions risked our missing some event crucial to the audience's understanding. In purely dramatic terms too, certain scenes were essential turning points in the unfolding narrative.

Many of the disasters of filmmaking, while seeming serious matters at the time, often take on a more comical aspect in retrospect. If they are sufficiently unrelenting, they may even produce a fatalistic outlook on the part of the filmmakers. If things seem to be going well, it is perhaps only an illusion, with some new disaster just over the horizon. So it was with *The Wedding Camels*, which may be taken as a lesson of encouragement to any neophyte filmmakers who feel daunted and dogged by bad luck. It is foolish to expect everything to go right but, as in this case, in the end one's misfortunes may prove less catastrophic than they appeared at the time.

The Wedding Camels was one of three ethnographic films in which we explored the institution of marriage among the Turkana, a pastoralist people of north-west Kenya. The project had its origins in films we had made earlier about the Jie people in nearby Uganda. Its purpose was to try to gain a better understanding of the complexities of marriage in a group very similar to the Jie. As with the Jie, it was evident that for the Turkana, marriage and family alliances underpinned almost everything of importance in social and economic life. It provided security and helped redistribute wealth in a region in which drought could destroy a family's herds at one stroke.

We arrived in Kenya with our three-year-old son in July 1973. Our filming equipment arrived a month later. At this point we had no idea what marriage or marriages would take place in Turkana District, but we hoped that in the months ahead we would be allowed to film one in all its complexity. Our objective was not to film a marriage purely as an event. What interested us were its larger implications, not just in a sociological sense but as it affected the lives of the individuals involved.

What we hadn't properly taken into account was that Turkana marriages generally take place only in the rainy season, and even then only in years of good rainfall – and we had arrived at the beginning of the dry season in northern Kenya. Thus we had many months to wait. Even if it rained, no marriages would take place if the rainfall was poor. As it turned out, the waiting was both useful and necessary. We needed time to find a place to live, to meet people, to gain permission to film and to improve our limited knowledge of the Turkana language, which was almost identical to that of the Jie. We reasoned that once we had found a marriage being planned, we would be able to film its preparations in some detail.

Our reasoning in this last matter was faulty. For the Turkana, arranging a marriage is as much (or more, in fact) about connecting two families as about the two individuals who will marry. It requires complex transfers of livestock from the husband's family to the wife's family, and the livestock must be gathered gradually from a host of relatives. Very often the bride will joint several other wives of her prospective husband, and they will have had an important say in choosing her. All these preparations take months, and for the most part they remain tentative up till the end, since they depend on the coming rains. Every family therefore wants to keep their options open, even as to who might marry whom, and the offers and negotiations are carried on largely in secret. Rumours abound. One rumour slips away into another. Pity the filmmaker who would like to know what is going to happen.

During our first weeks in Nairobi we went about the business of getting official permission to film in Kenya. It may seem strange that we had to do this even before meeting any Turkana families or asking their permission to film, but that was the case. I had applied for the necessary documents well before coming to Kenya but had received only non-committal replies. It seemed that a personal appearance was necessary to start the process rolling. It required a Licence to Film, granted by the Ministry of Information and Broadcasting, and a Research Authority, granted by the Office of the President. The problem was that the latter would not grant the Research Authority until the former had granted the Licence to Film, and the reverse was equally true. I therefore began what seemed an endless round of visits to the two offices, in each of which I was assured that the document I wanted would be issued once I had secured the other. When it seemed that this might go on forever, I went in desperation to the director of the National Museums of Kenya, where I had had the foresight to be made a visiting research associate. In ten minutes, with one telephone call to each of the offices, he resolved the problem. The documents were issued in a matter of days.

Once in Turkana, we travelled widely, camping in many places and meeting many people. We finally settled in an area at the southern end of the Lotikipi Plain. There we began a more sedentary life, enjoying the peace of familiar surroundings and familiar faces. These included not only the local Turkana families but Catholic fathers at a nearby mission, who appeared more interested in improving health and education than making converts. Our little boy quickly made Turkana friends of his own age. We felt safe in this environment, despite its relative isolation and occasional attacks on Turkana homesteads by armed Dodoth and Toposa cattle raiders. We slowly began the process of finding out what we could about any marriages that might take place in the area. This meant getting to know as many people as possible and listening in on all the latest rumours.

There is insufficient space here to list here all the steps that this took, or to describe how we finally found the marriage we eventually filmed, and how we were allowed by the families to film it. I shall therefore focus on more practical matters. Some eight months after we arrived in Kenya, heavy rain began to fall in Turkana and reports of negotiations about marriages began to be heard. We were overjoyed that what we had hoped for was finally getting under way.

At this stage there was only one slight worry. We had filmed a series of camera and lens tests after our arrival, but in the complications of shipping the film to and from the processing laboratory in London they had become lost, and we had never seen them. We were not unduly worried, for all the equipment had been tested before shipping, and the tests were just a further precaution. We began filming preliminary material with one of the families we had come to know well, and in which there was the possibility of a marriage taking place.

One day we were filming what promised to be a particularly important scene about Turkana attitudes towards marriage, the first of this kind we had witnessed. A group of elders were seated under a tree discussing a case in which a young man had got a girl pregnant and her father was demanding payment of livestock in compensation. It seemed a valuable scene for the film, bringing together many of the key elements we had been tracing for several months. By now the elders knew us well and were content to have us film. The light was good and even inviting, with the sunlight slanting in and touching the leaves overhead. We felt ourselves lucky, but as I started filming the camera went dead.

At first we thought it was the batteries, but back at our quarters we discovered it was the camera motor that had burnt out. What to do? It happened that a few days earlier I had been invited to Australia for a job interview, an invitation that in today's more straitened times would be unlikely. As we were in the midst of making the film, leaving just then was unthinkable, and I was about to decline. It then occurred to me that I might have the camera motor repaired in Australia more quickly than if I tried to send it to Britain or Switzerland (where it was made) or America. There would be delays, and we might miss filming crucial events. I sent a telegram to Australia accepting the interview invitation. I sent a second telegram to a filmmaker friend in Sydney. If I brought the motor with me, would he please try to have it repaired within a few days, while I had the interview?

I left Turkana in the Land Rover the next day on the two-day drive to Nairobi, taking the motor with me and 4,700 feet of freshly exposed film, to be shipped to the laboratory in London. A week later I reached Sydney via Bombay and was met by my friend at the airport, who undertook to have the motor repaired for me. I continued on to Canberra. The following morning I was awakened by the telephone ringing in my hotel room, for I had overslept the interview. Arriving late, I was duly interviewed and, as it turned out, offered the position.[3] Two days later I collected the repaired motor from my friend at Sydney airport and flew back to Nairobi.

I would have liked to have driven immediately back to Turkana, but the roads were cut by flooding rivers. It wasn't until five days later that I managed to get back, having been away for three weeks. Three long weeks, but fortunately nothing crucial had happened in the marriage plans we had been following most closely. The next day we started filming again. On this day the prospective bridegroom, Kongu, was arriving for the first face-to-face negotiations with the bride's father, Lorang. It seemed I had got back just in time.

Lorang and Kongu were seated beneath a tree, beginning their conversation, which had of necessity to progress gradually in the delicate matter of how much livestock would be given by Kongu's family to Lorang's family if he married Lorang's daughter, Akai. As they talked I began filming. Almost immediately Judith noticed a small plume of smoke rising up from the camera, and I realised the camera was slowing to a halt. Rather to our hosts' surprise, we gathered up our equipment abruptly and went home to examine the motor. But there was nothing to be done: it had burnt out again. We decided to leave next morning for Nairobi to see if a replacement motor could sent from America.

One of the pleasures of living in Kenya, offsetting many of the frustrations of dealing with some of the bureaucrats, was the helpfulness and unexpected generosity of others. Eldoret is a highland town where we usually stopped for the night when driving between Turkana and Nairobi. We arrived after dark and began trying to make an international call to our colleague James Blue in America, who we hoped could arrange to have another motor sent to us. Even at the best hotel in town, however, no international calls were possible. It might be possible from the post office, but as it was late evening the post office was closed. We made some further enquiries. The postmaster, it seemed, might help us, but he was at a party. When we found him celebrating with his friends, he listened carefully to our tale and said he would open up the post office for us. We drove there and were astonished to find, on the second floor, a huge mahogany-panelled telephone exchange, complete with brass fittings and a wall of switchboards with plug-in cables. Our newfound friend, the postmaster, soon switched us through to America and our colleague, faintly, at the other end of the line, promised to have a new motor sent to us.

In Nairobi we received a telegram from Blue, saying the new motor had been ordered and was being sent (figure 14.1). We waited for it to arrive, but after a week of hearing nothing we sent a telegram to the company supplying it, asking when it had been sent and why it had not come. Four days later, it arrived. Sad to say, it was in poor shape: a second-hand motor with at least four things wrong with it, and even loose wires hanging out of it. We cabled the company protesting and demanding a replacement (figure 14.2). A local electronics expert thought he might be able to make it run if we could get a new circuit board sent from Switzerland. We tried to arrange this by telephone and telegram. A circuit board was indeed air-freighted to us, but later we learned it was sent to the wrong address and had therefore been returned to Switzerland.

The day after receiving the defective motor, the lens tests we had made six months earlier finally reached us. They told a sorry story. The zoom lens we had been using, which had been serviced and tested prior to our departure for Kenya, went out of focus at the wide-angle position, something not noticeable in the camera's viewfinder. (We learned later that during servicing one element had been put in backwards.) Much of the first 4,700 feet we had filmed would therefore be unusable. There was no alternative: we sent a radiogram to Turkana asking our Turkana assistant to send the lens to Nairobi on the next lorry. We would try to have it tested and see if it could be readjusted or repaired.

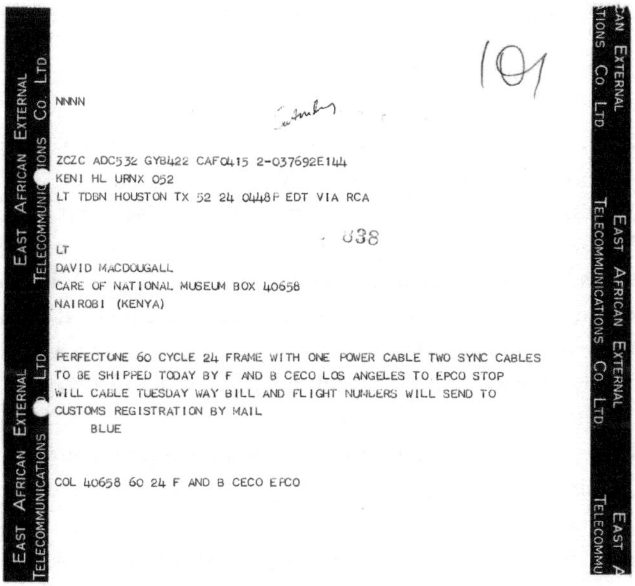

EAST AFRICAN EXTERNAL TELECOMMUNICATIONS CO. LTD.

NNNN

ZCZC ADC532 GYB422 CAF0415 2-037692E144
KENI HL URNX 052
LT TDBN HOUSTON TX 52 24 0448P EDT VIA RCA

LT
DAVID MACDOUGALL
CARE OF NATIONAL MUSEUM BOX 40658
NAIROBI (KENYA)

PERFECTONE 60 CYCLE 24 FRAME WITH ONE POWER CABLE TWO SYNC CABLES
TO BE SHIPPED TODAY BY F AND B CECO LOS ANGELES TO EPCO STOP
WILL CABLE TUESDAY WAY BILL AND FLIGHT NUMBERS WILL SEND TO
CUSTOMS REGISTRATION BY MAIL
BLUE

COL 40658 60 24 F AND B CECO EPCO

14.1 Telegram from James Blue to the filmmakers

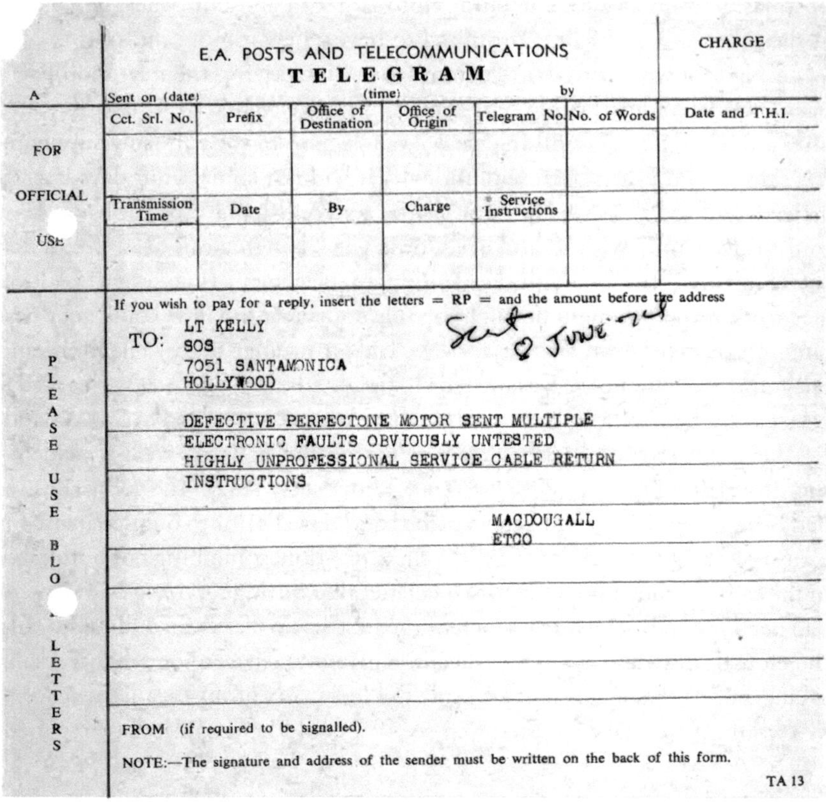

E.A. POSTS AND TELECOMMUNICATIONS

TELEGRAM

CHARGE

A Sent on (date) (time) by

Cct. Srl. No.	Prefix	Office of Destination	Office of Origin	Telegram No.	No. of Words	Date and T.H.I.
Transmission Time	Date	By	Charge	* Service Instructions		

FOR OFFICIAL USE

PLEASE USE BLOCK LETTERS

If you wish to pay for a reply, insert the letters = RP = and the amount before the address

TO: LT KELLY
SOS
7051 SANTAMONICA
HOLLYWOOD

Sent 8 June 74

DEFECTIVE PERFECTONE MOTOR SENT MULTIPLE
ELECTRONIC FAULTS OBVIOUSLY UNTESTED
HIGHLY UNPROFESSIONAL SERVICE CABLE RETURN
INSTRUCTIONS

MACDOUGALL
ETCO

FROM (if required to be signalled).

NOTE:—The signature and address of the sender must be written on the back of this form.

TA 13

14.2 Telegram from the filmmakers to an equipment supplier

Fortunately, we reassured ourselves, we had one small, older zoom lens still in Turkana which we could use if all else failed.

A week after the arrival of the defective motor, the replacement motor arrived in Nairobi. It seemed to work. By now we had been away from Turkana for over two weeks but we hoped against hope that nothing much had advanced in the marriage plans or, worse, that the marriage had now taken place. We would leave the next morning for Turkana, but first we sent a second radiogram to our assistant, telling him not to send the defective lens to Nairobi after all. We would use the smaller one instead.

To celebrate, we had dinner at Laverini's, an Italian restaurant in the centre of Nairobi. This proved misguided, however, for upon leaving the restaurant we found our Land Rover was no longer in its parking place across from the New Stanley Hotel. It had been stolen. Vehicles stolen in Kenya at that time were rarely recovered, because they were either driven immediately out of the country or dismantled for parts, to be sold through the many garages in

Nairobi and elsewhere. We walked disconsolately to the police station but were not encouraged by the police officers, who sadly shook their heads. But they would of course look for our vehicle.

The next morning I began walking around in the rougher, industrial parts of Nairobi, hoping to spot the Land Rover in some shed or go-down. I could see vehicles being worked on by mechanics, but not ours. It was more a vain hope than a real one, and all it earned me were a few suspicious stares. We returned to the police station later in the day. There some delighted police officers informed us that the Land Rover had been found. Apart from a dent in one fender and the theft of some tools, spare tyres and a drum of petrol stowed in the back, it was in good shape. After a day of buying replacement items, we set off for Turkana.

When we arrived we were relieved to find that the marriage negotiations had not advanced very far, but that our assistant had unfortunately sent both zoom lenses, not just the defective one, down to Nairobi, having failed to receive our second radiogram. After frantically sending messages to Nairobi to have the lenses returned, I rummaged around in our equipment cases and found one small lens with a fixed focal length that I had thrown in as an afterthought. It was not even supposed to fit our camera, having been made for a Bolex rather than an Éclair. However, it could be mounted on the camera, and I could see nothing wrong with it except that the optics were rather hazy, yellow and scratched. We could film with it, and we began to do so, starting with a group of women in a sorghum field chiding young men for their laziness. Eventually the other two zoom lenses came back from Nairobi and we were able to use the smaller one for the rest of the production.

Here ends the account of our technical disasters. And here, providentially, began for us a period of good fortune, which we had perhaps paid for excessively in the previous months. Kongu returned for further talks with Lorang about the bridewealth. There was much preparation of food. People began arriving from all over, having heard that a wedding and feasting were imminent. One day at last the wedding took place, and the bride, Akai, went to stay with her husband and begin her life among the co-wives of her new family. All this we managed to film. There was even an unexpected bonus. On the morning after the wedding, when all the guests had dispersed, we found Lorang seated with one of his oldest friends, and they spent the next hour quietly discussing everything that had taken place, apparently oblivious of our filming. Or were they? Perhaps it was simply a kindness to a pair of exhausted filmmakers.

There were further problems, of course, but they seemed minor and could be met with comparative equanimity. While Judith stayed on another week to complete some written translations, I drove the Land Rover back to Nairobi along the watershed route on the Kenya–Uganda border. On the way the radiator began leaking and I had to stop at each bore-hole along the way to refill it. Fortunately our son, now four, was with me, and he carefully held the jerry-cans under the pump while I operated the handle. A week later Judith returned to Nairobi, hitching a ride on a light aircraft and bringing our audio tapes with her, all the while fearing they might be erased by being too close to the engine. (Happily, they survived this.) There were later delays. Some of our translations went astray. It took months to sell the Land Rover, for less than we hoped to receive for it. But the laboratory did not lose the original footage, the editing went well, and the film, *The Wedding Camels*, and two long companion films were eventually finished, some eight years after we made our first journey into Turkana.

Notes

1 The film was *Imbalu: Ritual of Manhood of the Bagisu of Uganda* (1988), directed by Richard Hawkins with the anthropologist Suzette Heald.

2 We made the film as part of a Documentary Film Fellowship, awarded annually to independent filmmakers by the Australian Film Commission. We also received funding from the French television channel La Sept. The film was eventually broadcast on television by the Australian Broadcasting Corporation (ABC) and La Sept.

3 It is perhaps advisable to approach an interview jet-lagged, with lack of sleep and with other things on one's mind. I had been invited to be interviewed for the directorship of the Film Unit of the Australian Institute of Aboriginal Studies. After the principal of the Institute laid out his proposed filming programme, I gave my views, perhaps incautiously, disagreeing with him on almost every point and proposing a quite different programme. That evening, and in a jovial mood, he quietly let me know that I had got the job and, what was more, a job for Judith as well. We eventually made eleven films with the Institute from 1975 to 1987. Without the accident of the burnt-out motor it is unlikely we would have ended up in Australia.

15

Clearing customs

During the filming of *Photo Wallahs* (as described in chapter 14) it was necessary to clear our camera and sound recording equipment through Indian customs on two occasions. The second of these was in July 1988 on our return to India, after a lapse of four months. The following account was written on the evening of the same day and is reproduced here verbatim.

I arrive punctually at the Australian High Commission [in New Delhi] at 9.30 a.m. to begin this day, 12 July 1988, clearing the filming equipment through customs. At the gatehouse I sign the book and am given a grubby plastic pass. I note that Mr Gandhi, the shipping agent, has signed in just ahead of me. In the reception hall the two young women behind the counter are convulsed when I ask, quite innocently, 'Has Mr Gandhi arrived?' They thought I meant Rajiv Gandhi, the Prime Minister, they say, who is on an international tour. They point the way down the corridor, where Mr Gandhi is awaiting me with the High Commission's major domo in charge of shipping and logistics, Mr Sen.

Mr Gandhi is a short compact man in his thirties in a striped tennis shirt, carrying a thin grey attaché case. I try to size him up, but there's not much to go on so far. Mr Sen is a thin patriarchal figure. We look through the papers I've picked up from the front desk, left for me by the First Secretary, Brett Martin. There's a covering letter from him to customs, and copies of the officially stamped list of equipment and a letter from the Ministry of External Affairs requesting that the equipment be entered on a TBRE (Tourist Baggage Re-Export) form. It seems the Ministry has no authority to approve this importation; all they can do is kindly request customs' cooperation and hope that this will be acted on.

Mr Gandhi directs Mr Sen to type out one more letter, giving him authority to act for me and including a space for Mr Gandhi's specimen signature. The letter is typed and I form a first impression of Mr Gandhi as someone who knows his way about and prepares for the future.

We decide to leave Mr Gandhi's scooter at the High Commission and call a taxi, although I say I am quite prepared to ride on the back of the scooter. I decide Mr Gandhi would rather ride in a taxi when my offer is refused.

The young Sikh taxi driver seems to be in a state of deep lethargy, since he dawdles along at no more than 50 kph and waves all other traffic past with a

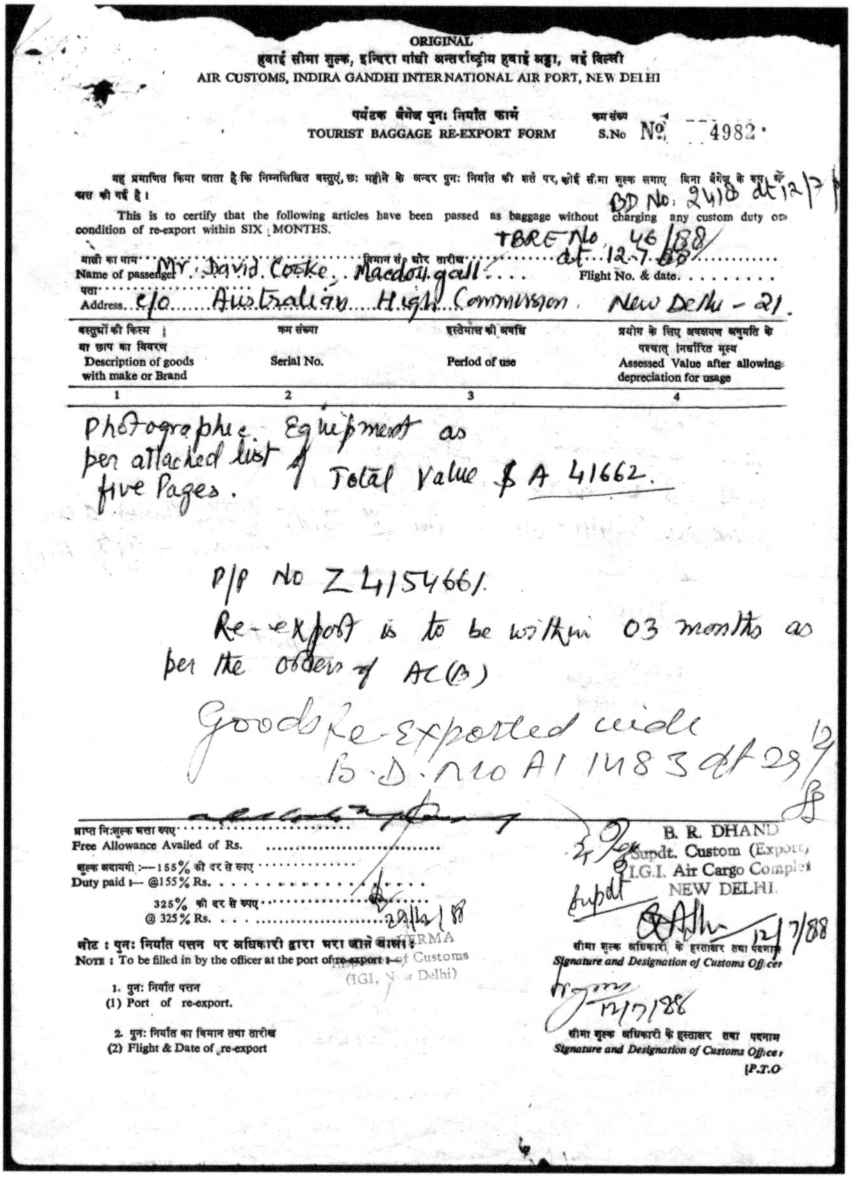

ORIGINAL
हवाई सीमा शुल्क, इन्दिरा गांधी अन्तर्राष्ट्रीय हवाई अड्डा, नई दिल्ली
AIR CUSTOMS, INDIRA GANDHI INTERNATIONAL AIR PORT, NEW DELHI

पर्यटक बैगेज पुनः निर्यात फार्म
TOURIST BAGGAGE RE-EXPORT FORM S.No No. 4982

यह प्रमाणित किया जाता है कि निम्नलिखित वस्तुएं, छः महीने के अन्दर पुनः निर्यात की शर्त पर, कोई सीमा शुल्क लगाए बिना बैगेज के रूप में पास की गई हैं।

This is to certify that the following articles have been passed as baggage without charging any custom duty on condition of re-export within SIX MONTHS.

BD No. 2418 dt 12/7
TBRE No 46/88/ dt 12.7.88

Name of passenger Mr. David Cooke Macdougall .... Flight No. & date.
Address c/o Australian High Commission New Delhi - 21.

Description of goods with make or Brand	Serial No.	Period of use	Assessed Value after allowing depreciation for usage
1	2	3	4

Photographic Equipment as per attached list of five Pages. Total Value $A 41662.

P/P No Z4154661.
Re-export is to be within 03 months as per the orders of AC(B)

Goods Re-exported vide B.D. No AI 1483 dt 29/12

Free Allowance Availed of Rs. ....
Duty paid :— @155% Rs. ....
@ 325% Rs. 29/12/88

B. R. DHAND
Supdt. Custom (Export)
I.G.I. Air Cargo Complex
NEW DELHI.
Supdt 12/7/88

Note : To be filled in by the officer at the port of re-export :—

(1) Port of re-export.

(2) Flight & Date of re-export

Signature and Designation of Customs Officer
12/7/88
Signature and Designation of Customs Officer
[P.T.O

15.1 An equipment importation permit for *Photo Wallahs*

gesture of one finger out the window. I think maybe the car – an old, solid Ambassador – has a sick motor. Mr Gandhi casts a few nervous glances at his watch. He wants to get started as early as possible.

We leave the taxi at the roadside and walk past the guard post into the grounds of the cargo terminal. Ahead of us, across the yellow earth and frizzy green grass, stretches the terminal itself, a long and high concrete warehouse.

We haven't talked much in the taxi, but I've told Mr Gandhi we hope to start shooting when we've got our equipment up to Mussoorie in a week or so.

'You must say,' he now instructs me, 'that you need to start filming at once, today. You must ask for a priority.'

I feel like an actor being coached before I am pushed on stage.

We reach the steps of the terminal, where a disorderly queue waits near a grilled window. Other people stand or sit about. 'Give me two fifty rupees,' says Mr Gandhi, handing me a hundred rupee note. I have only one and give it to him. He waves my explanation aside; he will collect the rest later.

'I have to buy a place in the queue,' he says. 'A hundred and fifty rupees. Then we may get to the window by twelve o'clock.'

I look at my watch. It's only a little past ten.

Mr Gandhi points to his attaché case and dashes off down the open side of the terminal, which is like a great railway platform. At first I think I am to follow him, so I pick up the case and set out after him, only to see him disappear through a doorway marked 'Gents'. I sit down and wait.

Nothing much is happening. Officials, agents, clients lounge about waiting for something to happen. Suddenly a rat shoots out of the darkness of a doorway and makes a dash along the platform, next to the wall. At the end a man is pouring water from a bottle into a glass just as the rat reaches him and tries to run up his leg. Water goes everywhere and the rat disappears through another dark doorway.

Mr Gandhi is back, but no sooner does he make contact with me than he is off again. We go up a staircase and into a room with a set of grilled windows facing us. Mr Gandhi takes my passport and the waybill number of the shipment, which I have written on a card. He thrusts these through one grille. The young and cool woman in a sari on the other side begins looking through huge tomes of waybills. Next she looks through trays on a desk. Then she looks through some more bound files. Finally she finds our waybill on a desk, just being processed by someone.

'Give me twenty rupees,' Mr Gandhi says to me. He takes it to another grilled window, pays, receives a stamped yellow form, returns, hands it through the grille and collects the passport and the waybill, which in fact is a thick sheaf of pink and white pages.

We head back down the concrete stairs. Mr Gandhi disappears briefly through the doorway where the rat had gone, leaving me with his case. Then we head back along the terminal to a new set of grilled windows, surrounded by young men who look hopelessly through them with papers clutched in one hand and the other hand hooked through a window or holding someone else's shoulder. Mr Gandhi pushes his way through the crowd and thrusts his papers – my papers – deep inside the window. I am beginning to gain in my admiration for Mr Gandhi and lose my disgust for queue-jumpers.

I hang around in the background watching old friends greet each other as they wait at the windows. Nothing much seems to be going on inside. I glance up at a huge silo-like building across from us, with steps running zigzag up its side. A bored monkey of enormous size leans out on the third storey and surveys the scene below. When I look back again he is gone. Now along the shaded platform on which we stand comes a starved and gaunt young man with a lurching walk. His face suddenly lights up in a smile and I see that he is drooling. He comes and stands beside me, and although I look studiously away from him I know he is smiling and staring at me. He moves away down the platform and then comes back tapping a matchbox. I shake my head. He smiles back, no less pleased than before, and wanders away.

Mr Gandhi has now got what he wants and we head back the way we came and through a wide doorway with a guard posted beside it. We are in a gigantic warehouse, most of it fenced off behind wire mesh. There are racks that go up to the highest part of the roof, filled with boxes and packing cases. Closer to us are offices, partitioned off from the rest of the building as an afterthought, and counters on which cargo can be inspected. There are mountains of cargo waiting behind them, surrounded by porters in identical yellow T-shirts and a few white-clad customs officers. Overhead a few fans are cutting through the air without discernible effect.

We go upstairs onto a kind of balcony overlooking the warehouse. At the far end is a waiting room with chairs facing a closed wooden door. Mr Gandhi taps on the door, opens it a crack and peers in. A uniformed guard steps out – an old man nearing retirement. Mr Gandhi whispers in his ear, gives him the papers and my passport and urges him back inside with them. We sit and wait.

'I have asked for a priority and for a TBRE.'

The guard steps out again and with barely a nod sits down in a chair beside the door. I have caught a glimpse of the great man inside at his desk, papers in front of him, talking on the phone.

After ten minutes Mr Gandhi has another word with the guard, who disappears inside. Other agents have joined us and handed their papers in too. We all wait and look through the window at the hazy steaming day outside. A tall woman in a green sari walks back and forth, trying to console her two-year-old daughter, who is having a tantrum.

The guard comes out and sketches a gesture of pen-writing in the air. Mr Gandhi gives him a nod and sits back in his seat, relieved. At length the guard brings us out our papers and shows Mr Gandhi a page clipped to them, covered in writing. This it appears is the authority to issue a TBRE, based on the letter we have provided from the Ministry of External Affairs.

'Give me ten rupees,' says Mr Gandhi as he reads the page. I fish out a note and hand it to him. Satisfied with the wording, he turns to the guard with a smile and a nod and jams the ten-rupee note into his hand. No one has seen. Then we are off at break-neck speed back along the corridor. At the bottom of the stairs Mr Gandhi disappears inside an office and comes out again.

We wait, seated on worn fibreglass form-fit chairs. Mr Gandhi has handed his papers – my papers – over to an official in one of the offices. As we wait, Mr Gandhi says, 'See that man? He's the boss of everything here.' At first I don't see whom he means, but then I notice a slight, tall figure moving unhurriedly through the crowd, a man with a calm, finely chiselled face. He bestows a word here, a word there. He has none of the 'boss' about him; rather he looks like a retired schoolmaster visiting his old pupils and fellow teachers.

We wait some more and then there is a diversion. Mr Gandhi jumps up and greets a fat smiling man and a dramatic, dark-haired woman who seems dishevelled by the heat and humidity. I am introduced but don't catch the names. 'He is from the Italian embassy,' says Mr Gandhi, clapping his friend on the shoulder, and it's clear he's glad to see him – a fellow professional among so many weary and ignorant clients, so many adversaries among the officialdom. Across from us now sits a group of Germans in shorts. They have five o'clock shadows and knobby knees. They look as if they have just got off a train or a two-day aeroplane flight. For a while I think they are on their own, but then they are joined by their shipping agent, a hatchet-faced man with a sheaf of papers.

Mr Gandhi gets his sheaf back from the office and we go along the inspection counters to a desk manned by a customs official in a dirtier white outfit than most of the others. He looks like an ice-cream salesman, but he is busy reading and stamping forms and tearing into people's luggage. The porters in yellow shirts haul the luggage around and do most of the sorting for him, leaving him free to rummage with one hand in a suitcase or pull out a shirt by the sleeve.

His first victim is the dishevelled woman from the Italian embassy, accompanied by the smiling fat man who is no longer smiling as much. Her suitcase lies open on the counter, with a cylindrical cardboard package next to it.

'How much longer do we stay here?' she gasps. 'I cannot stay here much longer. I am going to die!'

The customs official has a kindly face and steel-grey hair. He ignores her completely and rummages with one hand in the suitcase. Then he directs a porter to begin taking out the clothing.

'My God! How can you do this?' exclaims the woman. 'Can't you see they are clothes, not a bomb! Is this the way you treat a guest of the Indian government? I should never have come to India!'

The customs official keeps his kindly smile and directs that more clothes be taken out.

Beside me on the bench I'm now sitting on are the Germans. The one next to me is a gangly creature with a red nose.

'How do you do?' he says.

'Slowly,' I say.

He looks blank, then finds this a great joke. When he stops laughing he says, 'We are coming in the mountains to climbing.' I nod. He points to the raving Italian woman. 'It is very … very *difficile*,' he says, and then his face clouds over. He stares moodily at the customs desk.

By now one porter is pulling apart the cylindrical package. Another is pulling out silk blouses, drops of sweat from his forehead falling into the suitcase.

'What the hell are you doing!' She snatches the last blouse from him and then turns to the customs officer.

'They are being touched. They are getting dirty. Will you handle my underpants? Do you want to handle my underpants too?'

A curious Italian-style lamp with many joints is being removed from the paper cylinder. It looks like a miniature piece of planetarium equipment.

'It is a lamp!' she shouts impatiently. 'They do not make lamps like this here.'

The customs inspector looks as though he wonders if it is a lamp at all. Another officer is called over to give an opinion. Mr Gandhi is now arguing quietly with the woman and the fat man. Somehow he seems to have got behind the counter, beside the customs man.

'My God! Five thousand rupees' duty?' exclaims the woman. 'It is only worth a thousand rupees. We will get the money back. My ambassador will write a letter….'

When they have gone away we get down to the business of the film equipment. I hope that none of it will look like a lamp, or that our case will have been tainted by Mr Gandhi's association with the Italians. For myself, I have been sitting as quietly as possible on my bench. I think of some of the items like silica gel that are not on the manifest. Will they think it is heroin? But in a moment my confidence is back. We could hardly do as badly as the prima donna. In fact, I think we will win through by sheer reasonableness.

Mr Gandhi comes and goes with the sheaf of papers. The Germans go away again. At last Mr Gandhi gestures to me over the counter. He has had the equipment brought in from a distant warehouse and now it sits behind the counter, all seventeen cases of it. The customs inspector looks at the list.

'This is all photographic equipment?'

'Filming and sound recording equipment,' I say.

'How many cameras are there?'

I count the cameras and show him on the list – two film cameras and five still cameras.

'Let me see the cameras.'

We find out the case numbers and open the cases with the help of a porter, who has a knife. I pull out the Aaton case and open it. The camera lies there on its bed of silk and the inspector stares at it. I take it out for him and show the serial number. He seems barely convinced it is a camera. Next I take out the Eclair and show him how the magazine comes off.

'Ah ... the film is inside ... there.'

I explain about magazines, taking my time. Mr Gandhi is looking nervous and we rip open the plastic cooler containing the still cameras. He begins to unpack it and I have to slow him down. The inspector begins to tick off what he has seen on the list. We go through one more cooler, full of recording equipment, and then the inspector asks to see a case with only one item in it. He is clearly impatient with bits and pieces. I decide upon the tripod case, with only the wooden tripod legs in it. This seen, we return to the desk, where the inspector asks me to read out the items we have seen and their values. He writes this laboriously on a form with a purple ball pen. We add up the values. Then he asks us to make a list of everything else. Mr Gandhi waves the list.

'Everything is on the list! It is having everything on the list.' But the inspector shakes his head patiently. No, he must write down the items he has seen and then the items he has not seen. Mr Gandhi and I get on with it, and I quickly see that the trick is to summarise everything under a few headings. We find the value of this list by subtracting the value of what he has seen from the total.

The porters are banding up the opened cases with plastic bands which they tighten with a hand-operated machine. Other porters are running around with pots of red sealing wax.

When the inspector has finished writing out his form he looks at it proudly. I am asked to sign a statement that he has seen the first lot of items. Since he has seen more than that, in fact, as we went through the cases, I scrawl 'inspected' instead of 'seen.' I also add that the items are 'as per the approved list.' Then we have to write in the total value and sign that, and I sign something in a ledger.

I am under the impression that we are finished here as we race off through the crowd to the office at the corner, near the entrance. Its door is ajar and we slip in behind a group of people waiting around a desk. Behind the desk sits a man in shining white uniform with gold epaulettes, another schoolmaster. He is sitting bolt upright and writing on some forms. He wears thick glasses.

Mr Gandhi pushes our papers under his nose through a break in the crowd and keeps his hand on them, even though he is standing behind three people. He mutters a few words of apology to them for this pushy behaviour, implying that this is continuing business and not something on the order of what they are waiting for. As the officer ceases writing, Mr Gandhi points with his forefinger at a corner of the paper. I am beginning to see how experienced he is at getting signatures.

'It is just approval of TBRE,' he says, but the official leafs through the pages sadly as though much work lies ahead for him. He looks at his watch and dismisses the others, telling them to come back after lunch. All go except a young woman in red who says, 'It is just a simple signature I am waiting for, and I have priority.'

We have priority too. The official looks back and forth at us and the woman in red and tells us all to come back after lunch. As we go out Mr Gandhi explains to me, 'Because she had a priority too he could not give us a priority.'

Anyway, we have only a half hour to wait. I wonder how the official eats his lunch. He must lock his door and sit at his desk.

Mr Gandhi suggests we get something to drink and we walk over to a building that looks like a concrete bunker but turns out to be the canteen. Inside is a jostling sea of men, spilled food, and battered steel tables which tilt perilously if anything is put on them. Mr Gandhi wades in and gets cold drinks and two buns with vegetable pakoras in them. The fat man from the Italian embassy has arrived and trades jokes with Mr Gandhi as we sit around one of the tables. I ask about the lady.

'I sent her home,' the fat man laughs.

'Has she not travelled much before?' I ask.

'Oh no, she knows everything. She has been everywhere. She has been here three years. She was just grumbling.' I had thought they would be annoyed with her, but they seem to have taken her histrionics in their stride, as something normal.

'I have seen all kinds of people,' says the fat man. 'I have been at the Italian embassy twenty-two years.'

While the others sit talking I wander outside, hoping it will be cooler. I sit on the concrete steps but they radiate heat around me like a stove top. I get up and walk over to a patch of dusty earth and grass, thinking how this soil, now surrounded by airport buildings, is part of the great Gangetic plain. Until a few years ago it was probably part of a peasant holding, farmed over centuries. But the earth seems as hot to stand on as the concrete, so I walk to the shade of one of the cargo buildings and sit on a metal railing. It is cooler here and there is even a little breeze.

When I get back to the canteen it has cleared out a little. Mr Gandhi and the man from the Italian embassy have been joined by two others. We have another cold drink. Mr Gandhi looks at his watch and we make our way back to the cargo terminal. The office door is ajar and we find the office already full of people. Overhead a big fan makes the room seem cooler than the sticky air we have just left. The epauletted official is writing a long document, and it is ours. He also seems to be copying out portions of the Ministry of External Affairs letter. When he finishes it he signs firmly and hands the stack of papers to Mr Gandhi. As we go outside Mr Gandhi says wonderingly, 'He was working on it during his lunch.'

But now he looks at his watch with a troubled air.

'We have to finish and take the money to the bank by three. The bank closes at three.' It is already after two. We go upstairs again for a wait outside the big brown door with the uniformed guard attending it.

I ask about this money that has to go to the bank. What is it for? I have visions of having to post a bond or pay duty.

'It is for the airport handling charges,' says Mr Gandhi, and I realise that the 'bank' is only the cashier. 'It will be something like eighty rupees only.'

It appears that this highest of officials may be out to lunch. But then the guard makes talking-over-the-phone gestures. Mr Gandhi is trying to get our papers in order. One of them is torn at the corner and he is worried that the whole lot may be rejected because of this. He neatens the tear with his thumbnail and slips a white card behind it, where it is held tight by the paper clip.

The papers finally go inside and come out with a signature. We hasten downstairs, where we must get another signature from the official with the epaulettes. Once again I am amazed at how Mr Gandhi insinuates himself into the situation and gets the papers on the desk. The official is still as upright and uncreased as a naval officer in his white uniform. We go back to the customs inspector, whom I thought we would never have to see again. Apparently the final, the real TBRE has not been issued.

The inspector scrutinises the papers, then pauses to complete some other business. He is going through the luggage of a middle-aged Sikh man, who seems to have an unending supply of bedspreads. Last in the pile is a thin mattress covered with material in a floral pattern. The inspector gestures and a porter begins ripping the material at a seam. Inside is another floral pattern, and this is ripped and taken off too, revealing another cover. I begin to wonder if the entire mattress is in reality a series of covers, a crafty way of smuggling in cloth. But who would smuggle cloth *into* India?

Now the inspector reads our papers again and with a little smile says that the TBRE can only be issued with an 'undertaking' from the leader of the party to export the equipment within three months. His finger points to the word 'undertaking' on the Ministry letter and the hand-written document that came from the official behind the brown door. Despite the inspector's steel-grey hair and kindly expression I find I am beginning to dislike this man. Will he always be able to find a problem in our papers? I am beginning to suspect he takes a professional delight in sniffing them out.

I can tell Mr Gandhi is worried by the time passing, but he keeps himself in check. He pulls out the TBRE that was issued to us when we brought in the film stock with our personal baggage. But the inspector slowly shakes his head. I offer to write a new undertaking on the form, but this too seems unacceptable. Mr Gandhi snatches up the papers and we head back to the office at the corner. Mr Gandhi thrusts them between waiting bodies onto the desk and explains rapidly to the official, who tells him something and writes a squiggle on the form. We take it back to the inspector. He appears to disagree with what Mr Gandhi tells him.

'An undertaking is an undertaking,' says Mr Gandhi. But he asks if I have a sheet of paper. I have only a small one, so he rummages in his case and brings out a full-sized one. I write a letter to the Deputy Collector of Customs, undertaking to re-export the equipment within three months. The inspector signs it and the senior official from the corner office, passing by, initials it. He has a brief argument with the inspector, who appears to give in. But I guess he has further objections in store for us.

Finally, however, he begins to make out the TBRE form and copy its number on each page of the equipment list. He signs each page too. Mr Gandhi grabs the fat book of forms and carries it away to the corner office for signing. He brings it back and the form is signed again by the inspector and me. Then a page in my passport is annotated, with reference to the TBRE. Mr Gandhi looks hopelessly at his watch. It is after three.

He leaves me seated near the customs counter and goes off determinedly with a counter-plan. The Germans have come back with their agent, who is trying to get them to place separate values on their foodstuffs and climbing gear. They look perplexed.

Mr Gandhi returns triumphantly. He has managed to pay the fees directly, so now all we have to do is get a gate pass. The equipment will be taken to the delivery area. Already I have seen it being carried off on dollies. We walk out of the building and back to one of the outside grilled windows where we waited earlier in the day. It seems we need more than a gate pass. Our papers must be approved for delivery of the goods. Mr Gandhi coaches me about the gate pass and makes me wait by one window while he waits at another. Our papers are signed and passed along the desk to another window, where they are signed again. Then I am asked to sign a ledger, which I do, reaching through the grille, the book turned half-way around.

Mr Gandhi coaches me on the next step:

'You must ask for a gate pass straightaway. You must say you must have the equipment today.'

He calls through the window, which is covered with glass except for a slit at the bottom. I hear the world 'diplomat' and Mr Gandhi pushes me forward, displaying me like a ventriloquist's dummy. Then I have to speak my part. I lean down to the open slit and say, 'Can you please give me a gate pass? We must have the equipment today.' The man fills out a form in duplicate, twitching a toothbrush moustache as he writes. We are given our copy.

The pressure now seems off Mr Gandhi as we walk along the side of the building towards the delivery zone.

'It is very good,' he says. 'We cleared it in one day.' I look at my watch. It's after three-thirty.

There is a big commotion at the delivery dock. Porters rush in and out of the wide doorway, guarded by two men in khaki uniform. They inspect every item that comes out and check it against the papers that came with it. Mr Gandhi drops his briefcase among a pile of thirty or more others just outside the door. I stand by, keeping a watch on it, as he goes inside. But no one seems worried about anyone stealing anything. In the dim light inside I can see Mr Gandhi presenting his papers at a counter. Then he comes out and gestures to an old porter who appears to know him. He gives him a white docket and sends him inside.

'Now we wait a little,' he tells me. 'Shall we get another cold drink?' We stroll over to the canteen.

Over the drinks Mr Gandhi tells me about his family.

'I am awake since five o'clock this morning. My little girl is ten months old. She wants to play with me. I have two hours in the morning with her, two hours in the evening, each day.'

I ask how many children he has.

'Just this one. I also have no parents living, and my wife has no parents living.'

'But you have aunts and uncles?'

'Of course.'

I tell him it's good the child will have some older relatives, and he agrees.

'I am the last of fourteen children,' he goes on. 'My oldest brother has a child my age. We had a full team. Fourteen children. But only five are living. Nine have passed away.'

He tells me he was born in Haryana but came to Delhi after his schooling.

'And it was very tough. But now I own my house, I am the manager of the business with twenty-six people under me, I make a good salary, so I am satisfied with my life. If I make four thousand rupees a month, I save one or two thousand. I have no encumbrances. I have no younger brothers or sisters because I am the last one.'

He acts like a satisfied man, I think, and he is good at what he does. I ask him about the work.

'It is all in knowing the procedures. There are so many channels. Someone from outside cannot know them. The other day I had an Englishman. I said, "You sit here. Read or write or do what you want. When I need you I will call you."'

But I think Mr Gandhi has enjoyed my participation today. I have tagged after him like a spaniel, but I haven't got in his way. And most of the time I have been ready with a signature or a banknote at the right moment. When Mr Gandhi speaks of 'many channels' I feel I have the beginning of an idea of what he means. Each channel is separate from the others, like railway lines spreading out into the countryside. The officials of each must be satisfied. But somewhere the lines are interconnected; you can't move from one to the next unless someone throws the switch.

The old porter is at our elbow. The shipment is waiting to be delivered. We go back to the delivery shed, where a forklift truck is edging a huge packing case through the doorway with only inches to spare. Behind it I can see our equipment cases on two baggage carts.

'Go in and sign,' says Mr Gandhi.

I enter and go over to the guard. The porter gives me a white paper.

'The green paper, the green paper!' says the guard. I go out to Mr Gandhi, who gives me the green copy, which in fact is powder blue. When I have signed this and signed a ledger at the desk the cargo is waved through.

Mr Gandhi has organised a lorry from a number that are parked nearby, waiting for business. There is a driver and four young men. They make short work of loading the cases on the truck. I climb in front with Mr Gandhi and the driver. At the barrier we present the white gate pass. Looking through the rear window, Mr Gandhi shouts at one of the men who is sitting on a cardboard box.

'It would be a pity to sustain damage after coming all this way from Australia', he says. 'We must be careful.'

When the equipment has been delivered and safely stored at the house where we have taken it, Mr Gandhi and I take an auto rickshaw into town. On the way he pushes a receipt book across to me with a slip of carbon paper flapping in it. I sign his company receipt for the goods, and he asks me to sign the duplicate too.

'I think you are good at getting people to sign things,' I say. He laughs, but as soon as I've said it I'm not sure the joke is in good taste. There is a space for 'Comments' on the receipt, which he points to. I write, 'Thanks for your expert and professional assistance.' He turns the page so that I can write it on the duplicate. He glances at what I have written and acknowledges it with the slightest of nods. After all, it is only his due.

Note

This chapter was first published in *Visual Anthropology* 30:1 (2017): 78–87, copyright Taylor & Francis, http://www.tandfonline.com, DOI: 10.1080/08949468.2017.1255515.

Filmography

Titles are listed alphabetically in the form by which they are generally best known in English-speaking countries, with the original title or translation in parentheses.

51 Birch Street. 2005. Doug Block. Copacetic Pictures/HBO-Cinemax Documentary/ZDF Enterprises. USA/Germany. 90 mins.

The 400 Blows [*Les quatre cents coups*]. 1959. François Truffaut. Les Films du Carrosse/SEDIF. France. 94 mins.

The Act of Killing. 2012. Joshua Oppenheimer. Final Cut for Real/Piraya Film A/S/Novaya Zemlya. UK/Denmark/Norway. 117 mins.

The Age of Reason. 2004. David MacDougall. Centre for Cross-Cultural Research, Australian National University/Fieldwork Films. Australia. 87 mins.

Akazama. 1985. Marc Henri Piault. Centre National de la Recherche Scientifique (CNRS) AV. France. 52 mins.

All My Babies. 1953. George C. Stoney. Georgia Department of Public Health. USA. 55 mins.

An American Family series. 1973. Craig Gilbert. WNET New York/PBS. USA. 12 episodes of 60 mins.

The Angelmakers. 2005. Astrid Bussink. University of Edinburgh. UK/The Netherlands. 33 mins.

À propos de Nice. 1930. Jean Vigo. France. 29 mins.

An Argument about a Marriage. 1969. John Marshall. Film Study Center, Harvard University. USA. 18 mins.

Arnav at Six. 2012. David MacDougall and Arnav Koshy. Fieldwork Films. Australia. 28 mins.

Attica. 1974. Cinda Firestone. Attica Films, Inc. USA. 80 mins.

The Auction House: A Tale of Two Brothers. 2014. Edward Owles. Native Voice Films. UK. 85 mins.

Awareness. 2010. David MacDougall and Judith MacDougall. Fieldwork Films/Rishi Valley Education Centre/Research School of Humanities and the Arts, Australian National University. Australia/India. 67 mins.

Basic Training. 1971. Frederick Wiseman. Basic Training Company. USA. 80 mins.

Bataille sur le grand fleuve. 1952. Jean Rouch. CNRS/IFAN/CFE. France. 35 mins.

Beppie. 1965. Johan van der Keuken. Independent production. The Netherlands. 36 mins.

Berlin: The Symphony of a Great City [*Berlin: Die Sinfonie der Großstadt*]. 1927. Walter Ruttmann. Deutsche Vereins-Film. Germany. 65 mins.

Between the Tides. 1958. Ralph Keene. Shell Film Unit. UK. 21 mins.

Bicycle Thieves [*Ladri di biciclette*]. 1948. Vittorio De Sica. Produzioni De Sica. Italy. 89 mins.

The Birds. 1963. Alfred Hitchcock. Alfred J. Hitchcock Productions. USA. 119 mins.

Bowling for Columbine. 2002. Michael Moore. Salter Street Films International/Vif Babelsberger FilmprodUK.tion/Dog Eat Dog Films. USA/Germany. 120 mins.

Bread Day. 1998. Sergei Dvortsevoy. Jane Balfour Films. UK/Russia. 55 mins.

Breathless [*À Bout de souffle*].1960. Jean-Luc Godard. Les Films Impéria/Les Productions Georges Beauregard/Société Nouvelle de Cinématographie (SNC). France. 90 mins.

Bright Leaves. 2003. Ross McElwee. Channel 4 Television/Homemade Movies/WGBH Boston. UK/USA. 107 mins.

Burden of Dreams. 1982. Les Blanc. Flower Films/SDR Fernsehen. USA/Germany. 95 mins.
Canal Zone. 1977. Frederick Wiseman. Basic Training Film/Zipporah Films. USA. 174 mins.
Celso and Cora. 1983. Gary Kildea. Independent production. Australia. 109 mins.
The Chair. 1963. Robert Drew. Drew Associates/Time-Life Broadcast. USA. 59 mins.
Children Who Draw [E o Kaku Kodomotachi]. 1956. Susumu Hani. Iwanami Productions. Japan. 38 mins.
The Child's Eye. 2018. David MacDougall and child filmmakers in India. Fieldwork Films/Ronin Films. 12 films from 8 to 19 mins. Australia. 107 mins.
Chronique d'un été [*Chronicle of a Summer*]. 1961. Jean Rouch and Edgar Morin. Argos Films. France. 90 mins.
The City. 1939. Ralph Steiner and Willard Van Dyke. American Documentary Films, Inc. USA. 43 mins.
The City Beautiful [*Sunder Nagri*]. 2003. Rahul Roy. Independently produced. India. 78 mins.
The Civil War series. 1990. Ken Burns. Florentine Films/WETA Television. USA. 9 episodes of 62–99 mins.
Coal Face. 1935. Alberto Cavalcanti. GPO Film Unit. UK. 12 mins.
Cocorico! Monsieur Poulet. 1974. Jean Rouch, Damouré Zika and Lam Ibrahima Dia. CNRS/Les Films de l'Homme/CFE. France. 90 mins.
Collum Calling Canberra. 1984. David MacDougall and Judith MacDougall. Australian Institute of Aboriginal Studies. Australia. 58 mins.
Contes et comptes de la cour [*Tales and Tallies of the Courtyard*]. 1993. Éliane de Latour. La Sept/CNRS Audiovisuel/Aaton/ORTN. France. 98 mins.
Crisis: Behind a Presidential Commitment. 1963. Robert Drew. ABC News/Drew Associates. USA. 52 mins.
The Days Before Christmas. 1958. Terence Macartney-Filgate, Wolf Koenig and Stanley Jackson. National Film Board of Canada. Canada. 88 mins.
Dead Birds. 1963. Robert Gardner. Film Study Center, Harvard University. USA. 84 mins.
De Grands événements et des gens ordinaires [*Of Great Events and Ordinary People*]. 1979. Raoul Ruiz. L'Institut National de l'Audiovisuel. France. 65 mins.
Demolition [*Chaiqian*]. 2008. J. P. Sniadecki. Film Study Center, Harvard University. USA. 62 mins.
Dial M for Murder. 1954. Alfred Hitchcock. Warner Bros. USA. 104 mins.
Diaries 1971–1976. 1982. Ed Pincus. Independently produced. USA. 200 mins.
Diary of a Maasai Village series. 1984. Melissa Llewelyn-Davies. BBC Television. UK. 5 episodes of 50 mins.
Disappearing World series. 1970–93. Granada Television. UK. 490 films of 52 mins.
Diya. 2001. Judith MacDougall. Centre for Cross-Cultural Research/Australian National University/Fieldwork Films. Australia. 55 mins.
Don't Look Back. 1967. D. A. Pennebaker. Leacock-Pennebaker Inc. USA. 96 mins.
Doon School Chronicles. 2000. David MacDougall. Centre for Cross-Cultural Research, Australian National University/Fieldwork Films. Australia. 108 mins.
Le Doulos [*The Finger Man*]. 1962. Jean-Pierre Melville. Compagnia Cinematografica Champion/Rome Paris Films. France/Italy. 109 mins.
Eaux profondes [*Deep Water*]. 1981. Michel Deville. Hamster Productions/Gaumont/France 3/Elefilm. France. 94 mins.
Emak-Bakia. 1926. Man Ray. Independently produced. France. 18 mins.
Essene. 1972. Frederick Wiseman. Zipporah Films. USA. 86 mins.
Être et avoir [*To Be and to Have*]. 2002. Nicolas Philibert. Canal+/Centre National de Documentation Pédogogique/Grimages 4/Les Films d'Ici/Maïa Films/Arte France Cinéma. France. 102 mins.
The Family series. 1974. Franc Roddam. BBC Television. UK. 12 episodes of 30 mins.
Farrebique, ou les quatre saisons. 1946. Georges Rouquier. Les Films Etienne Lallier/Écran Français. France. 90 mins.
Fenlands. 1945. Ken Annakin. Greenpark Productions/Ministry of Information. UK. 17 mins.
Fine Cut series. 1992–93. Series 1. BBC Two. UK. 10 films of 90 mins.

Fitzcarraldo. 1982. Werner Herzog. Werner Herzog FilmprodUK.tion/Pro Ject FilmprodUK.tion. West Germany. 158 mins.

The Fog of War: Eleven Lessons from the Life of Robert S. McNamara. 2003. Errol Morris. Sony Pictures Classics/RadicalMedia/SenArt Films. USA. 107 mins.

Forest of Bliss. 1985. Robert Gardner. Film Study Center, Harvard University. USA. 90 mins.

Gandhi's Children. 2008. David MacDougall. Fieldwork Films/Centre for Cross-Cultural Research, Australian National University. Australia. 180 mins.

The Gleaners and I [*Les Glaneurs et la glaneuse*]. 2000. Agnès Varda. Ciné Tamaris. France. 88 mins.

The Glorious Sixth of June. 1934. Alberto Cavalcanti. GPO Film Unit. UK. 10 mins.

Grass: A Nation's Battle for Life. 1925. Merian C. Cooper and Ernest B. Schoedsack. Famous Players-Lasky Corporation/Paramount Pictures. USA. 71 mins.

The Hadza. 1966. James Woodburn. Hogarth Film. UK. 40 mins.

Haida Carver. 1964. Richard Gilbert. National Film Board of Canada. Canada. 12 mins.

The Honey Ant Ceremonies of Ljaba. 1956. T. G. H. Strehlow. Australian Commonwealth Film Unit. Australia. 32 mins.

Hospital. 1970. Frederick Wiseman. Osti Films. USA. 84 mins.

The House-Opening. 1980. Judith MacDougall. Australian Institute of Aboriginal Studies. Australia. 45 mins.

Housing Problems. 1935. Arthur Elton and Edgar Anstey. British Commercial Gas Association. UK. 15 mins.

The Hunters. 1958. John K. Marshall. Film Study Center, Harvard University. USA. 72 mins.

Ika Hands. 1988. Robert Gardner. Film Study Center, Harvard University. USA. 58 mins.

Imaginero – The Image Man. 1970. Jorge Prelorán. Tucuman National University/Film Study Center, Harvard University. Argentina/USA. 52 mins.

Imbalu: Ritual of Manhood of the Bagisu of Uganda. 1988. Richard Hawkins and Suzette Heald. University of California at Los Angeles. USA. 69 mins.

Indians and Chiefs. 1967. Judith MacDougall. University of California at Los Angeles. USA. 40 mins.

Innocence Unprotected [*Nevinost bez zaštite*]. 1968. Dušan Makavejev. Avala Film. Yugoslavia. 78 mins.

The Iron Ministry. 2014. J. P. Sniadecki. Cinder Films. USA. 82 mins.

I Shot My Love. 2009. Tomer Heymann. Heymann Brothers Films/Lichtblick Film/Westdeutscher Rundfunk (WDR)/Arte. Israel. 56 mins.

J. Lee Thompson: Director. 1967. David MacDougall. Columbia Pictures. USA. 15 mins.

Jaguar. 1968. Jean Rouch. Les Films de la Pléade. France. 110 mins.

Jane. 1962. D. A. Pennebaker. Drew Associates. USA. 53 mins.

Joe Leahy's Neighbours. 1988. Bob Connolly and Robin Anderson. Arundel Productions. Australia. 93 mins.

Le joli mai. 1963. Chris Marker and Pierre Lhomme. Sofracima. France. 165 mins.

Juvenile Court. 1973. Frederick Wiseman. Zipporah Films. USA. 144 mins.

Karam in Jaipur. 2001. David MacDougall. Fieldwork Films/Centre for Cross-Cultural Research, Australian National University/Fieldwork Films. Australia. 56 mins.

Kenya Boran. 1974. James Blue and David MacDougall. American Universities Field Staff. USA. 66 mins.

The Kids Grow Up. 2009. Doug Block. Copacetic Pictures/Hard Working Movies/ZDF-Arte. USA. 90 mins.

Kino-Nedelya [*Cinema Week*] [Кино-Неделя]. 1918–19. Dziga Vertov, Elizaveta Svilova, Mikhail Kaufman and others. USSR. 43 newsreels of varying lengths.

Kino-Pravda [*Cine-Truth*] [Кино-Правда]. 1922–25. Dziga Vertov, Elizaveta Svilova, Mikhail Kaufman and others. USSR. 23 newsreels of varying lengths.

Km 400. 1966. David MacDougall. University of California at Los Angeles. USA. 12 mins.

Koriam's Law: And the Dead Who Govern. 2005. Gary Kildea and Andrea Simon. Gary Kildea Films. Australia. 110 mins.

The Land Dayaks of Borneo. 1966. William Geddes. University of Sydney. Australia. 38 mins.

Land without Bread [*Las Hurdes*]. 1933. Luis Buñuel. Ramón Acin. Spain. 30 minutes.
The Last of the Cuiva. 1971. Brian Moser. Granada Television. UK. 52 mins.
Law and Order. 1969. Frederick Wiseman. Osti Films. USA. 81 mins.
The Leader, His Driver and the Driver's Wife. 1991. Nick Broomfield. Lafayette Films. UK. 85 mins.
Leviathan. 2012. Lucien Castaing-Taylor and Veréna Paravel. Arrète Ton Cinéma/Harvard Sensory Ethnography Lab. USA. 87 mins.
Link-Up Diary. 1987. David MacDougall. Australian Institute of Aboriginal Studies. Australia. 86 mins.
Un Lion nommé l'Américain. 1968. Jean Rouch. Les Films de la Pléiade/CFA. France. 20 mins.
Listen to Britain. 1942. Humphrey Jennings and Stewart McAllister. Crown Film Unit. UK. 21 mins.
Lonely Boy. 1962. Roman Kroiter and Wolf Koenig. National Film Board of Canada. Canada. 27 mins.
Lorang's Way. 1979. David MacDougall and Judith MacDougall. Fieldwork Films. Australia. 70 mins.
Louisiana Story. 1948. Robert J. Flaherty. Robert Flaherty Productions Inc. USA. 77 mins.
The Lumière Brothers: First Films. 1996. Thierry Fremaux, ed. Commentary by Bertrand Tavernier. Institut Lumière/ Association Frère Lumière. France. 103 mins.
Madame l'eau. 1992. Jean Rouch. BBC/Comité du Film Éthnographique/NFI-Productions/ Nederland Film/Nederlands Film Instituut. France/The Netherlands. 120 mins.
Man of Aran. 1934. Robert J. Flaherty. Gaumont-British Picture Corporation Ltd. UK. 77 mins.
Man with a Movie Camera [*Chelovek s kino-apparatom*] [Человек с кино-аппаратом]. 1929. Dziga Vertov. VUFKU. USSR. 68 mins.
Maragoli. 1976. Sandra Nichols. Document Film Service. UK. 58 mins.
The March of Time. 1935–51. Multiple directors. Time Inc. USA. c. 209 episodes of 20–30 mins.
Masai Women. 1974. Chris Curling. Granada Television. UK. 52 mins.
Mayank's Family. 2014. Mayank Ved. Fieldwork Films/Australian National University. Australia. 19 mins.
Meat. 1976. Frederick Wiseman. Zipporah Films/Corporation for Public Broadcasting. USA. 112 mins.
Miao Year. 1968. William Robert Geddes. University of Sydney. Australia. 62 mins.
Moana: A Romance of the Golden Age. 1926. Robert J. Flaherty. Paramount Pictures. USA. 64 mins.
Moi, un Noir. 1960. Jean Rouch. Les Films de la Pléiade. France. 70 mins.
Mokil. 1950. Conrad Bentzen. University of Southern California. USA. 61 mins.
La Montée au ciel [*Ascent to the Sky*]. 2009. Stéphane Breton. Les Films d'Ici/Arte. France. 52 mins.
The Mosquito Problem and Other Stories. 2007. Andrey Paounov. Agitprop/Filmtank Hamburg/ITVS. Bulgaria/Germany. 100 mins.
The Mursi. 1974. Leslie Woodhead. Granada Television. UK. 55 mins.
My Eyes as a Stranger. 1984. Toni de Bromhead. ARTE. France. 53 mins.
My Funny Film. 2012. Aniket Kumar Kashyap. Fieldwork Films/Australian National University. Australia. 16 mins.
My Lovely General Store. 2012. Ravi Shivhare. Fieldwork Films/Australian National University. Australia. 15 mins.
My Survival as an Aboriginal. 1979. Essie Coffey. Goodgaban Productions. Australia. 49 mins.
N!ai, The Story of a !Kung Woman. 1980. John K. Marshall and Adrienne Miesmer. Documentary Educational Resources/Public Broadcasting Associates. USA. 58 mins.
Naim and Jabar. 1974. David Hancock and Herb di Gioia. American Universities Field Staff. USA. 50 mins.
Nanook of the North. 1922. Robert J. Flaherty. Revillon Frères. USA. 70 mins.
Nawi. 1970. David MacDougall. University of California at Los Angeles. USA. 22 mins.

Netsilik Eskimos series. 1963–68. Asen Balikci and Guy Mary-Rousselière. Educational Development Center/National Film Board of Canada. USA/Canada. 9 films in 21 parts of 26–36 mins.

The New Boys. 2003. David MacDougall. Centre for Cross-Cultural Research, Australian National University/Fieldwork Films. Australia. 100 mins.

Night and Fog [*Nuit et brouillard*]. 1956. Alain Resnais. Argos Films. France. 32 mins.

Night Mail. 1936. Harry Watt and Basil Wright. GPO Film Unit. UK. 25 mins.

Los niños abandonados [*The Abandoned Children*]. 1975. Danny Lyon. Bleak Beauty. USA. 63 mins.

North Sea. 1938. Harry Watt. GPO Film Unit. UK. 24 mins.

On the Poll: Eddie Sachs. 1961. D. A. Pennebaker and Richard Leacock. Drew Associates. USA. 61 mins.

Ongka's Big Moka. 1974. Charlie Nairn. Granada Television. UK. 55 mins.

Onórino il fabbro! 1993. Lorenzo Brutti. Museo degli Usi e Costumi della Gente Trentina (MUCGT)/Institut Méditerranaen de Recherche et de Création (IMEREC). Italy/France. 28 mins.

Pacific 231. 1949. Jean Mitry. Tadié Cinéma. France. 10 mins.

Paul Tomkowicz: Street-Railway Switchman. 1954. Roman Kroiter. National Film Board of Canada. Canada. 9 mins.

People of the Australian Western Desert series. 1966–70. Ian Dunlop. Australian Commonwealth Film Unit/Australian Institute of Aboriginal Studies. Australia. 16 episodes of 5–53 mins, totalling 314 mins.

People on Sunday [*Menschen am Sonntag*]. 1930. Robert Siodmak and Edgar G. Ulmer. Filmstudio 1929. Germany. 74 mins.

People's Park. 2012. Libby Dina Cohn and J. P. Sniadecki. Sensory Ethnography Lab, Harvard University. USA. 78 mins.

Petit à Petit [*Little by Little*]. 1971. Jean Rouch. Les Films de la Pléiade. France. 96 mins.

Pett and Pott. 1934. Alberto Cavalcanti. GPO Film Unit. UK. 31 mins.

Photo Wallahs. 1991. David MacDougall and Judith MacDougall. Fieldwork Films. Australia. 59 mins.

Police series. 1982. Roger Graef and Charles Stewart. BBC Television. UK. 11 programmes of 50 mins.

Portrait of Jason. 1967. Shirley Clarke. Shirley Clarke Productions/Graeme Ferguson Productions. USA. 105 mins.

Power and the Land. 1940. Joris Ivens. Rural Electrification Administration/Department of Agriculture/United States Film Service. USA. 38 mins.

Primary. 1960. Robert Drew, Richard Leacock, D. A. Pennebaker, Terence Macartney-Filgate and Albert Maysles. Time-Life Broadcast/Drew Associates. USA. 54 mins.

Primate. 1974. Frederick Wiseman. Zipporah Films. USA. 105 mins.

Psycho. 1960. Alfred Hitchcock. Shamley Productions. USA. 109 mins.

La Pyramide humaine [*The Human Pyramid*]. 1961. Jean Rouch. Les Films de la Pléiade. France. 90 mins.

Les Raquetteurs. 1958. Michel Brault and Gilles Groulx. National Film Board of Canada. Canada. 15 mins.

Rats in the Ranks. 1996. Bob Connolly and Robin Anderson. Arundel Productions/Film Australia. Australia. 93 mins.

Rear Window. 1954. Alfred Hitchcock. Patron Inc. USA. 112 mins.

Los Refrigeradores. 2012. Thomas Lehner. Independently produced. Austria. 95 mins.

The River. 1938. Pare Lorentz. US Farm Security Administration. USA. 31 mins.

The Road to Button Bay. 1962. Hope Ryden and James Lipscomb. Drew Associates. USA. 55 mins.

Roger & Me. 1989. Michael Moore. Dog Eat Dog Films. USA. 91 mins.

Rome, Open City [*Roma città aperta*]. 1945. Roberto Rossellini. Excelsa Film. Italy. 103 mins.

Royal Family. 1969. Richard Cawston. BBC1/BBC2/ITV. UK. 90 mins.

Salesman. 1969. Albert Maysles, David Maysles and Charlotte Zwerin. Maysles Films. USA. 85 mins.
Le Sang des bêtes [*Blood of the Beasts*]. 1949. Georges Franju. Forces et Voix de la France. France. 22 mins.
SchoolScapes. 2007. David MacDougall. Fieldwork Films/Centre for Cross-Cultural Research, Australian National University. Australia. 77 mins.
Seven Up series. 1964–. Paul Almond and Michael Apted. Granada Television for ITV and BBC One. UK. 40 to 150 minutes each.
Sherman's March. A Meditation on the Possibility of Romantic Love in the South During an Era of Nuclear Weapons Proliferation. 1985. Ross McElwee. Independent production. USA. 157 mins.
Shoeshine [*Sciuscià*]. 1946. Vittorio De Sica. Alfa/ENIC. Italy. 93 mins.
Sicko. Michael Moore. 2007. Dog Eat Dog Films. USA. 123 mins.
Sifinja: The Iron Bride. 2009. Valerie Hansch. Independent production. Germany. 70 mins.
Sisters in Law. 2005. Florence Ayisi and Kim Longinotto. Vixen Films/Film Four. UK. 104 mins.
The Song of Ceylon. 1934. Basil Wright. Ceylon Tea Propaganda Board/GPO Film Unit. UK. 40 mins.
The Space between Words series. 1972. Roger Graef. BBC 2/KCET-TV. UK/USA. 5 films of 59 mins.
Spend It All. 1971. Les Blank. Flower Films. USA. 41 mins.
Stravinsky. 1966. Roman Kroiter and Wolf Koenig. Canadian Broadcasting Corporation/ National Film Board of Canada. Canada. 50 mins.
Sulfur [*Soufre*]. 2005. Florian Geyer. Arte. France. 52 mins.
Sunny and the Dark Horse. 1986. David MacDougall and Judith MacDougall. Australian Institute of Aboriginal Studies. Australia. 85 mins.
Sweetgrass. 2009. Ilisa Barbash and Lucien Castaing-Taylor. Sensory Ethnography Lab, Harvard University. USA. 102 mins.
Takeover. 1980. David MacDougall and Judith MacDougall. Australian Institute of Aboriginal Studies. Australia. 87 mins.
Tempus de Baristas [*Time of the Barmen*]. 1993. David MacDougall. Fieldwork Films/BBC Television/Istituto Superiore Etnografico della Sardegna. Australia/UK/Italy. 100 mins.
Theremin: An Electronic Odyssey. 1993. Steven. M. Martin. Kaga Bay/Channel Four Films. USA. 83 mins.
The Things I Cannot Change. 1967. Tanya Ballentyne. National Film Board of Canada. Canada. 55 mins.
Three Domestics. 1971. John K. Marshall. Documentary Educational Resources. USA. 32 mins.
Three Horsemen. 1982. David MacDougall and Judith MacDougall. Australian Institute of Aboriginal Studies. Australia. 54 mins.
Till We Meet Again. 2013. Rahul Roy. Aakar. India. 78 mins.
Titicut Follies. 1967. Frederick Wiseman. Bridgewater Film Co. USA. 84 mins.
To Live with Herds. 1972. David MacDougall. University of California at Los Angeles. USA. 70 mins.
Touchez pas au grisbi. 1954. Jacques Becker. Les Films Corona/Del Duca Films. France/ Italy. 94 mins.
Tourou et Bitti, les tambours d'avant. 1971. Jean Rouch. CNRS. France. 12 mins.
Triumph of the Will [*Triumph des Willens*]. 1935. Leni Riefenstahl. Reichsparteitagsfilm/L. R. Studio-Film. Germany. 120 mins.
Turkana Conversations trilogy. David MacDougall and Judith MacDougall. 1977–81. Fieldwork Films. USA/Australia: *The Wedding Camels* (1977). 108 mins. *Lorang's Way* (1979). 70 mins. *A Wife among Wives* (1981). 75 mins.
Two Laws. 1981. Carolyn Strachan and Alessandro Cavadini. Independent production. Australia.140 mins.
Umberto D. 1952. Vittorio De Sica. Rizzoli Film/Produzione Films Vittorio de Sica/Amato Film. Italy. 89 mins.

Under the Men's Tree. 1973. David MacDougall. University of California at Los Angeles. USA. 15 mins.

Under the Palace Wall. 2014. David MacDougall. Fieldwork Films. Australia. 53 mins.

Vermont People series. 1971–75. David Hancock and Herb Di Gioia. University of California at Los Angeles/Vermont Center for Cultural Studies. USA: *Duwayne Masure* (1971). 40 mins. *Chester Grimes* (1972). 50 mins. *Peter Murray* (1975). 50 mins. *Peter and Jane Flint* (1975). 120 mins.

Victory at Sea. 1952–53. M. Clay Adams. NBC Television/US Navy. USA. 26 episodes of 30 mins.

La Vie est immense et pleine de dangers [*Life Is Boundless and Full of Dangers*]. 1995. Denis Gheerbrandt. Les Films d'Ici/La Sept/Arte, l'INA. France. 80 mins.

Le Voyage dans la lune [*A Trip to the Moon*]. 1902. Georges Méliès. Star-Film. France. 14 mins.

Waiting for Fidel. 1974. Michael Rubbo. National Film Board of Canada. Canada. 50 mins.

Waiting for Harry. 1980. Kim McKenzie. Australian Institute of Aboriginal Studies. Australia. 58 mins.

Warrendale. 1967. Allan King. Allan King Associates/Canadian Broadcasting Corporation. Canada. 100 mins.

The Wedding Camels. 1977. David MacDougall and Judith MacDougall. Rice University Media Center/Fieldwork Films. USA/Australia. 108 mins.

Welfare. 1975. Frederick Wiseman. Zipporah Films. USA. 167 mins.

Who Killed Fourth Ward? 1977. James Blue, Brian Huberman and Ed Hugetz. Rice University Media Center. USA. 3 parts of 55 – 61 mins.

Whose Is This Song? [*Chia e tazi pesen?*]. 2003. Adela Peeva. Adela Media Film and TV Productions. Bulgaria. 70 mins.

Why Not a Girl? 2012. Anshu Singh. Fieldwork Films/Australian National University. Australia. 16 mins.

A Wife among Wives. 1981. David MacDougall and Judith MacDougall. Fieldwork Films. Australia. 75 mins.

With Morning Hearts. 2001. David MacDougall. Centre for Cross-Cultural Research, Australian National University/Fieldwork Films. Australia. 110 mins.

The Women's Olamal: The Organisation of a Maasai Fertility Ceremony. 1984. Melissa Llewelyn-Davies. BBC Television. UK. 114 mins.

The World at War series. 1973–75. Jeremy Isaacs. Thames Television. UK. 26 episodes of 50 mins.

The Yellow Bank. 2010. J. P. Sniadecki. Film Study Center, Harvard University. USA. 27 mins.

Zerda's Children. 1978. Jorge Prelorán. Ethnographic Film Program, University of California at Los Angeles. USA. 52 mins.

Bibliography

Agee, James, and Walker Evans. 1960. *Now Let Us Praise Famous Men*. 2nd edn. Boston, MA: Houghton Mifflin.

Appadurai, Arjun (ed.). 1988. *The Social Life of Things: Commodities in Cultural Perspective*. Cambridge: Cambridge University Press.

Bach, Steven. 2008. *Leni: The Life and Work of Leni Riefenstahl*. New York: Vintage Books.

Barthes, Roland. 1977. *Image–Music–Text*. Stephen Heath (trans.). Glasgow: Fontana/Collins.

Bateson, Gregory, and Margaret Mead. 1977. 'For God's Sake, Margaret': Margaret Mead and Gregory Bateson on the Use of the Camera in Anthropology. *Studies in the Anthropology of Visual Communication* 4(2): 78–80.

Bazin, André. 1967. *What Is Cinema?* Hugh Gray (trans.). Berkeley, CA: University of California Press.

—. 1971. *What Is Cinema? Vol. II*. Hugh Gray (trans.). Berkeley, CA: University of California Press.

Behar, Ruth. 1993. *Translated Woman: Crossing the Border with Esperanza's Story*. Boston, MA: Beacon.

Blue, James. 1967. Jean Rouch in Conversation with James Blue. *Film Comment* 4 (2/3): 84–6.

Böhme, Gernot. 2016. *The Aesthetics of Atmospheres*. Oxford and New York: Routledge.

British Film Institute. 2008. *Addressing the Nation*, booklet accompanying the GPO Film Unit Collection, Vol. I. London: BFI Publishing.

—. 2009. *We Live in Two Worlds*, booklet accompanying the GPO Film Unit Collection, Vol. II. London: BFI Publishing.

Cevoni, Albert. 1965. Le Cinéma et l'Afrique. *France nouvelle* 1033: 17–19.

Cizek, Katerina, and William Uricchio. 2019. *Collective Wisdom: Co-creating Media within Communities, across Disciplines, and with Algorithms*. Cambridge, MA: MIT Press.

Crapanzano, Vincent. 1980. *Tuhami: Portrait of a Moroccan*. Chicago, IL: Chicago University Press.

de Bromhead, Toni. 2019. *Muddied Waters: The Fictionalisation of Ethnographic Film*. Aarhus: Intervention Press.

de Heusch, Luc. 1962. *The Cinema and Social Science: A Survey of Ethnographic and Sociological Films*. Reports and Papers in the Social Sciences 16. Paris: UNESCO.

Dovey, Jon. 2014. Documentary Ecosystems: Collaboration and Exploitation. In Kate Nash, Craig Hight and Catherine Summerhayes (eds), *New Documentary Ecologies*. Houndmills: Palgrave Macmillan, 11–32.

Empson, William. 1949. *Seven Types of Ambiguity: A Study of its Effects on English Verse*. 2nd edn. New York: New Directions.

Flaherty, Robert. 1950. Robert Flaherty Talking. In R. Manvell (ed.), *The Cinema 1950*. Harmondsworth: Penguin Books, 11–29.

Gardner, Robert, and Ákos Östör. 2001. *Making* Forest of Bliss*: Intention, Circumstance, and Chance in Nonfiction Film. A Conversation between Robert Gardner and Ákos Östör.* Cambridge, MA: Harvard Film Archive.

Goffman, Erving. 1962. *Asylums: Essays on the Social Situation of Mental Patients and Other Inmates*. Chicago, IL: Aldine Publishers.

Goldschmidt, Walter. 1972. Ethnographic Film: Definition and Exegesis. *PIEF (Program in Ethnographic Film) Newsletter* 3(2): 1–3.
Grimshaw, Anna. 2020. Telling Stories, Screening Lives: Notes Towards an Anthropological Biography. *Social Anthropology* 28(1): 168–83. DOI.org/10.1111/1469-8676.12732.
Grimshaw, Anna, and Amanda Ravetz. 2009. *Observational Cinema: Anthropology, Film, and the Exploration of Social Life*. Bloomington, IN: Indiana University Press.
Haddon, Alfred C. 1900. Letter to Baldwin Spencer dated 23 October 1900. Spencer Papers, Pitt-Rivers Museum, University of Oxford.
Haddon, Alfred C., W. H. R. Rivers, et al. 1901. *Reports of the Cambridge Anthropological Expedition to the Torres Straits, Vol. I*. Cambridge: University of Cambridge Press.
—. 1908. *Reports of the Cambridge Anthropological Expedition to the Torres Straits, Vol. VI*. Cambridge: University of Cambridge Press.
Heider, Karl. 1967. Comment. A Research Film Program in the Study of Changing Man by E. Richard Sorenson. *Current Anthropology* 8: 464.
—. 1974. Ethnographic Film. In *Learning Two-74*. Berkeley: University of California Press, 1–5.
—. 1976. *Ethnographic Film*. Austin: University of Texas Press.
Henley, Paul. 2004. Putting Film to Work: Observational Cinema as Practical Ethnography. In Sarah Pink, Lásló Kürti and Anna Isabel Afonso (eds), *Working Images: Visual Research and Representation in Ethnography*. London: Routledge, 109–30.
—. 2010. *The Adventure of the Real: Jean Rouch and the Craft of Ethnographic Cinema*. Chicago, IL: University of Chicago Press.
—. 2020a. *Beyond Observation: A History of Authorship in Ethnographic Film*. Manchester: Manchester University Press.
—. 2020b. From Vues to Ethnofiction: French Ethnographic Filmmaking in Africa before Jean Rouch. *Visual Anthropology* 33(1): 32–80.
Kline, Ronald R. 1997. Ideology and the New Deal 'Fact Film' *Power and the Land. Public Understanding of Science* 6: 16–30.
Levin, G. Roy. 1971. *Documentary Explorations: 15 Interviews with Film-makers*. Garden City, NY: Doubleday.
Lewis, Oscar. 1961. *Children of Sanchez*. New York: Random House.
Loizos, Peter. 1993. *Innovation in Ethnographic Film: From Innocence to Self-consciousness, 1955–1985*. Manchester: Manchester University Press.
MacDougall, David. 1975. Beyond Observational Cinema. In P. Hockings (ed.), *Principles of Visual Anthropology*. The Hague and Paris: Mouton Publishers, 109–24.
—. 1998. Whose Story Is It? In *Transcultural Cinema*. Princeton, NJ: Princeton University Press, 150–64.
—. 2001. Renewing Ethnographic Film: Is Digital Video Changing the Genre? *Anthropology Today* 17(3): 15–21.
—. 2006. *The Corporeal Image: Film, Ethnography, and the Senses*. Princeton, NJ: Princeton University Press.
—. 2019. *The Looking Machine: Essays on Cinema, Anthropology and Ethnographic Filmmaking*. Manchester: Manchester University Press.
—. 2020. Seven Types of Collaboration. *Studies in Documentary Film* 14(4). DOI: 10.1080/17503280.2020.1854150.
Marcorelles, Louis. 1973. *Living Cinema – New Directions in Contemporary Film-Making*. London: George Allen and Unwin.
Marshall, John. 1993. Filming and Learning. In Jay Ruby (ed.), *The Cinema of John Marshall*. Chur: Harwood Academic Publishers.
Menon, Siddhartha. 2008. *Writing Again*. Thiruvananthapuram: Folio Publishers.
Molenberghs, P., R. Cunnington and J. B. Mattingley. 2012. Brain Regions with Mirror Properties: A Meta-analysis of 125 Human fMRI Studies. *Neuroscience and Biobehavioral Reviews* 36: 341–9.
Moore, Alexander. 1988. The Limitations of Imagist Documentary. *Society for Visual Anthropology Newsletter* 4(2): 1–3.

Morin, Edgar. 1962. Preface. In Luc de Heusch (ed.), *The Cinema and Social Science: A Survey of Ethnographic and Sociological Films*, Reports and Papers in the Social Sciences 16. Paris: UNESCO, 3–5.

Murdock, George P. 1954. *Outline of World Cultures*. New Haven, CT: Human Relations Area Files Press.

—. 1957. World Ethnographic Film Sample. *American Anthropologist*, New Series 59(4): 664–87.

Nichols, Bill. 1991. *Representing Reality*. Bloomington, IN: Indiana University Press.

Pink, Sarah. 2004. Conversing Anthropologically: Hypermedia as Anthropological Text. In Sarah Pink, László Kürti and Ana Isabel Alfonso (eds), *Working Images*. London and New York: Routledge, 166–84.

Radin, Paul. 1920. *The Autobiography of a Winnebago Indian*. New York: Appleton.

Ramchandran, V. S. 2010. *The Tell-Tale Brain: A Neuroscientist's Quest for What Makes Us Human*. Noida: Random House India.

Riegl, Alois. 1985 [1901]. *Late Roman Art Industry*, Rolf Winkes (ed. and trans.). Rome: Giorgio Bretschneider Editore.

Rosenthal, Alan. 1971. *The New Documentary in Action: A Casebook in Filmmaking*. Berkeley, CA: University of California Press.

Rouch, Jean. 2003. *Ciné-Ethnography*. Steven Feld (ed. and trans.). Minneapolis, MN: University of Minnesota Press.

Ruby, Jay. 1975. Is an Ethnographic Film a Filmic Ethnography? *Studies in the Anthropology of Visual Communication* 2(2): 104–11.

—. 1989. The Emperor and His Clothes. *Society for Visual Anthropology Newsletter* 5(1): 9–11.

—. 2000. *Picturing Culture*. Chicago, IL: University of Chicago Press.

Seger, Linda. 2018. *The Collaborative Art of Filmmaking: From Script to Screen*. London: Angus and Robertson.

Shostak, Marjorie. 1981. *Nisa: The Life and Words of a !Kung Woman*. Cambridge, MA: Harvard University Press.

Sorenson, E. Richard. 1967. A Research Film Program in the Study of Changing Man. *Current Anthropology* 8: 443–69.

Spencer, Walter Baldwin. 1928. *Wanderings in Wild Australia, Vol. I*. London: Macmillan.

Spiegel, Pauline. 1984. The Case of the Well-Mannered Guest. *The Independent: Film and Video Monthly*, April: 15–17.

Srivastava, Sanjay. 1998. *Constructing Post-colonial India: National Character and the Doon School*. London and New York: Routledge.

Stevenson, Robert Louis. 1910. *Prayers Written in Vailima*. With an introduction by Mrs Stevenson. Designed, written out and illuminated by A. Sagorski. London: Chatto and Windus.

Tavernier, Bertrand. 1996. Commentary on the Lumière Films. In *The Lumière Brothers First Films* (DVD). Lyon: Institut Lumière/Association Frères Lumière.

Turner, Victor W. 1986. Dewey, Dilthy, and Drama: An Essay in the Anthropology of Experience. In Victor W. Turner and Edward M. Bruner (eds), *The Anthropology of Experience*. Urbana, IL: University of Illinois Press.

Vaughan, Dai. 1983. *Portrait of an Invisible Man: The Working Life of Stewart McAllister, Film Editor*. London: British Film Institute.

—. 1999. *For Documentary: Twelve Essays*. Berkeley, CA: University of California Press.

Young, Colin. 1975. Observational Cinema. In Paul Hockings (ed.), *Principles of Visual Anthropology*. The Hague: Mouton Publishers, 64–80.

Zimmerman, Patricia R. and Helen De Michiel. 2018. *Open Space New Media Documentary*. New York and London: Routledge.

Index

Note: page numbers in *italic* refer to illustrations.